797,885 Books

are available to read at

www.ForgottenBooks.com

Forgotten Books' App
Available for mobile, tablet & eReader

ISBN 978-1-331-08050-3
PIBN 10142232

This book is a reproduction of an important historical work. Forgotten Books uses
state-of-the-art technology to digitally reconstruct the work, preserving the original format
whilst repairing imperfections present in the aged copy. In rare cases, an imperfection in
the original, such as a blemish or missing page, may be replicated in our edition. We do,
however, repair the vast majority of imperfections successfully; any imperfections that
remain are intentionally left to preserve the state of such historical works.

Forgotten Books is a registered trademark of FB &c Ltd.
Copyright © 2017 FB &c Ltd.
FB &c Ltd, Dalton House, 60 Windsor Avenue, London, SW19 2RR.
Company number 08720141. Registered in England and Wales.

For support please visit www.forgottenbooks.com

1 MONTH OF
FREE
READING

at

www.ForgottenBooks.com

By purchasing this book you are eligible for one month membership to ForgottenBooks.com, giving you unlimited access to our entire collection of over 700,000 titles via our web site and mobile apps.

To claim your free month visit:
www.forgottenbooks.com/free142232

* Offer is valid for 45 days from date of purchase. Terms and conditions apply.

English
Français
Deutsche
Italiano
Español
Português

www.forgottenbooks.com

Mythology Photography **Fiction**
Fishing Christianity **Art** Cooking
Essays Buddhism Freemasonry
Medicine **Biology** Music **Ancient
Egypt** Evolution Carpentry Physics
Dance Geology **Mathematics** Fitness
Shakespeare **Folklore** Yoga Marketing
Confidence Immortality Biographies
Poetry **Psychology** Witchcraft
Electronics Chemistry History **Law**
Accounting **Philosophy** Anthropology
Alchemy Drama Quantum Mechanics
Atheism Sexual Health **Ancient History**
Entrepreneurship Languages Sport
Paleontology Needlework Islam
Metaphysics Investment Archaeology
Parenting Statistics Criminology
Motivational

JOURNAL

OF A

Staff=Officer in Paris during the Events of 1870 and 1871

BY

M. LE COMTE D'HERISSON

London
REMINGTON & CO., PUBLISHERS
HENRIETTA STREET, COVENT GARDEN, W.C.

1885
All Rights Reserved

CONTENTS

I.	NEW YORK TO PARIS	1
II.	THE CAMP AT CHÂLONS	16
III.	ACROSS PARIS	29
IV.	THE FOURTH OF SEPTEMBER	53
V.	THE JOURNEY OF THE EMPRESS	82
VI.	IN THE HOME OF THE EMPRESS	95
VII.	THE EMPRESS AND THE GOVERNOR	123
VIII.	PARIS BLOCKADED	131
IX.	AN AMATEUR DIPLOMATIST	143
X.	FROM THE CAPITOL TO THE TARPEIAN ROCK	157
XI.	TROCHU AT HOME	167
XII.	THE THIRTY-FIRST OF OCTOBER	181
XIII.	ELECTIONS AND NEGOTIATIONS	206
XIV.	PARIS	219
XV.	VILLIERS CHAMPIGNY	242
XVI.	BUZENVAL	269
XVII.	AT VERSAILLES	282

PREFACE

TWO DOCUMENTS

I

Extract from the *Gouvernement de la Defense Nationale,* by Jules Favre.

'At half-past four I was still without any reply. The day had been foggy and cold; night was falling. The cannonade from the forts and ramparts resounded with greater intensity than ever. Shells rained over the city; the works which covered Saint Denis, and even Saint Denis itself, were wreathed in flames. Innumerable anxieties were torturing me. I was at a loss to account for this inexplicable delay unless, indeed, the Chancellor refused to treat with us at this decisive moment. At length, at five o'clock, the door of my room opened, and my envoy handed me a letter from M. de Bismarck to the effect that he would see me on the morrow, or that very evening if I so preferred.

'The young officer who brought me this despatch, Captain d'Herisson d'Irisson, was on the Head-quarters Staff of General Trochu, and had brought himself into prominent notice by his polished manner, his courage and intelligence. Gifted with a special aptitude for languages, he spoke English perfectly, and German with facility, not to mention Chinese, which he had rapidly acquired while serving with the brilliant expedition under General de Montauban. When the war with Prussia broke out he was in the heart of America; he returned in hot haste to place himself at the service of his country, and to shut himself up in the town which he believed was in the greatest danger. The Governor willingly confided the most dangerous missions to him, and he acquitted himself of these important duties with equal coolness and intrepidity. I had asked for him because I knew that I should find in him the qualities of which I stood in need. He was my staunch, discreet, and faithful companion during these long and painful negotiations. I am glad to have an opportunity here of recording my appreciation of the affectionate zeal which he never ceased to display in regard to me.'

II

LETTER ADDRESSED TO THE AUTHOR BY GENERAL SCHMITZ, COMMANDING A *Corps d'Armée.*

'The undersigned Schmitz (Pierre-Isidore) General of Division, Commander-in-Chief of the 12th *Corps d'Armée,* Grand Officer of the Legion of Honour, late Chief of the Staff of the Armies of the National Defence, hereby certifies that M. (Maurice) d'Irisson d'Herisson was attached, as Captain of the *Garde Mobile,* to the Staff of the Governor of Paris during the whole of the siege.

' The Governor of Paris on many occasions expressed his
entire satisfaction with the services rendered by M.
d'Irisson, notably in the affairs of L'Hay, Chevilly, Villiers,
and Champigny; this officer, indeed, did his duty with
admirable zeal and devotion, and when, at the end of the
siege, negotiations were going on between M. Jules Favre
and Count de Bismarck, he rendered eminent services; he
obtained from the Germans the concession that the colours
should not be handed over to them, and several military
points were, at his instance, erased from the Convention.

' Profoundly recognising the services rendered by M.
d'Irisson, the General, Chief of the Staff, would have been
happy to have conferred upon him the Cross of an Officer
of the Legion of Honour, but he was in too close contact
with the Governor to receive that reward.

' We all of us considered that our services, under such
lamentable circumstances, ought to be gratuitous.

' The only exception to this rule was in the case of
Captain Thory, upon whom the Minister of War caused
the Cross of an Officer to be conferred at Bourdeaux, after
the disbanding of the armies and the conclusion of peace.

' *Given at Head-Quarters, at Limoges, December 1st,* 1879.

'SCHMITZ,

' General Commanding the 12th Corps d'Armée.'

The officer who accompanied Jules Favre, and was his
discreet, faithful, and devoted companion, the officer to
whom General Schmitz did the honour of addressing the
foregoing testimonial, is about to recount to the public his
impressions of the period from July 1870, to February 1871.

This officer is not a historian; he endeavours to be a
narrator. Moreover, history is, as it were, a case which is

ever under hearing. The historian is a species of president who sums up a discussion. The narrator is a witness who recounts what he has seen.

From the historian, as from a president, are demanded, above all, strict impartiality and a succinct classification of facts.

From the narrator and the witness are demanded candid evidence and genuine impressions.

I am going, then, to describe, with frankness and sincerity, not all that happened, but everything that I saw during these terrible days, so full of catastrophes from which France has not even now recovered.

D'HERISSON.

PARIS, *January*, 1885.

JOURNAL OF A STAFF OFFICER

CHAPTER I

NEW YORK TO PARIS

Prévost-Paradol—His Despondency—His Suicide.—The Germans in America.—
Irish and English.—The Treaty of Tien-Tsin.—In France.—The *Marseillaise.*
—With the Minister of War.—*En route* for Châlons.

On the 10th of July, 1870, I was in Washington and
soliciting a short interview with Prévost-Paradol, who
had recently been appointed Minister Plenipotentiary of
France in the United States. As I was entrusted by the
Minister of Commerce with an official mission to North
America, I was really somewhat dependent upon the new
Ambassador, and he was good enough to give me an early
appointment.

Before I left France I had been presented to the
brilliant writer, won over from the old to the Imperial
régime, a trophy of Cæsar converted into a Member of
Parliament. He lived in a modest suite of rooms in the
Rue Saint-Georges, and at the date of our first interview

he had only just received his diplomatic appointment, and was preserving an unflinching demeanour under the angry sarcasms which were being hurled at him by his old friends for what they called his apostacy. He then appeared to me to be full of confidence in his own future and in the star of the liberal empire.

In Washington he was no longer the same man. He had fallen away, had aged even in so short a time, was melancholy, undecided, and as if he were borne down by the sense of having made an irreparable mistake—what the *boulevards* in their highly imaginative language call a *boulotte*. Such was my impression of the trenchant journalist, the witty talker, and the frank diplomatist, happy in airing his newly won distinction and in hearing himself styled Your Excellency, whom I had met only a month previously.

'Ah, my friend,' he said, as he welcomed me, 'what a misfortune, what an irreparable misfortune!'   ·

'What do you mean? What misfortune?' I replied in astonishment.

'Well—but—I mean this war.'

'What war?'

'The war with Germany.'

'Where do you get that idea from?'

I began to wonder within myself whether his brain was affected, or if he had already fallen under the spell of the 'evil eye' of the White House. I must explain that at Washington—a horribly wearisome place, seeing that it only contains the Capitol, the residence of the President, and the public offices, all of them institutions which act directly on the spleen—there is a current belief that the White House, the modest palace of the President, brings misfortune to those who enter it for the first time.

He read my thoughts and sadly replied to them:

'No, I am not mad. You evidently are in the dark as to what is going on. Learn, then, that General Prim took it into his head four days ago to offer the crown of Spain to Prince Antoine of Hohenzollern, of the Royal Family of Prussia; that France has protested in most energetic terms against what she calls the resurrection of the empire of Charles V; that at this moment curt and angry notes are being exchanged between Saint-Cloud and Ems, where the King and M. de Bismarck now are, and that there can only be one fatal result of all this—war, within a week, to-morrow, possibly to-day.'

'It will blow over, you will see, just as in the Luxembourg affair.'

'It will not blow over, for two reasons. The first is that Prussia wants to go to war with us. Indirectly for the last sixteen years, and directly for four, she has been preparing for it. Her army needs fighting just âs locomotives need to be used, lest it should become rusty. That is the first reason, and it is a peremptory one. The King and M. de Bismarck are wise enough to retreat even now, perhaps, if they were not afraid that some general, more sagacious than Niel, might arise in France to compel the Chamber to vote a fundamental re-organisation of our army on the model of their own. But the second reason, alas, is more absolute. The Empire needs a war, it wishes for one, and it will make one.'

And, lowering his voice, he added, in a tone of despondency,

'There were fifteen hundred thousand *Non* in the *plebiscite.*'

'Very well, then let us admit a war. And I thank you for having given me timely warning. I shall pigeon-hole my figures and reports. France has no more need of statisticians; she wants soldiers. I am a captain of *Mobiles*. Is it time to pack up? After all, I should not be sorry to take a trip through Germany. I speak German as well as old Arminius himself. I shall pay a visit of inspection to the libraries of the conquered towns.'

The Minister interrupted me abruptly.

'What a grand thing it is to be young and to believe,' he said. 'But, unhappy youth, not only will you not go to Germany, but you will be overwhelmed in France. Believe me, I know the Prussians. We are deficient of everything that we need in order to struggle against them—generals, men, and supplies. We shall be ground to powder.'

And then, as if he were speaking to himself and had forgotten that I was there, he added,

'France will be in a state of revolution before six months are over, and the Empire will be in the dust. Ah! I had good need'——

He did not complete the sentence, but I understood that in the catastrophes which he foresaw, he was not entirely forgetful of himself.

'Are you pleased, at all events,' I asked, 'with your reception here?'

'Passably. These people do not love us,' he replied. 'They have never forgiven our attempt upon Mexico. And as far as I am personally concerned—why should I not confess it privately?—I have noticed a certain amount of astonishment, almost amounting to disapprobation, in regard to my changed attitude. America is German to the backbone, and how should it be otherwise? There are certainly more Germans than English here, and not one of them, in betaking himself to a new country, has forgotten his old one. I tell you that from the moment rumour hinted at a rivalry between France and Germany, families who settled in America three generations ago, began to look askance at the French, and you may rest assured that many of them would abandon their commerce, their manufactures, their situations, to take up arms against us, even though they might stay here in peace. Their country, the Fatherland, as they call it—with such a feeling as that they would go to the end of the world. To speak frankly, I am discouraged, extinct, annihilated. Most undoubtedly was I wrong to leave Paris and lay aside my pen.'

He then apologised for not asking me to stay to dinner. He was not settled, but was still like a bird on a twig. Later on I left him in an agitated frame of mind, but I nevertheless could not bring myself to share his delusions and his fears. France defeated, the Empire done away with—what nonsense, said I to myself. 'Dress up a clever man in official costume and he will be frightened of his shadow.'

I was coming down stairs from my room on the following morning when I was accosted by a *table d'hôte* companion.

'You are a Frenchman, sir.'

'Yes. What of it?'

'Have you not heard the news?'

'No. Is war declared?'

'Your Ambassador committed suicide during the night.'

I rushed off to Prévost-Paradol's house. I was denied admittance. The eyes of the servant who refused me were full of tears. I pushed him aside and went upstairs. On his bed and fully dressed I saw the Minister, with a large stain of blood on his shirt front, where the bullet had entered his body. The police were engaged in drawing up their report.

During the night Prévost-Paradol had placed himself before the glass, and feeling with his left hand for the beating of his heart, he had placed a pistol with his right hand to the spot, and shot himself.

His valet, who hastened to the room on hearing the report, found him standing up, with his elbows on the mantel-piece and his head between his hands.

' Did you hear ? ' his master said to him.

' Yes, sir. I thought you had fallen. If you are ill you had better go to bed.'

And he fell dead almost in the arms of his servant.

I offered to take back the children of the unhappy man. A friend of the family undertook their removal to France. The fatality which dogged their steps is well-known. The son followed in his father's steps. One daughter, I believe, went mad, and the other went into a convent, where she prays to that God who was so cruel to them all.

It was with the greatest difficulty that we succeeded in obtaining the prayers of the Catholic Church for the suicide. The priest of the Church of St Matthew only opened the gates to the corpse on the express order of the Grand-Vicar of Baltimore, who was acting for his Bishop, absent at Rome for the Council. He pronounced a touching funeral oration over the coffin, from which the following very remarkable passage has been often quoted :

' However extraordinary, however unchristian, and even anti-christian, may appear the manner in which an end was put to this earthly existence, however diverse may be the opinions of the world in regard to it, and particularly in regard to the moral and religious sentiments of the deceased at the terrible moment of his death, let us remember that judgment does not belong to us.

' No men, and no class of men, have any right to judge their fellows after they have departed this life.

' The Church herself, chosen by Christ to explain His doctrines and precepts, and to watch over His sacred constitution, does not take upon herself to condemn a soul that has taken its flight to the other world, because her ministerial authority does not extend beyond the tomb.'

On the day following the obsequies the newspapers announced the declaration of war between France and Germany. I had nothing more to do in America, and I hastened to New York to secure a cabin on board the first steamer—a Cunard boat—for England.

During the few hours preceding my departure I was enabled to realize that Prévost-Paradol had not exaggerated the anti-French sentiments of the American people. At the drinking bars, in the streets, in the squares, in the places of business, everywhere there were manifestations in favour of Germany. It needed much self-restraint to avoid coming to blows, and I well remember in what a state of furious exasperation I spent in the solitude of my cabin the last moments of my stay in the United States. Unhappily, I found the same feelings rife on board the boat. Every corner was full of Germans on their way to rejoin the army. I longed to commence hostilities on my own account, and the ten days of the voyage were one long spell of enervating excitement. We had on board the American General, Burnside, who was going to attach himself, as a looker-on, to the German Staff, in order to follow the military operations, to gain some instruction, and to see the great war. He himself had a certain military reputation which he had acquired during the war of the Secession. We had also Major Kodolisch, an Austrian, who subsequently was destined to attract public attention in France as Military *Attaché* to the embassy of his country.

But when I reached Ireland the scene changed, and I was delighted to find at last some people who loved France. At Queenstown first, and afterwards at Cork, I was stopped without ceremony in the streets, in the hotels, everywhere.

'You are a Frenchman, sir?'

'Yes, I am.'

'Ah! So much the better. Good luck and courage to you!' and then followed a shake of the hand, a slap on the back, and a cordial look of sympathy.

Some of these good fellows who imagined that as a Frenchman I should be sure to be on intimate speaking terms with the Emperor, used to get me into a corner to impart *sotto voce* confidences, something after this fashion:

'Be sure you tell your Emperor that as soon as he has gamed his first victories we shall rise here. And, above all, don't let him forget us when he comes back from Berlin.'

In the principal towns of Ireland our early successes, fleeting and insignificant as they were, were received as national victories. Flags and illuminations were the general rule. This enthusiasm had the effect of startling the English government, and the uneasiness it caused in official circles was not without its influence on the surreptitiously hostile attitude which England held towards France during the whole of the war.

At the end of the siege she sent us cheeses, there is no doubt about that—the lesson was worth their cost. We were no longer to be feared, and she could without danger display her gastronomic commiseration towards a nation which a little diplomatic commiseration might possibly have saved.

I do not like the English, I confess. I fully recognise

their grand qualities as a nation, their tenacity, their spirit of enterprise, and their magnificent solidarity. But all this appears to me to be spoiled by their selfishness, which is both monstrous and somewhat unscrupulous in regard to ways and means. I admit that nations should be selfish ; it is, we are told, their duty, and selfishness is, perhaps, only a species of patriotism. But let them be honestly selfish, for honesty spoils nothing, not even patriotism.

And on this point I will ask permission of my readers to recount to them, by way of example, a personal reminiscence, an entirely unknown and unpublished anecdote, the authenticity of which I guarantee.

The incident happened in China. Following on the first operations conducted by General de Montauban, a treaty was signed at Tien-Tsin, not on this occasion by the captain of a man-of-war, but by Lord Elgin on behalf of England, and by Baron Gros on that of France.

This treaty, duly signed and drawn up in duplicate— one copy in English, the other in French—was entrusted to the Mandarin who had discussed its provisions, and— nothing more was ever heard of it.

When it became apparent that China was not acting in accordance with the treaty, an enquiry was set on foot as to what had become of it, and I have still a vivid recollection of the laughter of the Commander-in-Chief, and the quips of his Staff, when he received the cool, calm reply that the Mandarin with whom he had been negotiating had no powers whatever, nor had he been entrusted with any mission ; that he was an amateur diplomatist, merely a private individual who happened to be in our neighbourhood, and had amused himself and filled up some measure of his time by treating directly with us.

We advanced to Palikao, and then to the Summer

Palace, where we arrived quite by chance, without knowing anything about it. In fact, we might just as easily have found ourselves anywhere else, for the maps in possession of our Staff were most imperfect, and on none of them was there an indication of the locality of the famous building—a fact which did not in any way prevent the Paris gossips from saying that Montauban was a rogue, and that he knew exactly where to put his hand on the hoarded treasures of the Son of Heaven.

When we arrived at this sumptuous residence, a collection of magnificent palaces, we were received by half-a-dozen rounds from as many guns defending the gateway, and we found that the palace had already been half-sacked by the populace of the surrounding district, who were delighted at the opportunity of displaying their hostility to the conquering race, the Mougol dynasty.

The soldiers dispersed in all directions, and a sergeant of a line regiment soon brought General de Montauban some papers which he had found in the Emperor's private apartment. They were our celebrated treaty of Tien-Tsin. The General sent for me, and out of curiosity, as well as in accordance with his extremely methodical habits, he took the French copy and gave the English one to me to translate. We set to work to collate them, and I had not gone very far with my reading before he interrupted me.

'D'Herisson, that is not there.'

'Indeed it is, sir.'

'You are quite sure?'

'Certain.'

'Strange; but go on.'

In a word, the English treaty was not word for word with the French treaty. It was not a literal translation.

The English had stipulated for all kinds of private advantages for themselves alone, stating that we were mercenaries in their pay, and that they would settle with us in due course.

These two curious papers ought to be found somewhere or other in the archives, public or private. But however that may be, I had them in my hands. I assert that as a fact, and pass on without further comment.

The trip across the arm of the sea which separates Ireland from England, St George's Channel, sufficed to plunge me once more headlong into America. In England no attempt was made to conceal the general longing for the success of the German armies.

I hope, I may say I am convinced, that the day will come when the English will regret having been passive spectators of the overthrow of their rivals, so long resigned to the thankless *rôle* of allies of Great Britain. But we can hardly ask nations to display perspicacity, and in this month of August, 1870—it is a fact—the subjects of Queen Victoria had but one fear, that of seeing us in Berlin. Their anxiety was destined to be short-lived.

At last I reached France. I thought that when I set foot in my native land I should find a nation in arms, silent, calm, conscious of the serious nature of what is called a Continental war, master of itself and prepared as one man for a supreme effort. Alas! I was speedily disenchanted.

Scarcely had I commenced my journey by rail, at the very first stations on the Northern line, when I found myself surrounded by unhealthy excitement and inexpressible confusion. The soldiers who were rejoining their regiments sang the *Marseillaise.* The crowds who escorted them gave themselves up to childish manifestations. They shouted 'To Berlin!' They were drunk with words and wine. I expected a very different sight. Beside me the more serious and reflective part of the population looked into each others' eyes, and in that mute language exchanged the saddening reflections they dared not express. Not in this fashion did the great armies of days gone by, who crowned our glorious colours with so many victories, set out for war. To use a barrack-room expression, 'It smelt nasty.' I reasoned with myself, nevertheless; I thought of the nerves of the French nation, and I said to myself that all this excessive excitement was perhaps a good thing, that the high spirits would work wonders. And I breathed a sigh of relief and confidence as I felt under my feet the pavement of Paris, that pavement which seems to be alive beneath the soles of your boots, and strikes you as at once elastic and firm.

I am not a historian. That title suits neither my inclinations nor my powers. I have not undertaken to give an account of the Franco-German war; not even of the siege of Paris. What I have promised my readers and what I shall strive to give them are my own genuine impressions. I have not a word to say as to why or wherefore the insignificant success at Sarrebruch was followed by the repulse at Wissembourg and the disaster at Reichshoffen; how or why Bazaine, amid the applause of the Left of the Chamber, was appointed Generalissimo; how or why the Left of the Chamber, from the moment of our earliest defeats, commenced to wage a war against the Imperial dynasty, which, thanks to the disaster of Sedan, culminated in the revolution of September; how or why the Ollivier ministry succumbed under the weight of the very first misfortunes brought about by the war; how or why the Emperor, without command or prestige, driven

out of Paris by the Empress-Regent and repulsed from the
frontier by Prussia, wandered a pale phantom of an already
half-dethroned Cæsar, between his capital and the advance
guard of the enemy; nor, last of all, how or why General
Palikao undertook the difficult and patriotic task of forming
a Cabinet, and enjoyed a certain amount of popularity even
at the hands of the Left.

I saw nothing of all this, and I am only going to record
what I saw.

An hour after my arrival in Paris, on the 13th of
August, I called upon General the Comte de Palikao,
Minister of War and President of the Council. I had conscientiously employed the hour in getting myself a complete uniform, equipping myself from head to foot, transforming myself, in a word, into a presentable soldier.

To those who may be astonished at the idea of a simple
captain of *Mobiles* boldly knocking at the door of a
Minister's office, I must explain once more that during the
Chinese campaign relations had been established between
the General and myself, partaking of almost paternal kindness on his side, and of absolutely filial devotion on mine.
I may also explain that the General had given me an even
greater mark of his favour after the war, by sending me
home to the Emperor as the bearer of his despatches and
reports, among which was a rather curious document.

The General had received an official intimation that the
Emperor was desirous of conferring upon him a title
commemorative of his victories, and a pecuniary grant as a
recompense for his services. The Chamber, it will be remembered, refused the grant, and the Emperor supplied the
omission by a private gift of 500,000 francs from his privy
purse. The General was worried by an idea on the subject
of a title. He was afraid that the Emperor would make

him Duc de Pekin. 'Duc de Pekin,' he would say over and over again, half jokingly and half in earnest, 'that would not sound well for a soldier'; and he was created simply Comte de Palikao.

After this explanation it will be understood that as I was on the unemployed list, I was not doing anything very extraordinary in asking my old chief, who had always shown himself desirous of continuing to be my protector and my friend, for a company.

In addition to this I promised to take up very little of the time he had to devote to his immense labour.

'You are to wait for the General; he will take you with him in his carriage to the Chamber,' was the intimation I received after a short sojourn in the ante-room. And a few moments later the Minister emerged in civilian attire, with his portfolio under his arm, and pushing me into his carriage he sat down beside me.

'Well, my dear boy,' said he at once, 'what are you doing here?'

'I am a captain of *Mobiles* on the unemployed list, sir; I should like a company.'

'Very well; go to Châlons. All the *Mobiles* are there.'

He scribbled a few words in pencil on a slip of paper and added,

'Give this to Berthaut, who is in command there, and if he has not a company at his disposal he will form one for you.'

Then, as we were whirled rapidly along, he plunged forthwith into old reminiscences, and went on so say:

'Ah, we had a good time in China! But now, what can I do! I do my best, but it is very late in the day to do anything as it should be done. We have been neither lucky nor clever. I am like a cook who has to wait for the company to sit down to table before he can make his preparations and get the dinner ready. It is a terrible task and one devoid of glory; but I am doing what I can.'

And pointing to the Palais-Bourbon, which had the appearance of springing out of the Pont de la Concorde, which our carriage was crossing, he said:

'They have been glad to get me after all, although in days gone by they behaved so badly to me. Ah! I assure you I am not working for them, but for France first of all, for she must be our chief care, and also for that poor Empress, who is so energetic, and so touching withal.'

We arrived at our destination.

'Will you be present at the sitting?' said the General to me. 'You do not care about it? You are quite right. They pass their time, and make me lose mine, by continually cross-examining me, asking me preposterous and useless questions, and gargling their throats with big words which mean nothing. Well! Well!'

He disappeared, and I never saw him again during the war. Furnished with my scrap of paper and its scrawl I hastened to the station to find a train for Châlons.

Very late in the evening I managed to find a seat in one of the compartments of an immense train, drawn by two engines, crowded with troops of all arms, officers and soldiers hurried off in small detachments, and dragging behind it I don't know how many trucks laden with munitions of war.

CHAPTER II

THE CAMP AT CHÂLONS

A Thirty Hours' Journey.—A Military Train.—Yesterday and To-Day.—The *Isoles* MacMahon.—My brother.—At the Theatre.—The Emperor and his *Mobiles*. —A Despatch.—General Schmitz.—The Staff of the 12th corps.—The Emperor's Chocolate.—Horses.—Faithful Joseph and English saddles.—General Trochu, Governor of Paris.—An unfortunate Word.—Journey with the *Mobiles*.

WE were thirty hours in accomplishing the distance between Paris and Châlons, a distance done by an express train in three-hours-and-a-half.

I must confess that the behaviour of the troops conveyed by the train was deplorable. It was impossible to induce them to remain quietly in their seats. Overexcited by the copious libations in which they had indulged before starting, and which were supplemented by the relays of drink they had brought with them; impatient too, as all travellers are by reason of continual stoppages, uncomfortable carriages, and a snail's rate of progressing, they rushed to and fro, piled themselves up in the same compartment, made excursions on the baggage trucks, along the foot-boards, tore their uniforms, and shouted out that strident *Marseillaise* which hovered in 1870 over all our defeats and all our shame, and which I can never hear without feeling sick.

The officers dared not say a word, or if they did open their mouths, they gave the word of command with that timidity which is so sure a sign of a defeated and demora- lized army, and of leaders who are reduced to endeavour by dint of platitudes to gain the forgiveness of their inferiors for hardships borne in vain and battles unskilfully fought. It was heart breaking.

And yet with what rejoicing were they received by the inhabitants of the places through which we passed. At each station, and indeed whenever the train pulled up, the wives of the landed gentry followed by their servants in livery, and of the middle-class accompanied by their *bonnes*, with the women of the lower orders by themselves, rivalled each other in fuss and generosity. There were baskets of provisions, piles of fruit, litres, the never failing litres, of liquor served out profusely, and better than all these demoralizing provisions, there were the warm shakes of the hand, the modest kisses of the women, and the frank salute of the men. These effusive marks of sympathy made my eyes fill with tears, and I resolutely refused to see, even in thought, beyond these good and lovable people, the hordes of spiked helmets which were destined to spread like a black torrent in their midst, and to exact by intimidation what brotherly love was pouring forth, willingly and in profusion, before me.

We reached Mourmelon on the morning of the 15th of August. What a 15th of August! Once upon a time, in the midst of this smiling landscape, regiment upon regiment dressed its ranks on parade, while the bayonets of its men

B

glistened in the sun in honour of their Sovereign's birthday, and to and fro, among the white and cheerful tents, soldiers passed in full uniform, spick and span and well set up, while joyous salvoes of artillery saluted Saint Napoleon, and Generals with their Staff, gilded like the archangels on the high altar, exchanged visits and congratulated each other on the honours and rewards which had been gazetted the same morning in the *Moniteur*.

Instead of this order, disorder reigned supreme in the camp, which appeared as if it were given over to pillage. All the little attempts at ornamentation, the small gardens, bust, statues, fountains, shrubberies—everything which the fancy of the soldiers had devised—were ruthlessly ravaged, destroyed, or torn up by the roots. Instead of be-gilt Generals there were commanders in dirty uniforms, who seemed afraid of showing themselves to their men. Instead of the fine regiments of other days, there was a mass of beings without discipline, cohesion, or rank, the swarm of dirty unarmed soldiers known as the *isolés*.

There, outside the tents and huts, there was no room for them inside, squatting or lying round the bivouac fires, without any regular telling off, without arms, and with their uniforms in shreds, were the *isolés* of Macmahon, the fugitives from Reichshoffen, the remnants of regiments overwhelmed and dispersed by defeat; soldiers of the line without rifles or ammunition pouches, Zouaves in drawers, Turcos without turbans, dragoons without helmets, cuirassiers without cuirasses, hussars without sabretaches. It was an inert world, vegetating rather than living, scarcely moving when kicked, and grumbling at being disturbed in its sleep of the weary. The majority of these *isolés* were Zouaves and Turcos, who had suffered more severely than the other corps.

And, last of all, instead of the joyous salvoes of artillery of former days, there was the hum of the murmuring crowd. Indeed, if we had heard the sound of artillery at that hour, it would have been the guns of Gravelotte mowing down whole companies of the *Garde Impériale.*

In the interior of the camp there was the same disorder. The battalions of the Paris *Mobiles* were lodged as they arrived, wherever there happened to be room at the time, and if you asked a passing soldier where such and such a company was quartered, he would pretend to know nothing about it, and would give himself the pleasure of telling you to go to ——

My first object at the Camp of Châlons was to see General Berthaut, and next to find my brother, a Secretary of the Embassy recalled in consequence of the war, and now orderly officer to the General. With a tongue in one's head and good boots on one's feet there is not much difficulty in going anywhere, and so in the end I found the General. I handed him the Minister's memorandum, and he promised to attend to it. As for my brother, I ran him to ground in a tent where he was sleeping the sleep of the just, with a pair of pistols, loaded and cocked, at the head of his bed. All the officers did the same.

I commenced operations by taking possession of his pistols, and then I awoke him and gave him a lecture on the utter futility of his military precaution, since all the world might have done as I had—disarmed him while he was asleep.

He laughed at my lecture, and we spent the day together. In the evening we went to the theatre. It is almost incredible, but is a fact that in the midst of the unruly camp and men crushed by defeat, the old French spirit of gaiety had still some flickerings of life. There was a theatre in camp, devoted to tragedy and comic opera. Among other actors there were Barreti, of the Opera Comique, and a youth named Ange who had that very year carried off a first prize at the Conservatoire. To say that the performance was well managed would be a slight exaggeration. The foot-lights were scaled and everybody sang whatever he happened to know. Plays were invented, cues improvised, and there was much reviling of the Prussians. And every now and then the hateful *Marsaillaise* resounded. Many a victory must needs be won to the strains of that anthem before it can be pardoned for the defeats to which it has served as prelude and accompaniment.

On the following day, Tuesday, August 16, towards evening the Emperor arrived unheralded by drum or trumpet, and installed himself in his quarters without anybody except the Staff having been warned of his coming.

Only in the morning after his arrival was it known that he was there by the increased animation in the neighbourhood of head-quarters, the sentries at their posts, and the lacqueys in all their splendour of green and gold at the entrance.

I never expected his presence to excite such enthusiasm as his uncle inspired even in the days when he possessed no more of France, so to speak, than his horse could stand on, but neither did I expect to hear the insults that were heaped upon him.

I witnessed exhibitions of feeling such as I never could have believed if I had not seen and heard them. The *Mobiles* were employed on fatigue duty in parties of nearly a thousand men at one time. When one of these parties approached the Imperial quarters this is what happened:

A wag would call out in his shrillest tone, '*Vive l'Empereur*,' and the whole party as one man would count, one, two, three, and reply,

'M——!' Here insert the famous expression used by Cambronne. And the officers dared not say a word.

This did not prevent the publication of the following despatch in Paris two days afterwards.

'CAMP OF CHÂLONS, *August* 20, 6 P.M.

'The Emperor yesterday on horseback inspected several *Corps d'Armée*. Everywhere the troops surrounded him, imploring him to put himself at their head.

'True copy.
'The Minister of Interior.
'HENRI CHEVREAU.'

So much for despatches!

On the morning of the Emperor's arrival I was walking in a melancholy frame of mind in the neighbourhood of the Imperial head-quarters. I was still out of temper by reason of the stupid manifestations I had just witnessed, thinking sadly that in all probability General Berthaut had forgotten all about the insignificant *Mobile* who had handed him the minister's memorandum, having eaten nothing since my very meagre dinner the previous evening, and quite ignorant of where I should get breakfast, seeing that provisions were running short and the canteens were completely sold out, when I heard my name called out by a general officer.

'What are you doing here, my poor d'Herisson?'

It was General Schmitz, who was destined during the siege to put his name to so many documents, preceded by the two letters, P.O., signifying *par ordre*, but under-

stood by the Parisians as meaning that the names given
him in baptism were Paul and Oscar. General Schmitz
went to China as colonel and chief of the staff to General
Montauban. He was an old acquaintance of mine, and he
remains my best friend; if I may use the term to express
the cordial relations existing between a man of my age, a
mere private individual, and a General as distinguished
and eminent as he was.

'I am here, sir, in search of a company of *Mobiles*, and I
am experiencing some difficulty in finding one.'

'So much the better, because I want you. I am Chief
of the Staff of the 12th Corps, commanded by General
Trochu. I am going to attach you to the Staff of the
General commanding. Besides, it is the destiny of both of
us to serve with Trochu, for you know that he was
originally named for the command of the Chinese Expedition. He declined, and the Emperor appointed Montauban.
Do you agree? I will go and make out and sign your
appointment. Wait for me, I will be with you in three
minutes.'

And I resumed my walk, with my stomach still empty,
but with a far more cheerful mind.

Just at this moment I saw a magnificent green lacquey
emerge from the central headquarter tent; he was
majestically carrying on a silver salver smoking hot
liquids, flanked by buttered toast. As he passed me on
the other side of the palissade I addressed these simple
words to him:

'Twenty francs?'

'It is the Emperor's chocolate,' he replied. 'His
Majesty does not want any breakfast. He is not hungry.'

I took a louis out of my pocket, and the faithful
servant immediately opened a small door, and telling me to

go in, installed me in an office, where I drank I don't know
how many cups of chocolate, supplemented by toast,
sandwiches, and cakes. I was making what might be
called an imperial breakfast, when General Schmitz,
amused by my adventures and by the sight of me at home
with the Emperor, came to crown the feast with my
appointment, signed 'Trochu.' I was attached to the 12th
Corps d'Armée as orderly officer to the general commanding. I had the right of adding gilt epaulets to my uniform.

'That is not all,' said General Schmitz to me, 'There
will be no basking in Capuan luxury. Have you any
horses? You will need a couple. Off with you to Paris
and buy them.'

'I need not do that, sir. I will send my servant to buy
them.'

'Oh, you have a servant, have you?'

Indeed I have a servant, and what is more, an English
servant, who, however, will appear but seldom in these
reminiscences. I forgave his nationality on account of
his fidelity, and I never called him by any other title than
faithful Joseph. He was a sort of jockey, about fifty years
of age and looking fifteen. Small, thin, wiry, and fair-
complexioned, without a vestige of hair on his face, he was
as clever in the kitchen as in the stable; he was a treasure.

'Will you tell him also,' added General Schmitz, 'to
bring me two English saddles. I have not enough for
campaigning.'

Faithful Joseph was therefore promoted to the rank of
remount officer. I said good-bye to him at the railway
station, provided with all that he wanted for the purchase
of the horses and saddles, and I resumed my walk.

Two hours afterwards I saw at some distance from me a
knot of soldiers hustling what seemed to be a ragged urchin.

I drew near, and to my astonishment I recognised in the victim my faithful Joseph.

The wretched fellow, whilst waiting for the train, had unfortunately got into conversation with the bystanders, chattering about his mission, of which he was very proud, and conscientiously murdering our language with his horrible English accent.

That was quite sufficient; he was taken for a Prussian spy. To his entreaties and his explanations that he belonged to a neutral nation, there was but one reply, ' Do not play the rogue. If you speak English, you must be a Prussian.'

And he was accordingly driven before them, jostled, knocked about, maltreated generally; his feet bare, and holding—I could never discover why—a boot in each hand. I verily believe that his persecutors were going to shoot him summarily in a corner, without council of war or benefit of clergy.

As for reasoning with the excited soldiers or using my authority as an officer to make them relinquish their prey, both methods were out of the question. I tried a different system. I began to swear like a templar, and to box like a Londoner, and I let out right and left among the crowd. The plan was efficacious. My Joseph was released. He has never forgiven me for this accident.

I was attempting to console him when General Schmitz appeared on the scene once more.

' My dear fellow,' he shouted, as he came up, ' no more horses, no more English saddles. Telegraph to your servant not to buy anything. What does it all mean? We are going back to Paris. General Trochu is appointed Governor, and takes me with him as chief of his staff. The decree is signed.'

And he showed me a paper on which I read,

' Napoleon, &c.

' ART. 1. General Trochu is appointed Governor of Paris and Commander-in-Chief of all the forces entrusted with the defence of the city.

' ART. II. Our Minister of War is charged with the execution of this decree,

　　　' *Done at Châlons, August* 17, 1870,

　　　　　　　　　　　　　' NAPOLEON.

' By the Emperor,

　　' The Minister of War,

　　　' COMTE DE PALIKAO.'

' And what is to become of me ? '

' You are most probably coming with us. In the meantime I have a mission for you. General Trochu is sending the *Mobiles* back to Paris. Go to Reims, make all arrangements with the railway authorities for the organization of the necessary train service, and take the command of the first train yourself. Come and see me in Paris as soon as you have accomplished your task.'

The very first act of the new Governor, as a matter of fact, was to recall the *Mobiles* to Paris. And in the proclamation wherein he announced their return to these young troops, there was one word which made some of us prick up our ears. ' You have,' said the General, ' the right to defend your homes.' In the midst of the disasters which were beginning to overwhelm us, in the midst of the serious troubles, moral and material, born of our catastrophes, there were not a few, and I was one of them, who thought that the slightest blow struck at a discipline already too severely shaken was neither more nor less than a veritable national misfortune. And to talk of their rights to a turbulent mob, already too prone to forget their duty, was a direct attack on discipline. A soldier has no more right to be here than there. It is his duty to go where he is sent. To admit that the Parisian *Mobiles* had a right to be in Paris, was to admit that the *Mobiles* of Ardèche had a right to be at Privas. Imagine what an army would be like with such theories as these! It is nevertheless but fair to say, in justice to the Governor, whose words were frequently not up to the level of his ideas, that the return of the *Mobiles* and his wish to flatter them, formed part of a plan concerted with the Emperor, a plan which explains the conduct of the General up to the 4th of September inclusive, and about which I will give a few details, which are curious, and, as far as I know, have never been published.

I started at once in a light cart for Reims, and on the following morning a train, got together by the railway company's people, was in readiness for the first detachment of the Paris *Mobiles*, who marched from Châlons. The entrainment and departure were carried out without a hitch. But the journey had no charm for me. The isolated bodies of troops whose behaviour had scandalised me between Paris and Châlons, were little saints compared with these devils of *Mobiles*. The train was like a swarm of ants in disorder. Running along the roofs of the carriages, at the risk of being decapitated by a bridge; passing to and fro along the footboards, at the hazard of being crushed by a way-post or a train coming the other way—all this was mere child's play. They swarmed on the tender and even on the engine. At the least stoppage—and we stopped frequently—they scoured the fields, stole vegetables, pulled down palings, smashed windows, and committed every imaginable folly. As one result of my service in the regular army I had acquired certain ideas as to strict discipline which were in ill accord with disorderly soldiers and passive officers, and at one moment, when I was exasperated at my authority being slighted, I quietly drew my sword with a settled determination to use it, even at the risk of being cut to pieces. The demonstration, however, happily sufficed, and comparative order reigned until we reached Paris, where I gladly handed over to the proper officers, who were in readiness at the station, the task of conveying these lunatics to the camp of Saint-Maur.

It must not be assumed, in reading these opinions of mine on the Paris *Mobiles*, that I despise the special qualities of which these troops gave proof, or rather, the qualities which existed in them in an embryo state and might have been developed. There were in the Paris *Mobiles* . first-rate elements, orderly and devoted men, some charming little soldiers, and even some modest heroes. But their improvised battalions were neither properly formed, nor welded together, nor in regular order. They had not even an idea of military discipline, and had not had time to contract those habits of patience, self-denial, and self-efface-ment, without which an army cannot exist. Their leaders, brave youths, but for the most part novices in service, were afraid of them, and they dared neither repress the license of their men, nor firmly insist on outward signs of respect being paid to themselves. The ordeal of battle is not re-quired as a means of discovering if troops are good ; the experiment would be too costly. There are certain outward signs, certain minor details which never deceive. If you see soldiers who are careful of their appearance, their uniform and their arms, and who salute their officers re-spectfully, you may unhesitatingly put yourself at their head and lead them no matter where. They are good soldiers. It may be said that cleanliness and respect are infallible signs of military healthiness. But cleanliness, a taste for trimness in appearance, and respectful salutes, are not to be acquired in an hour, or even a week. They are the fruit of education, and the *Mobiles* had not had time to complete their education. Was it their fault? Was it not rather the fault of the Opposition, whose incessant nagging prevented any serious organization of these young troops, and who, when they came into power, had nothing wherewith to oppose a seasoned and disciplined enemy but a lot of soldiers whose temperaments they had, so to speak, spoiled to begin with. I remember that the first speech made by Gambetta in the Chamber was in defence of two soldiers of the line who had been punished for having taken part in a public meeting where the assassination of the Emperor was under discussion. I rather think that he would have been glad to recall and destroy that speech, when at Tours he approved of the just severity of D'Aurelles, who had dozens of bad soldiers shot every morning by way of example.

What lessons—the greater part of them, alas! lost—did that cursed war teach! What instructive sights! What retorts uttered by the reality of events against human sophistry! And was it not extraordinary to see those very men who had protested against the general armament of the nation, who had cried out that France was being turned into a barrack, was it not extraordinary to see them compelled to transform their country into a camp with their own hands, and later on to vote compulsory military service?

CHAPTER III

ACROSS PARIS

At the Louvre.—The Green Room.—General Schmitz's Office.—Inventors.—Paris in a Fever.—The False Despatches.—At the Bourse.—Girardin's Bet.—German Spies.—An Old Woman who is a Man.—The Enrolment.—Patriotic Enthusiasm.—The Irregular *Corps*.—The Free Ambulances.—The Firemen.—M. Thiers Agitates.—Negra and Metternich.—Review of the *Mobiles*.—The *Francs-Tireurs*.—The Depopulation of the Suburbs.—Trochu an Orator.—Moral Force.—In the Chamber.—Paris Asleep.

I TOOK good care not to forget the kind promises of General Schmitz, and scarcely had the new Governor of Paris arrived, preceding, as he said in his proclamation, the Emperor—who, by the way, was destined never to see Paris again—than I betook myself to the Louvre, where he had taken up his quarters, with his Chief of the Staff. I came out again armed with my appointment as Orderly Officer attached to the Headquarter Staff of the Governor. I took up my duties at once.

General Trochu had installed himself in the premises now occupied in the Louvre by the Ministry of Finance. Access to it is gained by the Rue de Rivoli. After having passed through the spacious inner courtyard, there is a small flight of steps to be ascended, and then you find yourself in the offices of the Headquarter Staff. There is no exit by the Place du Carrousel. But as provision had to be made for every eventuality, as a good general ought always to have his line of retreat secure, as we were favoured with all sorts of sinister predictions, and as we had been informed that one fine day we should leave the place not by the doors, the windows looking into the interior of the Carrousel, and formerly condemned, were re-opened.

To reach the Governor's office, it was necessary to pass first of all, through a spacious ante-room, and then through the room allotted to the orderly officers, called the green room, on account of the colour of its hangings and furniture. The office occupied by General Schmitz opened out of this green room. The Chief of the Staff passed his life seated, almost night and day, behind a desk laden with reports and despatches, issuing all sorts of orders in every direction, providing against every eventuality, drawing up his instructions with that just appreciation, clearness and precision of expression, which never failed him for one single day throughout the siege, which then called forth the admiration of his subordinates, and which the officers of his *Corps d'Armée* still appreciate.

Although there were very many of them, the duties of the Orderly Officers of the Governor were most fatiguing. Two were always on duty in the green room, whose special mission it was to make a preliminary weeding-out from among the innumerable people who requested speech of General Trochu ; who wanted to submit to him their grievances, their observations, their criticisms, their plans, and their inventions. The least serious of these were shown the door, and the remainder shown in to the Chief of the Staff, who, in his turn, served as the last screen between the public and the Governor.

I shall not surprise anybody when I say that the most diverse, the most unexpected, and sometimes the most ridiculous propositions were submitted to us day by day. I myself received and listened to more than one hundred and fifty inventions of systems, as infallible as they were different, for steering balloons, of bombs, of explosives warranted to result in suffocation, or to induce sneezing; inventions of extraordinary cuirasses, fantastic torpedoes, and Greek fire by the hundreds. I do not count those devoted spirits who volunteered to kill the King of Prussia or M. de Bismarck, or the real madmen, or the poor mothers who came in search of news of their sons, or the generous citizens who brought presents in their hands, or the talkers, pure and simple, who came to us to while away their own time and waste ours. All these colloquies were interrupted by deputations to be received and answered, and we thought ourselves fortunate if we had not to leave everything else and rush to one of the windows looking on the Carrousel, and harangue the crowd. We lived in this Babel as in a dream for more than five months, and our only moments of distraction and recreation when on duty were when we rode behind the Governor. Subsequently, when the investment was complete, I had to talk more frequently and at closer quarters with the Prussians, in my capacity as interpreter and envoy, than with my fellow-citizens.

During the early days I took advantage of the few leisure moments left me by my duty, to make some excursions in Paris on my own account, strolling about, noting, observing, reading the newspapers, and entering into conversation with the passers-by.

Paris had the appearance of preparing for a revolution rather than a regular defence. It was a prey to the most extraordinary and intense excitement, which manifested itself in all sorts of different forms; in the Chamber, by perpetual questions addressed to Ministers, by incessant demands for the armament of the *Garde Nationale,* and by continual attacks on the unfortunate dynasty; in the centres, the squares, and on the Bourse by mobs who collected without rhyme or reason, by pushings here and there, by shouting and disputes. In the day-time the Bourse was black with heads. The Rentes executed fantastic leaps and bounds, the speculators cried out one against the other, and the public cried out against the speculators. In the evening, the boulevards glittered with lights and the *cafés* were filled to overflowing. From time to time somebody, nobody knew who, was cheered, or some absolutely unknown person was hooted, much to his own astonishment. The troops were cheered, and so were the *francs-tireurs* and the ambulance corps. Marie Sass, who was compelled to sing the *Marseillaise,* received an ovation, together with Capoul, who had to appear with her. At the opera the same kind of thing went on; now it was Marie Sass, as the Goddess of Liberty, and now Dévoyod, as a Zouave, who sang the patriotic song.

There was a general rush for the newspapers, which published edition after edition, and whose correspondents, spread abroad hap-hazard in the midst of the armies, recounted their impressions and their adventures.

And in the midst of these excited crowds, came one despatch after another, at first obscure and letting our disasters leak out drop by drop; and then suddenly much clearer, mentioning some small success, enormous losses on the part of the Germans, their cruelties and their exactions.

At one moment there would be universal rejoicing, and a
rush to the windows to hang out flags and light lamps. Half-
an-hour later another despatch would arrive. Away went
the flags, and out went the lamps. In consequence of these
perpetual moral somersaults, there reigned in the midst of
the population, impressionable as a woman, a fever, a
nervous affection, a fearful intellectual disorder.—The
Prussians were not advancing. The people breathed again.
Nancy had been captured by four Uhlans. They recoiled
and were indignant—The White Cuirassiers had been exter-
minated at Borny, and not one of them survived. Alas!
there were far too many left—thirty thousand Prussians
had been engulfed in the quarries of Jaumont, where they
had been driven by Canrobert—everybody's head was in the
air. Nobody had ever heard of these quarries. On investi-
gation it was ascertained that they did not exist. Prince
Albert of Prussia was killed, and his coffin covered with
black velvet with silver stripes was crossing the Prussian
lines—another fable. Finally, on the eve of the very day
when they had to publish the news of the catastrophe of
Sedan, the Paris papers complacently announced that the
King of Prussia had gone mad. How was it possible to
avoid becoming absolutely epileptic under such circumstances? The wonder was that there were a few people who
retained their senses during those terrible days.

And not only among the lower orders was this unpleasant
effervescence manifest—the higher and educated classes
were not exempt from the nervous malady. One heard
serious, clear-headed, rich, intelligent men declaring that our
defeats on the Rhine were more or less providential, because
they had the effect of drawing on the Prussian armies, who
would find their sepulchre in France. And to the despatches
announcing eighty thousand Germans as being here, a

C

hundred and fifty thousand there, and two hundred thousand farther on, they would reply with imperturbable calmness, 'So much the better, so much the better! The more that come in, the fewer will get out.' Girardin bet a Prussian Colonel, Von Holstein, that the Prussians would not enter Paris. And the colonel wrote him a letter which seemed to sound the knell of the final defeat.

'We shall conquer,' said the Prussian, '1st, because we have the moral support of Europe; 2nd, because of the superiority of our artillery; 3rd, because we desire the union of Germany (the idea of annexation comes from your Emperor, who has as imitators, MM. Cavour and Bismarck); 4th, because our soldiers are well commanded, and we have among us no division of interest or of principle, and no insubordination like that of your *Mobiles*, whom we fear less than a band of students; each of our soldiers has as much instruction as one of your officers; 5th, because we are fighting for civilisation—that is to say, for the emancipation of mankind by means of instruction.'

In common justice to the Germans, it must be admitted that from the very outset they both knew what they wanted and where they were going. While Berlin, in strong contrast to Paris, wrapped itself up in austere calmness—in the anxious sternness of a mother whose sons are risking their lives on the field of battle—the press as well as the officers not only declared aloud that Germany would not lay down her arms until she had conquered Alsace and Lorraine, but they also gave proof of a strange perspicacity in regard to our situation, both moral and material, affirming that we were not ready; that we were deficient of everything; and that our political dissensions would be almost as profitable to the German army as victories.

There was an instinctive feeling that, of the two sovereigns who hurled battalion after battalion into the fray, the one who knew France best was, perhaps, not the Emperor of the French. We felt surrounded, watched denounced, and in a word, spied.

A spirit of exasperation against German spies consequently awoke in the minds of the Parisians with the rapidity of a train of powder. Were there any German spies? Unquestionably. Prussia had in her pay in Paris and throughout France people who were spies by profession, and 'it will not be news to anybody to recall the fact that one of them, captured and convicted, met his death firmly at the hands of a firing party, crying out with his latest breath, ' For my country.'

In addition to this, the German army abounded in unconscious spies, or rather, in officers and soldiers who knew our country better than we ourselves did, who had lived in it and studied it, and who, recalled to Germany by the exigencies of their military service, naturally turned their acquired knowledge to account. There are, perhaps, not three hundred people in all France who could traverse Berlin without losing their way. I assert 'as a fact that there were in the German army two hundred thousand men, who, by reason of their either having stayed or lived there, knew Paris as well as we did. A Frenchman travels little, and when he does travel he is so hampered by his ignorance of foreign languages that his observation is of the most limited extent. The German willingly changes his residence, and when he does change it, he does so for the purpose of gaining knowledge as much as for a livelihood. In Germany everybody, starting from a certain social level, looks upon intercourse with a Frenchman as a piece of good fortune. They speak to, and question him, never in German, but invariably in French. How do you say this? He serves as an unconscious and gratuitous private tutor. In France, to be obliged to talk to a German who cannot speak our language properly is looked upon as a bore. To sum the matter up, all the German Generals, and all the Staff Officers, spoke French, while in our Head-quarter staff there were not, perhaps, ten officers at the outside who could make themselves intelligible to a German. There is one excuse for this ignorance, I admit. The French language being recognised as the language of diplomacy, spoken by all those who aspire to govern their country, and considered as the necessary complement of an aristocratic education, Frenchmen had for a long time, and up to a certain point, an excuse for neglecting the acquirement of the language of the people who strained every nerve to learn French. But the disappearance of our military and even intellectual supremacy ought to have compelled us to gain a knowledge of foreign languages. We are only now beginning to understand that. In 1870 we still ignored it.

Every man who did not speak French with purity was, therefore, suspected, the masses being, besides, incapable of distinguishing between the various foreign languages spoken in their midst. Englishmen, like my faithful Joseph, Americans, Swedes, Spaniards, and Alsatians were arrested alike. A similar fate befell all those people who, either in their dress or their manner, betrayed anything unusual. Stammerers were arrested because they wanted to speak too quickly; dumb people because they did not speak, and the deaf because they did not seem to under-stand what was said to them. The sewer-men who emerged from the sewers were arrested because they spoke Piedmontese.

The German spies were likewise so numerous that, so to

speak, in drawing a bow at a venture, the arrow occasionally went straight to the proper mark. For instance, two spies were captured disguised as Sisters of Charity ; another, disguised as a beggar, was engaged in sketching the fortifications in his hat, but was careful to hold out his hand with a piteous air when anybody passed by. Another, in the uniform of a naval lieutenant, and armed with a regular permit from the Minister of War, made a very minute inspection of Mont-Valérien. When the telegram ordering his arrest came to hand, he had disappeared. But side by side with these well-merited arrests, what deplorable mistakes were made ! On one occasion an unfortunate priest had a narrow escape of being cut to pieces because, after having been appointed a military chaplain, he, accidentally and through awkwardness, fired off his revolver in a *fiacre* ; on another, a seller of lemonade, whose name had a German ring about it, very nearly had his shop sacked ; on a third, an inoffensive passer-by was pointed out by a facetious ragamuffin, and beaten unmercifully.

How many times at the Head-quarter staff did we have presented to us for immediate execution poor devils who had no idea why they were being maltreated, stray provincials, or strangers who had lost the way to their hotel ! One curious and unexplained incident, the remembrance of which haunted me like a riddle for a long time, happened under our very eyes in the staff offices.

It took place at the end of August; General Trochu had just received a deputation of the Garde Nationale, who had petitioned to be armed, and had been dismissed highly pleased with their reception, when a hideous uproar was heard beneath our windows. We opened them and saw a furious crowd surrounding a poor old woman who was carrying a basket and was already almost stunned. She

was standing on the edge of the pavement, watching the
drill of a battalion of the Garde Nationale, when a man
cried out, 'Here is a Prussian spy!' In a moment the unfortunate creature was cuffed with all their might by the
surrounding crowd. She would have been knocked to
pieces had not one of us called out of the window, 'Bring
your spy here: we will question her.' A few seconds later
she was bundled like a parcel into our famous green room,
and began to cry and protest her innocence. Suddenly she
uttered a terrible shriek; one of her persecutors had put
his hands under her petticoats, and called out triumphantly,
'Did not I tell you it was a man?' And it was a man in
very truth. We handed him over to the tender mercies of
M. Pollet, an intelligent assistant whom the Prefect of
Police had placed at our disposal, and who acted with us as
a sort of civil provost. The old creature gave his address,
and his neighbours were summoned; all of them, who, by-
the-way, called him *la mère une telle,* declared that he was
a good old woman, well known for more than forty years
in their neighbourhood, where she passed as a person of
independent, though small means. The man in woman's
garb was released. Why this citizen had conceived and
persistently carried out the idea of living under a borrowed
sex nobody could induce him to say. I resolved to clear up
this mystery one day when I could find time; but when I
asked M. Pollet for his address, he informed me that the
poor man only survived the scene I have just related two
days, and that he had died of the shock. I suspect the
buffeting he had received had no little to do with his sad
end.

There was one spectacle well calculated to console us for
all the wretchedness of which we were eye-witnesses, and
for all the scenes that passed before us, whether ridiculous

like the one I have just described, or bloody, like the criminal attack on the barracks of the firemen of La Villette—I mean the sight presented by the enlistment depôts. The most inoffensive citizens enrolled themselves with a single-mindedness and courage as extraordinary as they were sincere. Good-will and a desire to sacrifice themselves were evident in their bearing and conversation· It was really touching. I remember the Marquis Lafond de Candaval presenting himself and being refused; he was eighty-seven years of age and wanted to enlist as a private soldier in the line so that he might join his son in the army on the Rhine.*

The second half of August also witnessed the formation and equipment of many free corps. I have no hesitation in saying in all sincerity that I do not like these free corps, and I do not understand their *rôle* in time of war. As a rule— there were honourable exceptions and if I do not quote them it is simply because I might omit mention of some and consequently seem to include them in the category of the condemned—as a rule, the individual who raises a free corps is also an irregular in civil life, incapable of accommodating himself to the stern exigencies of military discipline, an ambitious fellow who wants to play the general, when he does not happen to be a light-fingered gentleman desirous of manipulating the contents of a well furnished chest. He naturally surrounds himself with others as irregular as himself; equips them, accoutres them more or less elegantly, and sallies forth with them in search of adventure, delighted to live a life as free as that of a New World trapper in the midst of an old and downcast nation, requisitioning right

* Captain Dancourt, Mayor of Montargis, aged seventy-eight, was more successful and actually joined the army. A man named Simeon Guillot, who was born in 1798 and had the St Helena medal, enlisted in the twenty-ninth regiment of the line.

and left, more exacting than the conquering foe, and more dangerous to the army of his own country than to the enemy. These *terra firma* corsairs fill me with unconquerable repugnance. When a man is really and seriously desirous of being useful to his country, of serving it and giving up his life to it, he does not indulge in such vagaries. He goes quietly to his district depôt and enlists in the active army, he becomes a soldier, a real soldier, and not a fancy or an amateur one. Those people must have been absolutely mad who dreamt that any damage would be inflicted on the Prussian masses by the free corps, *franc-tireurs*, and scouts of whom the enemy did not take the slightest notice, and who were only harmful to the French peasantry. It is one of two things—either the *franc-tireurs* are capable of becoming good soldiers, in which case they weaken the active army by their absence, or they are incapable of becoming so, in which case they would be doing far better by staying at home instead of encumbering the roads and exhausting the precious resources of the country. At the risk of appearing ferocious, brutal if you will, I declare—and all real soldiers whom I have met agree with me—that if I had been a general and had penetrated into Prussia, I would have done precisely what the Prussians did and would have shot every irregular who fell into my clutches. There is no other way of making war properly, that is to say, humanely; as humanely, I mean, as the momentary excitement of warfare will admit, and in accordance with the rights of men, the ordinary rules of humanity.

I might say almost as much in regard to voluntary ambulances, though the inconvenience caused by them is not nearly so considerable. But if you want to organise an ambulance, contribute your intended expenditure to the military chest, and enlist either as an army doctor, or hospital attendant, or in the administrative *corps*, as the case may be. You will have done your duty simply and strictly; it will then be the duty of the Government to utilize your contribution and your goodwill practically and methodically, as everything ought to be done in war. Otherwise, the responsible authorities, driven to distraction by all these military and benevolent experiments, lose their heads and do not know on whom to rely, and thus it is that disasters happen. If your Government is incapable and your administration defective, so much the worse for you, citizens, who placed the Government in power and made the mal-administration possible. But from the moment that the word 'war' is pronounced, you have no right as private individuals to substitute your individual action for public action; and if you persist in doing so, inevitable catastrophes will punish you, however pure and straight-forward your intentions may be.

In Germany, in time of peace, the Government knows, catalogues, and arranges all the efforts and sacrifices which private individuals are willing to make in time of war. And in such towns as are capable of sustaining a siege there is a conscription of beds, of doctors, of nurses male and female, just as their is a conscription of horses which must leave the coach or the plough to drag guns into action, or must quit the broughams and victorias of the wealthy to help to mount the cavalry.

The first condition of war is order, and whatever is not foreseen is disorder. The day these unpalatable truths are understood by every Frenchman, the country will be in a position, whenever she pleases, to become once more the military master of the world. While this book was being printed, I went more than once to the office to see to the correction of my proofs, and seated myself by the side of the

compositors who were setting up the type: I watched
their nimble fingers taking hold, almost as quickly as the
thought which influenced them, of the letters in the little
cases containing them, placing them one beside another in
the stick, and reproducing by these leaden signs the words
written in the copy by my pen.   To render their work possible, every letter must be in its compartment, just where it
ought to be, and if their trays were upset and the letters became mixed up, it would be impossible for them to compose·
'What would you do,' I asked one of them one day, 'if
somebody were to jumble up your letters?' "When, sir,"
he replied, "the letters are disarranged, or mixed, they are
said to have 'fallen into pie.' They are then sent to be melted
down again.   It is useless to try to sort them, it would be
time and trouble thrown away."   Well then, in the days
which I have just been describing, France, to borrow the
printer's peculiar and picturesque expression, had 'fallen
into pie.'   All the letters, that is to say all the citizens, had
become mixed up.   It was impossible to compose anything,
to do anything with them.   The whole unfortunate nation
required melting down.   Has it been recast? Alas!

Another idea, more ingenious than practical, and more
artistic than useful, was the summoning of all the firemen
to Paris.   The author of this idea was the amiable gentleman called Janvier de la Motte, the most popular of all the
prefects of the Empire, the man who was jocularly
christened the 'father of the firemen,' and who died not
long ago, after a brilliant administrative one, followed by
an equally brilliant parliamentary one, mourned by all,
even by his political opponents. At his summons the firemen
came from all parts of France.   Firemen from the towns,
neat and well set up, and firemen from the villages, dressed
like those we see at a masked ball, with wonderful

helmets most probably borrowed from the models of David, the painter of the Greek and Romans. Some of these fine fellows, who had left home without knowing why, on arriving in Paris asked, 'Where is the fire?' They were quartered in the *lycées*. A certain amount of money was spent in feeding and paying them, and then they dispersed, and nobody ever heard any more of them. As I have mentioned money, I may as well allude here, by way of parenthesis, to the success of the loan of 750 millions, and that of the patriotic subscription of the French press, initiated by the *Gaulois*, which in a few days reached a total of 1,500,000 francs.

Meanwhile, Paris was beginning to understand that it would have to sustain a siege, the duration of which nobody ventured even to guess. The most sanguine of the optimists could not have imagined that the capital would hold out as long as it did. The most despondent of the pessimists could not have supposed that its long resistance would have turned out so useless. In spite of the hope in Bazaine, upon whom everybody at that moment, looked as a hero and a great general, but of whom scarcely any mention was made after Gravelotte, in spite of the confidence still inspired by MacMahon even after Reichshoffen, it was necessary to victual the city in view of a possible investment, offers flowed in to the staff, and I had frequently to conduct corn-merchants and cattle-dealers, who had addressed themselves to the Governor, into the presence of Clement Duvernois, the Minister of Commerce, entrusted with the provision of supplies. The genius displayed by Clement Duvernois in carrying out this vast and complicated enterprise is now a matter of history. By a very strange coincidence, on each of the three occasions when I went to see him I met M. Thiers there. M. Thiers had not then acquired the popularity bestowed upon him by our defeats, foreseen by him; by his diplomatic tour across Europe; and above all, by the fact that among all the members of the Government of the National Defence, he seemed, with his past Cabinet experience, the sole surviving waif of the regular *régimes*. He was as restless as a squirrel in a cage. Silent in the chamber, he made up for it by his constant attendance in the offices of ministers, where he lavished his counsel and advice, frequenting the Embassies into which he had the *entrée*, or where he was listened to, questioning diplomatists, sounding the intentions of other Governments, active and full of business. He was ubiquitous, and one seemed to see nothing but him.   Two other personages, foreigners both of them, also passed their existence in running to and fro.   I mean MM. de Metternich and Nigra, the representatives respectively of Austria and Italy in Paris. I shall have something to say about the part they played when I come to the subject of what I saw of the 4th of September.   However, all these diplomatic comings and goings produced but little result.   It was already known that the Queen of England had written to the Empress to say that she could not interfere in the Franco-Prussian conflict.   No reliance could be placed upon Austria.   As for Italy, there was a report one day that a hundred thousand of her troops would cross the Alps and come to our assistance.   We believed it for the moment.   But Italy gave no thought to those who had made her.   She was arming for the conquest of Rome.

We were left to our own resources, and by degrees the soldiers of the regular army, still quartered in Paris, were despatched to the North.   The authorities dared not entrust these duties to the *Mobiles*, who were still encamped at St Maur.   On the 25th of August, the General reviewed these young troops amid the greatest enthusiasm. For two hours battalion after battalion marched past him to the cry of ' *Vive Trochu* !' He returned their salute with a smile. It seemed to me, nevertheless, that his amiability was forced, and that he would have preferred a silent march past. The shouting savoured of riot.

As we came back we met, almost at the gate of the Louvre, a stretcher on which an old general was being carried, as pale as death.

' Go,' said the Governor to me, ' and ascertain his name and where he was wounded.'

I put spurs to my horse, reached the litter, put my hand to my kepi, and made the desired inquiry. The poor General confessed in faltering tones, and with much embarrassment, that he had fallen from his horse. Trochu shrugged his shoulders and passed on.

The possibility of a siege, and the preparations for provisioning the city had brought about an extraordinary amount of animation. A double current ran through Paris, one going out, and the other coming in. The Governor had signed an order for the expulsion of all people who were without means of subsistence or were dangerous to public security ; it was a dead letter. A certain number of able-bodied people, perfectly capable of manning the ramparts and even of taking part in future sorties, took their departure whithersoever they pleased, to Italy, Spain, Belgium, or England, but the mass of what might be called useless mouths, old men, women, and children, having neither resources nor homes in the country, were perforce obliged to remain in Paris. A decisive step should have been taken at this particular juncture, and the whole of this description of inhabitants should have been transported to the South. As it was, nobody even thought of such a step.

As for the vagabonds and dangerous classes, the 31st of October proved that they had preferred to remain in Paris, where they found an admirable hiding-place amid the general disorder. By way of compensation, the environs were completely depopulated. Crops were hastily gathered in and loaded on waggons, and through every gate thronged interminable strings of vehicles laden with provisions, while barges on the Seine, and trains on the various railways brought coal, wine, grain, and cattle. The peasants and their families came with their crops. It is impossible to do justice in words to the spectacle afforded by the thousands of vehicles conveying goods and chattels, women and children, mixed up with cooking utensils, sacks of corn or potatoes, and with a cow and calf in tow. There were cupboards full of rabbits, and beds converted into hen coops. The motley procession marched to the accompaniment of oxen lowing, goats and lambs bleating, ducks quacking, cocks crowing, hens clucking, children crying, and men swearing. The small tradesmen who had built little boxes, which they called villas, by the thousand in the environs of Paris, were equally anxious to find safe house-room for their stocks of provisions and their summer furniture. But transport was lacking. A furniture van drawn by two horses cost 500 francs a day. I saw some instances of people who had been clever enough to get hold, how I know not, of mourning coaches and were cheerfully seated in hearses surrounded by their household gods.

It is extraordinary, but it is a fact, that at this very time, even before Sedan, the Germans reckoned upon the investment of Paris, and I recollect being told that M. Eugene Clicquot had received a letter requesting him to have his castle at Courcelles ready for the reception of the Prince Royal of Saxony. The mere name of Clicquot was enough to recall joyous memories in Prussia. In 1815 the allies who had taken up their quarters in the house of the great manufacturer of champagne emptied a vast number of bottles, for which they entirely forgot to pay. But when they reached home again they had a kindly recollection of the French nectar, and sent large orders to the firm of Clicquot. Orders poured in from every quarter where the invading regiments were stationed, that is to say, from every corner of Europe, and the story goes that this was the foundation of the large fortune made by the famous widow.

As Paris was not precisely adapted for the accommodation of much cattle, the beasts were herded in the Bois de Boulogne, the Bois de Vincennes, and the public squares, and the grass in the latter did not last very long. As the beasts came in the Governor ordered the expulsion of all foreigners—mouths evidently useless. This step, on the eve of a possible siege, was both legitimate and prudent. It was approved and carried out.

I find that up to this point I have scarcely mentioned the Chamber of Deputies, whose sittings nevertheless were continual and stormy, nor have I said a word about the Empress. I confess that as my duties did not lead me in the direction of the Chamber, neither did my tastes incline me that way during my rare hours of idleness. I have never been able to comprehend the use of a Chamber under such circumstances, and it seems to me that when the cannon speaks, members of parliament would do well to be silent. In addition to this, the obligation laid upon ministers to spend hour after hour under the fire of attacks from the Opposition benches, wearied them, made them lose their self-possession, and hindered them from working. As for the Empress Regent, I will in due course explain how she bore herself towards the Governor imposed on the

Emperor by the will of the people, and appointed by him with the secret and somewhat intelligible idea of profiting by his momentary popularity. It will be readily understood that between the Louvre, where General Trochu had taken up his quarters, and the Tuileries, there was a gulf seldom crossed by the General; and when he did cross it, it was much against the grain—from a sense of duty alone, and without the slightest inclination on his part.

In Paris the *rôle* of idol is subject to many vicissitudes, and already, towards the end of August, some timid carpings intervened amid the general chorus of eulogy and adulation which had greeted the Governor. Devoted to my chief, and proud of being attached to him, of being in attendance on him, and of riding behind him, I was indignant enough, and I fear all the more indignant because I could have wished that the malcontents had been less in the right. They reproached him with talking and writing too much. They began to call him 'Monsieur Trochu,' and even 'Monsieur Trop lu.'

It is quite certain that in this world of ours no man is perfect, and that the material of great qualities is composed of a mass of small defects, which holds the same position in regard to those qualities that the wrong side of the material does to the right. The General was a studious man. He wrote well, and was fond of writing. He spoke well, although, in my humble opinion, his sentences were always too long, and he was fond of speaking. Like all scholars, he had a weakness for explanation, and he thought proper, through the medium of a letter to a newspaper, to explain his proclamation to the Parisians. It was a mistake, and all the more stupid because the explanation was not expected. In it the Governor declared himself a warm partisan of moral force. He wished to govern by moral force. It is quite true that power derived from brute force, and sustained solely by it, is destined to rapid decay and inevitable defeat. It is quite true that the greatest of all forces is moral force. But, not only in France, but everywhere else, one is accustomed to seek for these beautiful ideas in the works of a philosopher—not in the proclamation of a General. And although we may not feel leniently disposed towards a wearer of the sword who proclaims himself an apostle of the sword, we cannot help being considerably astonished when we hear him sing the praises of persuasion and moral force. It seems to me that the gap between the trooper and the preacher is quite wide enough for a man of mind and talent—such as General Trochu was—to find ample room to move about as he pleases. Why did he always betray a tendency towards his office in preference to the saddle ? It surprised some and rendered others uneasy. Both the astonished and the uneasy, however, only formed an almost imperceptible minority, and if they were received with favour at the Tuileries, they had, on the other hand, to endure many a rebuff at the hands of the Comte de Palikao. This Minister supported the Governor most loyally, and to the early grumblers he replied curtly—

'He talks, it is true, but he acts.'

Towards the end of August, a month so full of events and feverish excitement, on the 29th, the first Council of War sat in judgment on the two principal authors of the abominable attack made, on the 15th, against the barracks of the Firemen of La Villette. A band of maniacs, whom public opinion persisted in calling accomplices, conscious or not, of Prussia, attacked the guard-room of the Firemen, demanding the surrender of all the rifles in the barracks, in order to march to the *Corps Législatif*, and proclaim the Republic.

D

The Firemen resisted. The rioters opened fire with their revolvers. A Fireman was killed. A civilian was wounded and then kicked to death. A little girl was killed by a random shot. Eudes and Brideau, the leaders of the prepossessing band, were condemned to death. They were to have been executed on the morning of the 5th of September. The Revolution of the 4th of September saved their lives.

This attempt, however, did not prevent MM. Ferry and Favre from urging the Chamber to agree to a general arming of the citizens, with an amount of persistence and obstinacy which, with them, was destined to survive the siege, and which gave us the Commune.

And now I have reached the fatal date—the 4th of September.

All through Saturday, and since the previous evening, reports had been flying about that MacMahon had suffered a fresh defeat. Messages had been received from Belgium to the effect that the battle had been furious, since from all the frontier towns telegrams came to hand announcing a terrific cannonade; and for forty-eight hours the destinies of France had been submitted to the wager of battle.

At half-past three on Sunday morning, General Palikao ascended the tribune in his Chamber, and, without giving any precise details, announced that a great battle had been fought between Sedan and Mézières, and that fortune had varied; that Bazaine, who had sallied out from Metz to effect a junction with MacMahon, had been compelled to retire after eight hours' fighting; that the movement had failed, and that the situation was grave.

Jules Favre at once ascended the tribune, and in ambiguous terms proposed that a sort of military dictatorship should be conferred upon General Trochu. General de

Palikao replied that he had too much confidence in the Governor to believe that he would, in violation of his oath, accept any such position.

The deputies remained in their committee rooms. The *grille* was closed. In the evening Gambetta harangued the crowds collected on the quays, implored the citizens to wait, and announced that there would be an evening sitting. Afterwards the *Sergents de Ville* and the *Gardes de Paris* cleared the immediate neighbourhood of the Palais-Bourbon.

At five o'clock the Empress received the succinct telegraphic account of the catastrophe of Sedan. She retired to her room alone to weep.

At 1.20 a.m. General de Palikao reascended the tribune. He announced that the semi-official news had become official, and, in a few curt words, which fell like so many blows from a sledge-hammer on the heads of the motionless and solemnly silent deputies, he recounted the disaster— MacMahon wounded, the capitulation, the Emperor a prisoner.

Then he asked the Chamber, under the exceptional circumstances, to adjourn the sitting until the following day, Sunday, at noon.

Jules Favre then rose, and laid on the table the motion for the deposition of the Imperial dynasty, and, accepting the adjournment proposed by the Minister, undertook to explain on the morrow his reasons for his motion.

This sitting, at which I was present, lasted ten minutes.

At the end of the Pont de la Concorde, in the Square, as I was going into the Louvre to report what I had seen to the Governor, I saw the white head of M. Thiers at the window of his carriage, which was surrounded by the crowd. He was telling them of Sedan, and they cheered him.

That night Paris slept under a lovely sky, and beyond her, in the background, behind the towers of Notre-Dame, behind the spire of Sainte-Chapelle, behind the turrets of the Palais de Justice, in the star-lit azure the moon glided calmly, and her shapeless mask seemed to me to be looking down, at one and the same time, on the capital, slumbering in ignorance of the blow with which it had been struck, and beyond, in the North, on our poor soldiers, bivouacked, without food, shoes, or arms, between the lances of the Uhlans.

As I crossed the Carrousel I glanced at the Tuileries. Above the illuminated vestibule, above the guard whose bayonets glittered in the light, a ray shining from a window marked the spot where were the private apartments of the Empress. And, sad at heart, I thought of that poor woman who, far from her captive husband, far from her isolated son, was weeping and keeping watch during her last night of royalty.

To-morrow, almost immediately, I said to myself, who knows! that woman, that Empress, will too be abandoned, perhaps, as she has been surrounded by courtiers, will be as wretched as she has been happy, as forgotten as she has been fawned upon. She may, perhaps, be reduced to such an excess of solitude and abandonment that she will have to seek the support of the arm of some brave man, the first at hand, some poor insignificant *moblot* like myself.

And I am not quite sure that I did not dream that night that I was saving the Empress.

We shall see by-and-by that the part I played in regard to her was far less imposing and less romantic.

CHAPTER IV

THE FOURTH OF SEPTEMBER

Paris awakes.—The Chamber Invaded.—The Deposition.—A Walk on the Quays.
—Jules Favre and the Crowd.—Apotheosis.—Universal Delirium.—And the
Empress?—Marie-Antoinette and Marie-Thérèsa.—Nigra and Metternich
again.—At the Tuileries.—The Empress flown.—At the Louvre.—At the
Hôtel de Ville.—The First Speech.—General and Lawyers.—Rochefort and
Trochu.—M. Thiers.

I WAS for duty on Sunday, the 4th of September. That
is to say, I was detailed on the previous evening to accompany the General on horseback in case he should have to go
out. Consequently, when I returned from the Chamber at
night and learnt that the General was in bed, instead of
going to my quarters, I lay down to sleep on a couch in the
green room.

At dawn the newspaper boys in the Rue de Rivoli
began to rouse the still slumbering city with the alarming
words, 'Napoleon III a prisoner!' The morning papers
explained and commented on the overnight sitting in the
Chamber, and gave tolerably accurate accounts, based on
those in the Belgian prints, of the catastrophe of Sedan,

already three days old.   At eight o'clock the immense
human hive was in an uproar.   From all sides a tide began
to run towards the centre of Paris, bearing onwards with it
the inhabitants of the outlying districts.

Under our windows the Rue de Rivoli and the Place du
Carrousel were black with people.   It was a lovely day,
and everybody knows that all Paris is out of doors on
Sunday.   Some strolled quietly under the arcades, or along
the footpaths; others hurried feverishly towards the
Palais-Bourbon, where they foresaw that there would be
work for them, and others again, massed in the squares or
at the corners of the pavement, waited and watched as they·
drank in the balmy air of a real summer's day.

I had told the General, who, however, had been able to
read for himself the account of the night sitting in the
Journal Official,

'They meet at noon to discuss the motion for the
deposition.'

The steps to be taken for the safety of the *Corps
Législatif* were no business of ours, the necessary orders
having been given directly by the Minister of War.
Nevertheless, it was but natural that the Governor of
Paris should pay attention to what was going on in his
command, and from half-past eleven the detachment on
escort duty was drawn up in the court-yard behind our
horses, which were saddled and bridled.   From time to
time General Trochu opened the door of his room and went
to that occupied by his Chief of the Staff, General Schmitz,
who was immersed in drawing up his orders, writing his
despatches, and annotating his reports, and as he crossed
the green room, where we were waiting, he would say to us,

'Anything new ?'

'Nothing, sir,' was our invariable reply.   Though within

shot of the Palais-Bourbon, we were utterly ignorant of what was going on. Everybody was going that way. Nobody came back ; and none of us had orders to make enquiries.

Towards one o'clock the sitting announced for noon was opened. General de Palikao had laid on the table a motion for the appointment of a Committee of Defence, consisting of nine members, and entrusting to the Minister himself the post of Lieutenant-General of the Committee. M. Thiers and several of his colleagues had drawn up another almost similar, but announcing the convocation of a Constituent Assembly as soon as circumstances should permit. These, with the motion for the deposition laid on the table on the previous night by Jules Favre, made a total of three perfectly unconstitutional and revolutionary motions, for not one of the three made mention of the still existing Government of the Empress-Regent. Urgency was voted for all three motions, and the deputies retired to their committee rooms to discuss them, according to the usual custom.

Nevertheless, by degrees the *Garde Nationale* relieved the Line Regiments on all the posts round the Palais-Bourbon. Regular battalions marched away, and citizen battalions took their place. At the same time, the cordon formed by the *Sergents de Ville* gave way, the points hitherto guarded were abandoned, and, last of all, mixed up, all of a heap with the *Garde Nationale*, came the crowd, who, with shouts of ' *La Déchéance* ' and ' *Vive la République*,' made their way, first of all to the seats, and then to the semi-circle of the Chamber. Gambetta and Jules Favre began to speak. General de Palikao endeavoured to make himself heard. He was driven back, and disappeared in the hubbub. Without any division having been taken on it, the deposition was an accomplished fact. At three o'clock President Schneider, recognising the impossibility of orderly discussion, declared the sitting at an end.

At this very moment General Trochu, impatient, and roused to a pitch of feverish excitement by long hours of waiting, mounted his horse, saying to us, ' Let us go and see what is going on over there.' I was, consequently, riding behind the Governor, when, emerging from the gate of the Louvre, he began to cross the Place du Carrousel. What struck me most forcibly was the circumstance that, in the midst of the crowds who turned round and gathered near us to cheer the General, I saw either hanging from, or clinging to the railings of the Tuileries, a considerable number of those ragged, sinister-looking individuals who emerge, whence no one knows, in times of disturbance, but seem to have vanished when times are quiet, and the national life is regular. They were silently gazing on the Imperial residence, and, looked upon as a whole, this portion of the populace resembled a species of gigantic wild beast crouching in readiness for a spring, and fascinating its prey before taking the fatal leap.

When we reached the quay, after having passed under the arch upon which the bas-relief of Napoleon III as a Roman emperor seemed, too, to be gazing on the *Corps Législatif* we turned to the right along the terrace by the side of the water.

Issuing from the Pont de la Concorde, a noisy crowd was surging along in front of us, howling and unruly, following, or rather pushing onwards a tall man who, with bare head and long, bushy, and dishevelled grey hair, appeared to be struggling in front of them. It was Jules Favre.

As soon as he caught sight of the Governor he came to him, and, the General having pulled up, they in very loud tones, so as to make themselves heard above the din around them, exchanged a few words which reached us very distinctly.

' Where are you going, General ? '

' To the Chamber.'

' It is useless. The Chamber of Deputies no longer exists. It has been invaded by the people. The deposition has been proclaimed, and if you are anxious to preserve order, your place is at the Louvre, at your Head-quarters, whither the deputies for Paris, constituted into a Government of National Defence, are going to seek you.'

' Ah ! ' said the General, and without another remark he turned his horse's head and retraced his steps through the midst of a crowd which increased every moment. As he turned to the left to get into the Carrousel, Jules Favre had resumed his walk, still surrounded by the unruly mob, who, as they made their way along the quays, appeared to wish to escort him to the Hôtel de Ville, whither MM. Gambetta, Crémieux, and de Kératry had already driven, and were haranguing the people who thronged upon them through the public and private rooms.

The Carrousel was crammed with people, and as he rode up the shouts of ' *Vive la République !* ' ' *A bas l'Empire !* ' mingled with those of ' *Vive Trochu !* ' broke out afresh with extraordinary force.

For nearly twenty years Napoleon III had inspired in the French in general, and the Parisians in particular, a feeling of confidence in his energy. He had lived on the reminiscence of his *coup d'état*. And the people instinctively said of him, 'He is no poltroon to escape in a

cab like Papa Philippe. He would blow himself up rather
than give in.' Consequently, even after the weak errors of
the last few years, even after Baudin had been endured, the
funeral obsequies of Victor Noir accepted, the press un-
muzzled and Rochefort tolerated, he was still feared. In
his absence he still had a weighty influence over the sayings
and doings of Paris. The first manifestations of insurrection were timid, and it was easy to see, from the somewhat
undecided manner of those who risked the., that they
were almost terrified and embarrassed by their own
audacity.

But now, when for three days it had been a fact beyond
dispute that the Emperor with the huge moustache was a
prisoner of war, and that he would never return to instil
courage into his shattered soldiers and vigour into his dis-
heartened *Sergents de Ville*, the populace of Paris were as full
of joyful enthusiasm as a band of schoolboys whose usher
has disappeared. Joyful enthusiasm! Yes, these words
are not one whit too strong, although they may seem
almost blasphemous. Joyous! And the Prussian, with all
obstacles swept from his path, had already resumed his
onward march! Joyous! With one of our two armies captured! Joyous! In spite of the fact that never for cen-
turies had we suffered such a military catastrophe.

Some there were who honestly thought that, with
Napoleon out of the way, peace would be concluded at
once. Others, who knew what they were about, did not
think that a shred of their country was too dear a price to
pay for the fall of a *régime* which they detested. At this
moment, at the time I am writing these words, there is a
man, a lawyer, high up in the public service and held
in much honour, who said in my hearing on the steps of the
Palais de Justice, 'The disappearance of the Empire is well

bought with Alsace and Lorraine.' And indeed why should not this individual have said it, when one of his masters not only said it with cynical calmness, but published it to boot?

How many were there of us that day, who, without wishing to grant an amnesty to the Empire, and even being disposed to make an effort to punish it for its faults when once peace should be made— how many of us were of opinion that it would have been wise and patriotic to permit it to continue the war or to make peace, and to leave ourselves free to settle our accounts between ourselves, after the stranger had departed from among us? We were not many, certainly, and we were carried away by the stream of universal delirium.

It was extraordinary. People belonging to the most diverse classes, those whose manners, occupations, and interests would have betokened an absence of familiarity with politics, became fanatics. The women, as usual, made themselves remarkable by their enthusiastic, violent, and hysterical demonstrations. They kissed our horses. They kissed our boots. We might have just performed the most glorious deed of arms, we might have been the saviours of the country, whereas we had only been for a short ride and had exchanged three sentences with an old lawyer.

As I went in I glanced towards the Tuileries. A band of about fifty men in blouses had succeeded, how I know not, in effecting an entrance into the court-yard of the Palace. Others were on their way to join them, some getting over the railings, and others, at a run, breaking through the line of sentries, who dared not use their rifles.

Those who, like myself, witnessed the Revolution of 1848, and the days of riot which succeeded it, could easily foresee that when this, as yet, harmless and simply inquisitive band should be increased by a few thousand men and a few hundred furies, there would be an end of the Tuileries. A regular, or, rather, an irregular, pillage would commence, and the throne of Napoleon III would, as happened to that of Louis Philippe, hasten to its destruction, and by the same road—the window.

What would become of the Empress amid all this confusion ? Would she be able to fly ? Would she be respected ?

At last we got back to Head-quarters, and I betook myself at once to the Chief of the Staff to report the state of affairs. Absorbed in his work, still seated before his desk, sealing and sending off his despatches, General Schmitz had absolutely no idea of what had taken place. I told him all in a few words—the Chamber invaded, the deposition accomplished, General Trochu's ride of no avail, a Government in course of formation at the Hôtel de Ville, and the probable pillage of the Tuileries in the evening, if not at once ; I added that I thought it most important that very energetic measures should be taken to prevent the populace from disgracing and dishonouring the new Government which would succeed the Empire by making it responsible for pillage and robbery, and possibly consequent danger to personal safety.

The General heard all I had to say, nodding his head by way of approval, but with the hesitating manner of one who does not know where to put his hand on the man he wants. I then said that my uniform as a *Mobile* was popular among the crowd, who looked upon the *Mobiles* as the first insulters and the first declared enemies of the Emperor ; that my uniform would probably enable me even to protect the Tuileries and the person of the Empress, provisionally at all events, and until regular steps could be taken for the safety of the unfortunate Sovereign.

I further added a rumour was current among the people in the streets that she was either going, or had gone, and that, should she wish to leave the palace openly and in the daytime, I would offer her my services to escort her and protect her carriage.

I imagined, I confess, that the Empress, who, by the way, was not disliked, and whose misfortunes were already enlisting the sympathies of the people, even in the intoxication of their easy victory, would be desirous of leaving in state. And this idea of mine after all was not so romantic or far-fetched, because by her side there was a Princess, her cousin, the daughter of a royal house, the Princess Clothilde, who refused to lower herself by leaving the capital of France in any manner less fitting than that in which she had entered it. She took her departure in an open landau and in state. When the people saw her driving off in the midst of a revolution, as calm and impassive as if she were on her way to the Bois de Boulogne, they said in their free and easy way, 'She is a good sort, all the same!' And everybody saluted her; some, indeed, laughed, but there was no rudeness in the laugh, which sounded as if it were intended as a mark of familiar and good-natured approval.

It was not to her birth, but to chance and the power of her charms, that Eugénie de Montijo owed her position as Sovereign of France. A marriage without alliances, the war in Italy, the Mexican campaign, and the minister Ollivier, were, before the war of 1870, the four great mistakes of the reign of Napoleon III; and it must be confessed that in these great mistakes the Empress played an almost essential, an almost preponderating part. She benefitted by the first, and advised the other three.   All the world knows by this time that she assisted, at all events equally with Marshal Lebœuf, to drag the fatal declaration of war in 1870 from the hesitating Emperor—from the Emperor who had no confidence, from the Emperor who knew better than anybody else what a formidable enemy he had to meet, and how many men and guns he could put in the field to oppose the Prussian army.

If her influence had ceased at the threshold of the Council Chamber, if she had been contented to be the Empress of charity as she was the Empress of beauty, we should, in all probability, still possess Alsace and Lorraine, and there would be a dozen thousands of millions of francs more in the French exchequer.   In all probability, too, the Prince Imperial would now be sitting on the throne, with a daughter of the Queen of England by his side.

Without any prejudice, and without wishing to plunge into politics, one may be allowed to maintain that, whether from the point of view of wealth at home or alliances abroad, that arrangement would have been worth more to our country than the reign of Monsieur and Madame Grévy.

Apart from this, and as before all things one ought to be just, I am convinced that during the lamentable days I am describing, the Empress would have known how to comport herself as befitted her position.   True to the example of Marie Antoinette, whom during the last year of her reign she chose as her model and her favourite heroine, she would have remained bravely in the Tuileries, and in case of need would have, I am sure, resolutely faced the rising.   And perhaps, pushing imitation to the level of heroism, after having copied Marie Antoinette in her pleasures, she would have imitated her in her courage, her pride, her disdain of suffering and death, and her sublime contempt for her insulters.

Who knows, after all, but that this Marie Antoinette, face to face with the impressionable and changeable populace of Paris, would have become a Marie Thérèse, for whom men died enthusiastically? Well, they died bravely for M. Crémieux, and he was infinitely less seductive.

Providence did not reserve these sublime and difficult parts for the Empress, but chose as the instrument of her will two diplomatists, the Prince de Metternich and Chevalier Nigra. M. Jules Favre, in the work he devoted to the history of the Government of the National Defence, states that when he took possession of the portfolio of Foreign Affairs after the 4th of September, he found no written trace of any alliances that France might have made, and which might have been brought to light and utilised at an opportune moment. M. Jules Favre has no doubt told the truth. But I would remark that, especially among monarchical governments, there are negotiations of exceptional gravity, and bound, if they are to be successful, to remain absolutely secret, which never furnish materials for protocols, and are not deposited in pigeon-holes or exposed to the indiscretion of anybody. If the office of the high chancellor of the German Empire, or even the Palace of Berlin itself, were invaded to-morrow by successful rioters, it is very probable that they would not find a trace of the words spoken or heard between the three Emperors during their interview of a year ago. And yet it would be childish to suppose that these monarchs met for the sole purpose of shooting deer or pheasants, or of reciprocating a change of costume.

I happen to have had opportunities of conversing with people infinitely more initiated than I am with what may be called the inner life of contemporary politics; with people who can go behind the scenes of the great European theatre of comedy and the drama, and be on easy terms with the actors. None of them has as yet seriously contested the point that Austria and Italy had entered into some engagements, contingent perhaps, with the Emperor Napoleon III. Many of them have stated that such was the case. It is exceedingly probable, though not absolutely proved, that Napoleon III had come to an understanding with these two Powers. It was the vital interest of one to profit by the Franco-German war in order to repossess herself of the position, the German supremacy, of which her rival had robbed her four years previously. The other was bound by the memory of benefits conferred and subsequently forgotten, but whose price she could not without embarrassment have refused to pay to her creditor.

A victory on the Rhine, that is to say, a substantial victory followed by the invasion of Germany, and not an insignificant parade like Sarrebruck, would have perhaps detached from Prussia the hesitating allies she dragged behind her, whom her success attached firmly to her standard and subsequently enslaved. Most assuredly would such a victory have made the Austrian and Italian trumpets sound the assembly. This possibility is perhaps the only excuse for the declaration of war, the only possible explanation of what now appears to us to have been an act of purposeless madness. Whatever may have been the mistakes made by Napoleon III, it is impossible to describe him as an utter idiot; that would, indeed, be hard upon the France he governed for twenty years and which believed in him all that time; and hard, too, upon the Europe which was influenced by him for fifteen years, and all that time acknowledged his supremacy. To describe him so would be unjust.

This consideration, even more than certain indiscretions and statements in connection with the subject, permits the belief that Austria and Italy were, at a given time, to intervene in useful fashion, and that the given time was the occasion of our first success.

Instead of success we had catastrophes, and such catastrophes that after Reichshoffen in some minds, after Sedan, in the minds of every competent person, the game was inevitably lost.

Thenceforward the play of the two Powers I have mentioned was very simple and clearly defined. Confronted by victorious Prussia, marching onwards and strengthened by her early victories, it was absolutely prudent, if not absolutely honest, to leave France to her unhappy fate. And as the words or letters had been exchanged with the Emperor alone, the most fortunate thing that could happen to these allies of an hour was the disappearance of the Emperor and the fall of the Imperial Government. The Emperor and his Government once got rid of, nobody was in a position to insist upon the fulfilment of promises the divulging of which—to say nothing of the proof of them—would have placed the Governments of Francis Joseph and Victor Emmanuel face to face with Prussia in the position, if not of avowed enemies, at all events of undignified rivals and disloyal adversaries.

With the Emperor a prisoner at Sedan, with the Emperor refusing to treat with William as sovereign with sovereign, and confining himself to the *rôle* of a defeated and downcast soldier, it was only necessary, in order to accompany the disappearance of the Imperial Government

E

with that of the irksomeness of engagements lightly undertaken, to advise the Empress to fly.

That was the mission voluntarily undertaken by the
Ambassadors of Austria and Italy, and in their successful
accomplishment of it, it may be safely stated that they
rendered a signal service to their respective Governments.

During the halcyon days of the empire these diplomatists had played the lucrative and pleasant part of ambassadors, ever willing and respectfully ecstatic slaves of
the woman even more than of the sovereign. From the
very beginning of our misfortunes they never left the
Tuileries, where they hid their national anxieties under the
guise of an apparent anxiety about the fate of their idol.
The last act of this diplomatic comedy was not difficult of
performance. They persuaded the Empress that the mob
were about to invade the Tuileries, and that she would be
massacred. They made her afraid. They did not even
give her time, as we shall see, to provide herself with the
things necessary for a journey. They pushed her in a state
of terror along the suites of rooms in the Tuileries, and
along the galleries of the Louvre, below which rolled onward the popular wave which bore Jules Favre on its crest
to the Hôtel de Ville. They made her emerge by the
colonnade fronting Saint-German-l'Auxerrois, found a *fiacre*
for her, and confided her to the tender mercies of a large
city in insurrection.

I can quite imagine how they must have rubbed their
hands after it was all over. Napoleon a captive, Eugénie
a fugitive; no longer any regular government, and consequently no longer any obligations in regard to it. No
longer a creditor, and consequently no longer any debts.
It was an admirable manœuvre admirably executed.

I have wandered far from the desk of General Schmitz,

on which I was leaning, while he, sitting back in his arm-chair, and playing with a pencil, listened to my little speech, my projects and my requests. I begged of him to give me a letter to the Empress, to whom I had never had the honour of being presented, and to write to her to let her know that she could dispose absolutely of me, and of my life, should that be necessary in order to save hers ; and to tell her that, at all hazards, our country must be saved the shame and disgrace of one of those great crimes which, unhappily, the history of France has so often had to record.

The General took up a pen, wrote the letter, and gave it to me with an injunction to watch the turn of events, and to issue immediate and stringent orders for the repression of any attempt at pillage.

This is the letter which, at a future period, during the proceedings at Versailles, was mentioned by M. Rouher, when General Trochu was accused, as if of a crime, of having taken no other measures for the safety of the Empress than the despatch of an insignificant Captain of *Mobiles.* Poor General Trochu! From this book only can he know that one of his Orderly Officers solicited and obtained the honour of such a mission. No further attention was paid to the insignificant captain of *Mobiles,* and the famous letter of General Schmitz became a weapon in the hands of those who wished to strike General Trochu.

Later on I shall prove, by means of irrefutable evidence, what the responsibilities of General Trochu in regard to the Empress actually were, and shall give an account of his discharge of them, which was afterwards made the subject of so much misrepresentation. I will content myself now with saying, in passing—1st, That the expressions of General de Palikao at the sitting of the Chamber on the 4th of September, the day in question, prove that the

Minister himself was making the necessary military dispositions for the protection of the Government and the
Chamber; 2nd, That the Governor had on that day no
business to call him into the presence of the Empress, who
disliked him and did not conceal her dislike, and that he
was ignorant of her departure until the newspaper boys
shouted it out, together with the news of the deposition, in
the streets.

Ten minutes after I left General Schmitz, I was at
the Tuileries armed with my letter. I went in by the
gate in the Rue de Rivoli without any attempt being made
to stop me, and without challenge of any kind either from
the bewildered sentries or the piteous-looking and disconcerted gatekeepers.

In the court-yard I found the same citizens whom I
had noticed when I rode behind the General across the
Carrousel, still preserving their attitude of timid curiosity,
and still at some distance from the building itself. I took
no heed of them, but pushed on to the main entrance, the
Pavillon de l'Horloge. There, too, I noticed the same
carelessness and discouragement on the part of the door-
keepers and other attendants. Only on the first floor,
almost at the door of the private apartments of the
Empress, an usher, clad in black, with knee-breeches, a
sword at his side, and a silver chain round his neck, asked
me what I wanted.

I replied that I had a letter to deliver to Her Majesty,
and that it was imperative that it should be delivered at
once.

'Her Majesty has gone away,' said the usher.

'Gone away! Where?'

He did not know. Some maid-servants, whose faces
were bathed in tears, came down the great staircase, on

the landings of which people were hurrying to and fro, some going up and some coming down. The terrified household were hastening along the corridors, looking for the keys to lock up the wardrobes. Doors were banged violently. Complete disorder and universal panic reigned throughout.

I spoke to one or two persons, who, however, did not condescend to pay the slightest attention to me, but went on their respective ways without replying to me. At length I met a maid-servant who was good enough to listen to me, just as I was beginning to be seriously annoyed, and consented to take my letter to Madame Aguado. She sent me word at once that the Empress had gone away, that nobody knew where she had gone, but that she hoped, nevertheless, to contrive that in one way or another my letter should be delivered that same day, and that, should there be any answer, it should be sent to me to the Head-quarters of the Governor.

I confess that I did not believe in her departure, but imagined that my letter, if it had not already reached its destination, was not far from it. I was wrong. The Empress had really left. We know now that the unhappy sovereign, laying aside all her pride, did Mr Evans, her dentist, the honour of asking his assistance and protection. In his carriage she managed to leave Paris and reach Deauville, whence she crossed to England.

To pursue the matter further would have been both out of place and useless. I went downstairs again and at the bottom of the staircase came upon a group of two men and three women, who were in a state of the greatest distress. The women wept like so many Magdalenes, for, to say nothing of their genuine sorrow on account of the departure of their mistress, the uncertainty of their future and the inevitable ' What will become of us ? ' sufficed to set all the fountains of their grief in motion.

'Then it is quite true ? ' I said to one of them. 'The Empress has gone away ? '

' Alas ! yes, sir. Scarcely a quarter-of-an-hour ago, and without even so much as a pocket handkerchief with her.'

And their sobs redoubled. It is a remarkable thing that very frequently, in the midst of the most important events, some trivial incident or other strikes you and becomes, as it were, impressed so indelibly on your brain that it never leaves you. Thus I recollect that at this moment the doors opening on to the Carrousel, and those leading to the private garden, were open, and there was a tremendous draught in the hall. To get out of it, I stepped into the private gardens, on the historical ground where the unfortunate son of Marie Antoinette played at gardening, where the son of the Duchesse de Berry played at soldiers with his little companions, and where the little Prince Imperial rode his velocipede.

Below me, at the entrance to the garden, the mob, which had effected an entrance into the Great Park, after having pulled down the four eagles surmounting the railing, was massed. Mounted on a chair, General Mellinet, governor of the palace, was haranguing them, and gesticulating vehemently. M. de Lesseps by his side was parleying with them. At the head of the invaders, who were orderly enough, I noticed the well-known face of Sardou, who was struggling like a demon. His strongly marked features, like those of an emaciated Cæsar, reminded me of Bonoparte when he entered the Tuileries for the first time, and said to Bourrienne, who was by his side, ' Now we are in here we must take care that we never go out again.' The Bourrienne of Sardou was a fine young fellow, pale and

with long black hair, who, as I afterwards discovered, was
M. Armand Gouzien.

The mass, which undulated behind them as if on the
top of a wave, suddenly shouted 'Ah!' and this was followed by '*Vive la République*,' as every arm was outstretched as if to point to something in the air behind me.
I turned round. The tricolor standard, which floated above
the Pavillon de l'Horloge when the sovereign was in residence in the Palace of the Tuileries, was being hauled down.

'Gone away without even a pocket handkerchief,' so
the weeping chamber-maid had said. That remark inspired
me with the idea of making the necessary arrangements to
send the Empress a supply of clothes and linen, the want
of which is positive suffering to a woman when travelling,
especially in the case of a woman who, like the Empress,
was not precisely accustomed to material worries.

I pictured her to myself as travelling like a pauper,
and though I quite recognised that the Head-quarter Staff
of the Governor was not chosen expressly to pack up
petticoats, I made up my mind, if I could get the necessary
permission, to devote all my leisure moments to this salvage
operation.

A few soldiers, summoned from the guard-room, sufficed
to clear the court-yard, and as I was going away I gave
strict orders that nobody except those belonging to the
household of the Palace should be admitted into the court-
yard or buildings under any pretext whatsoever.

This not excessively energetic act was probably the last
carried out by the soldiers of the *Garde Impériale*, for
very shortly afterwards they were relieved by the *Garde
Nationale*, who furnished the Tuileries guards throughout
the siege.

On my return to the Louvre, I had literally to elbow my

way to the orderly officer's room. Without and within, in every conceivable position, there was a dense, surging and excited crowd, flowing in a compact stream back from the Hôtel de Ville, where M. Gambetta had just proclaimed the Government of the National Defence, composed of MM. E. Arego, Crémieux, Jules Favre, Ferry, Gambetta, Garnier-Pagès, Glais-Bizoin, Pelletan, Picard, Rochefort and Jules Simon. These appointments had not been made in private. The work was publicly done by the entire crowd, and each one, in accordance with revolutionary tradition, shouted out the names of his candidates. Great partiality was shown for the deputies for Paris, and the Rochefort question came at once to the front. Rochefort was a deputy, but Rochefort was in Saint-Pélagie, and Rochefort was a somewhat fantastic personage in the eyes of the lawyers. There was, however, no way of getting out of his popularity, and the general opinion, I fancy, was interpreted by M. Picard when he said: 'We had better have him inside than out.' So they took him inside. A mob released him from prison and brought him forth in triumph.

There had never been any objection to General Trochu, and, by common consent, he was appointed President of the Government. It was this fresh state of affairs that caused the general reflux to the Louvre. As always happens with young Governments, the new power, and especially the man who seemed to be the dominating influence in it and to personify it, immediately had plenty of courtiers and flatterers. They crowded round him, were very energetic, and lost no opportunity of being seen. I really believe that, like Leporello, I might even have offered my protection, for everybody and everything that had access to the Governor had the appearance of partaking of his newly-acquired power.

By the time we got back to the Louvre, and as I went, as I have already said, to report myself to General Schmitz, it was a quarter to four. General Trochu, who had only just dismounted, had retired to his room, had taken off his uniform and resumed civilian attire. Then I learnt for the first time from a comrade the name of a person with long whiskers, whom I had noticed on the quay at the right hand of Jules Favre, and, like him, appearing to be leading the people to the Hôtel de Ville. His name was Jules Ferry. He seemed to be in a state of great excitement, conversed most familiarly with all around him, and continued to do so while his colleagues were conferring with the Governor.

Shortly afterwards, during my excursion to the Tuileries, General Trochu left for the Hôtel de Ville. The deputies assembled there had requested his presence in their midst.

At the Hôtel de Ville, he had scarcely set foot in the office of the Prefect of the Seine, where the Members of the Government were in conclave, before he was questioned by the deputies of the Seine. The Emperor was a prisoner, the Empress had fled; could they count upon him to form the Government which was so urgently needed?

Trochu was not in the least a man after the fashion of Tacitus. He could not be brief, and in these tragic circumstances he must needs make a speech on the spot.

'It is not,' he said, 'at a time when the country is in danger, and when every conceivable misfortune seems to be weighing upon France, that I can think of quitting my post, and fly from danger, or shirk responsibility. The more serious that responsibility is, the more earnestly do I believe that it is my duty to accept it; but going hand in hand with you, gentlemen, is quite another thing, and before answering you I beg your permission to ask you one

question. Do you intend to respect the three principles—
God, Family, and Property? Do you undertake to do
nothing against them? You agree to that? Good. In
that case I am with you.

'We ought only to have one idea—to repulse the
Prussians and maintain order at home. I must add, as
the *sine quâ non* of my acceptance, that I must be the
President of the Government you are about to form.'

He continued speaking; and Jules Favre, in his book,
has recorded his somewhat lengthy speech.

'It is indispensable that I should accept this post. As
Minister of War or Governor of Paris, I should not be able
to bring the army with me; and if we want to defend
Paris we must have the army within our grasp. I am no
politician—I am a soldier. I know the feeling of my
comrades. If they do not see me at your head, they will
hold aloof, and your task will be impossible. In this
resolve I am not actuated by ambition, but by the conviction that without it nothing can be even attempted. If
we have any chance of success it lies in the concentration
of power in our hand. As commander-in-chief of the army
my authority must be unlimited. I will in no way hamper
you in the exercise of civil power, but its action must be
co-ordinate with that of defence, which is our supreme
duty. No part of this double movement must be withheld
from me; it is a question of responsibility and safety.'

I am not inquisitive, but I would give much to have
seen the faces of these good apostles when the General
asked them whether, above all things, they would respect
God, Family, and Property. He must have appeared to
them wonderfully behind the age. Of course they promised
to respect them, they would have respected anything that
General Trochu wished—Trochu the soldier, the man of

order, duty and honour, who consented to enfold them, so to speak, in his own respectability.

He might have made them recognise the Syllabus, the Infallibility of the Pope, and the Immaculate Conception, had he so chosen. They accepted everything, and said Amen to everything.

He was elected President with acclamation and without the least reservation.

I should have liked, too, to have seen the astonishment of these lawyers, when they found themselves face to face with a General who could speak at as great length and quite as well, if not better than themselves, who rounded his periods as if he had been doing nothing else all his life, and who could have pleaded before any bench, or perorated from a tribune, in a manner considerably superior to their own.

It must have been wonderfully amusing.

Moreover, this oratorical display was only the prelude to an infinite number of similar sittings.

More than once it happened to one or other of us to have to accompany the General to the door of the room where the Government were deliberating, or to wait for him there. Each time the door opened to let a member in or out, we heard the voice of the Governor. The General spoke incessantly and well. The others only listened.

They were motionless and apparently under the influence of magnetism. He lulled them to sleep with their eyes wide open. I cannot describe them better than by comparing them to those birds which, when they are made to touch a chalk line with their beaks, remain in that position, motionless and in ecstasy.

The Governor had good reason to say that without him the task of the new Government was an impossibility.

He it was who shut the provincial and, to a certain extent, the foreign eye to the inherently illegal and revolutionary character of the new power.

There can be no question but that the Imperial Government had made mistakes, many mistakes, enormous mistakes, unpardonable mistakes, if you will. It is no less true that to leave the Chamber on the appearance of the populace there, to put yourself at the head of the so-called sovereign people, and then go and manufacture for yourself a Government at the Hôtel de Ville, is to do a factious work.

And yet, face to face with the country suffering from invasion, as he said, in presence of the frightful excesses which might break out in Paris—the Commune is a proof that one had a right to foresee them—the General thought it his duty to associate himself with the Government which had promised him to respect God, Family, and Property.

Some have said that ambition led him to act as he did. If he had been ambitious he would have remained at Châlons, and with his popularity and power of oratory, the force of events would have made him the first President of the Republic. Who knows even if, more fortunate than MacMahon, who was going neither to give way nor resign but who did give way and did resign, he might have succeeded in avoiding both at once ? I do not make a point of this, because I am afraid of having the celebrated phrase cast in my teeth, 'The Governor of Paris will not capitulate,' and I should be defending a bad cause if I were to maintain that handing the pen to somebody else, when the moment for capitulation arrived, is one way of not capitulating.

It is, by the way, a great pity that our language lends itself so thoroughly to theatrical phrases. It tempts us to say them, and they nearly always miscarry, to wit the memorable, 'I will only return dead or victorious,' which was sublime before the battle, and for which Ducrot might have been pardoned, had not death and victory shown themselves equally rebellious against his heroic efforts.

We have still one more saying, dating from the same day, and also destined to be handed down to posterity. In order to show that the new Government was not proceeding by way of disturbances, but by the deliberations of the representatives of the country freely consulted, the placard posted up in Paris began with these words, 'Frenchmen, the people have anticipated the Chamber.' Is not that idea of anticipation, which in reality consisted of pillage and dispersion, quite delicious?

The people anticipated the Chamber, meaning (and I hope I may be pardoned for the triviality of the expression) that they sat on the Chamber, a somewhat familiar way of anticipating people.

N.B. The representatives of the people, who had anticipated the Chamber, adjudged to themselves, at the first sitting, an indemnity calculated on the basis of 50,000 francs per annum. Not exorbitant, but comfortable enough in these early days for people to whom virtue was supposed to be its own reward. The only one who thought proper to decline this little civil list was Henri Rochefort. His colleagues never succeeded in persuading him to recede from his disinterested position, in itself a tacit reproach to them.

As I have already said, the members of the Government only accepted him in self-defence, solely to support their popularity by his before the crowd, who, to everything they said, replied, 'And Rochefort?' A grotesque post as grand master of barricades, or something of that sort, was invented for him, and the people were content to know that their idol would, when the proper moment should arrive, have something to do with the barricades. However, Rochefort was not likely to trouble his colleagues very long.

The most marvellous thing was that Trochu and he were on the best possible terms. The *Vaudevilliste,* accustomed to parody everything, listened without a quiver to the celebrated adjuration in the name of the three great principles—God, Family, Property ; and, whatever became of the Government, he invariably supported the Governor. The law of contrast, the meeting of extremes !

The only difficulty which arose on this first day of peaceful installation was in connection with the Ministry of Interior. Gambetta wanted it ; so did Picard. It was put to the vote, and Gambetta carried it off by a majority of two over Picard.

The first result of this appointment was the preponderance of Gambetta, who set the whole country aflame with the proclamations his duties allowed him to draw up, and the next was his departure for Tours and Bordeaux. It is possible, and I have frequently heard it contended, that if Gambetta had had the portfolio of Finance or any other portfolio than that of the Interior, he would have remained in Paris, and it is just possible that Trochu would have been sent to arouse the provinces.

And although it is an admitted fact that events make men to a greater extent than men make events, we may fairly ask what would have happened if Gambetta had remained in Paris, and if Trochu had been sent in his stead to the Departments ? What would not Gambetta have done with that enthusiastic and feverishly heroic populace whom his ardour and talent could sway at will ? On the other hand, what would Trochu not have done if he had been at Tours? An indefatigable worker, passing the night in his office without thereby affecting the work of the morrow; a methodical organiser, acquainted with the organisation of the French army as no one else was— what an amount of intelligent effort could he not have carried into effect!

Gambetta believed beforehand in the success of whatever he undertook; Trochu, and herein lay his great weakness, did not believe in the possibility of the defence. He thought that all was over after Châlons. He was too clear-headed to have any doubt on that head. He had no foregone belief in success, but he was sure of what would happen. Gambetta ought to have been in Paris, and Trochu in the provinces. In the one place the faith which works miracles, in the other the wisdom to turn every effort to good account. With Gambetta the diluvial sortie would undoubtedly have been attempted. Trochu would never have opposed the Prussians with any but armed, equipped, disciplined, and tolerably trained troops. For my part, I believe that Trochu was actuated by a sincere sense of duty, and I decline to look upon him as under the influence of ambition. The man who, elected by several departments at the end of the siege, voluntarily left the Chamber after having held it breathless and spell-bound under the power of his oratory, by a veritable parliamentary feat of strength during two consecutive sittings, that man was not ambitious.

When urgently solicited to take part in the labours of the National Assembly, he simply replied,

'If you have had hold of the handle of the frying-pan and have it in your hand, you need look no further to make an omelette.'

After having, fifteen years ago, retired to Belle Isle first of all, and subsequently to Tours, he now lives a life apart, seeking to be forgotten by all.   Although by no means a rich man, he has adopted several orphan relations and is educating them.   To be a Cincinnatus he lacks, alas! but one thing—that he should have saved his country.

To sum up and have done with the political incidents of this day, which a traveller arriving from the other hemisphere without having read the newspapers might have taken for a *fête* day—a *fête* under a cloudless sky and a brilliant sun, a *fête* with smiles and gaiety written on every countenance—it was the work of the entire Left of the Chamber, with the exception of two personages whose standing did not allow of their accepting inferior posts, and who, not being deputies of Paris, were not compromised in this fool-hardy Government, MM. Grévy and Thiers.

The former kept quiet, and in the back-ground; the latter kept himself neither the one nor in the other.   Even before night-fall he had seen General Trochu, he had seen Jules Favre, he had seen all the world.   Delighted, *in petto,* that his friends should have plunged him up to his neck in an undertaking which, as he knew as well as the Governor, could only have an inevitably fatal result, he had by the evening of the 4th of September elaborated a plan, placing him on the outskirts of the Government, in a position to benefit by all their successes, to wash his hands of all their reverses, and to profit alike by their ill and good fortune, by their labours as well as by their mistakes.   He proposed his great tour across Europe, and successive visits to Sovereigns and ministers.   He wanted to set out, to save his country if he could, but also to secure recognition in advance for his future Government, and then to return speedily into the midst of a young and enthusiastic Republic, with all the prestige of a man who has spoken to kings, has dined at their tables, and has treated with them.

If the General represented in the Government the respectability it lacked, M. Thiers represented in connection with the same Government those diplomatic and ministerial traditions which it lacked even more than it did respectability.

CHAPTER V

THE JOURNEY OF THE EMPRESS

The Farewells.—In a *Fiacre.*—At the house of Dr Evans.—The perplexities of an American.—In a Landau.—Through the Troops.—Washing.—At Deauville. —Sir John Burgoyne and the ' Gazelle.'—At Sea.—The Storm.—On *Terra Firma.*—The Empress at Hastings.

I MUST here insert a parenthesis in the midst of my personal reminiscences—in a word, I am going to sing the odyssey of the fugitive sovereign, and it will be based on the evidence of the least known but most authentic witnesses.

On the 4th September there were on duty at the Tuileries, General de Montebello, Admiral Jurien de la Gravière, the Marquis de la Grange, Mesdames de Renneval and de Saulcy, the Comtesse Aguado, the Marechale Canrobert, and Mesdames de la Poëze and de la Bedollière.

Shortly before her departure, or about two o'clock, for the exact hour of her departure was half-past two, the Empress, leaving MM. Nigra and de Metternich in her private room, went into her ante-room, where were assembled the persons I have just enumerated. She wore a brown dress, with a pelerine by Worth, of black cloth lined with violet silk and trimmed with fine gold lace. She had nothing on her head, and still held in her hand the cambric handkerchief with which she had dried her eyes, red with weeping, and had somewhat effaced, or smeared on her cheeks, the little touches of black crayon with which she was wont to line her eyes by way of making them appear larger—Spanish fashion.

The ladies in waiting, visibly affected, were standing up, and approached one after another to kiss the hand of their sovereign, who said to them, ' In France one has no right to be unhappy.'

After this kissing of hands and leave-taking, the Empress went back into her room, where she was anxiously awaited by the two Ambassadors, who were in a state of perpetual anxiety lest she should change her mind and refuse to depart, as they had advised her to do.

The last fortnight spent by the poor woman in the Tuileries had been neither more nor less than one long torture, veritable moral agony.

There had not been a single hour of those terrible days that had not brought a telegram announcing, or one confirming the news of a misfortune or disaster. Both mind and body had been on the rack during all these days devoted to tears, despair, and work, and followed by sleepless, restless nights.

She was only kept up by the aid of very strong coffee, and all her sleep was obtained by the use of chloral. She had, indeed, taken such a quantity of the drug that she suffered from fits of drowsiness, during which, with her large eyes wide open and fixed, she seemed to be oblivious of all that was going on around her, and to be incapable of understanding what was said to her.

The two Ambassadors, with their advice, their feigned alarm, and their exaggerated pictures of the pretended ills that threatened her, were not calculated to neutralize the effect which coffee and chloral had produced on her over-strained nerves.

They told her that the hour of flight and retreat had arrived. The too conspicuous pelerine by Worth was exchanged for a more sombre cloak, and the Empress hastily imprisoned her magnificent hair beneath a little black *capote* belonging to Madame Virot, the strings of which she feverishly tied under her chin. She took in her hand one of those little bags in which ladies carry their purses, handkerchiefs, and tablets, and taking the arm of Prince de Metternich, she followed M. Nigra, who had given his arm to Madame Lebreton, across the Louvre, this latter lady, reader to the Empress, having refused to leave her Imperial mistress. Madame Lebreton is, as may be remembered a sister of that gallant and often victorious soldier, Bourbaki.

In this order they reached the colonnade of Louis XIV., opposite the Church of Saint-Germain-l'Auxerrois, and at that spot, in front of the gilded gateway, the Empress and Madame Lebreton got into a *fiacre,* M. de Metternich giving the driver the laconic direction, ' Boulevard Haussmann.'

An urchin of fifteen, in blouse and cap, who was passing at the time, called out: ' Isn't she pretty !—It is the Empress ! '

Happily for the fugitives, the exclamation was drowned in the noise made by the wheels of the *fiacre*, which had already started in the direction of the Rue de Rivoli.

Towards the middle of the Boulevard Haussmann, the two ladies stopped the vehicle ; and while Madame Lebreton was paying the driver, the Empress took refuge under a carriage entrance. Another passing vehicle was hailed, and the new driver was told to go to the house of Dr Evans, Avenue Malakoff.

This practitioner resided in a splendid and comfortable mansion. Dr Evans was not merely a specialist who had made an enormous fortune and a European reputation; he was also a good man. Later on, when the sufferings and privations of the siege began, he instituted and maintained at his own expense the American Ambulance. And his fellow-countrymen, who had danced so indefatigably at the court balls and in the Paris drawing-rooms, who had eaten so much *foie gras* and imbibed so much champagne at our festivities, and who had handed over to us so many ' misses ' more or less rich—generally less—did not subscribe among them a total of 500 francs for the support of this ambulance, which was called American all the same.

Dr Evans bore the whole expense himself; and as he had not only the wounded to look after, but very frequently able-bodied men to support—his own minister, Mr Washburne, to wit—when accounts were made up it was discovered that, including his subscriptions in aid of the prisoners of war in Germany, this generous American citizen had made the French country a present of 1,200,000 francs. That, it must be confessed, was paying right royally for the reception accorded him by Paris; and he by himself atoned for all the meanness of his fellow-countrymen, their demonstrations against us, and the real harm they did us.

When she reached the doctor's house, and had been shown into his drawing-room, the Empress said to him, in a voice broken with sobs—

' My dear Dr Evans, you alone can save me. Everybody

has abandoned me. I can no longer rely upon anybody. I want to escape, to leave this ungrateful city, and I have come to beg you to furnish me with the means to cross to England.'

Dr Evans knew the Empress when she was only Mdlle. de Montijo, and had rendered her several small services before she reached her lofty position. He was consequently allowed to go in and out of the Tuileries, and to visit his Imperial patient, pretty much as he pleased; and in their intercourse there was not only confidence, but also cordiality. He was quite as much agitated as his visitor; and he was completely overcome by the unexpected spectacle of so much human grandeur thus laid low, and of a sovereign betaking herself to him for aid and protection.

He, nevertheless, was fully alive to the responsibility he was asked to assume. As a foreigner and merely a guest of France, he recoiled from playing a political *rôle* for which he might be called sharply to account, and there was no disguising the fact that to facilitate the flight of an Empress-Regent was decidedly a political act. But anxiety in regard to his own personal interests simply crossed his mind and did not remain there a moment. We are all made alike. Placed opposite an unexpected danger, we all of us, first of all, become unconsciously on the alert in regard to our personal safety. We all have that feeling. Ordinary men obey it; strong men conquer it, and so did Dr Evans, who speedily became possessed of one idea alone —to devote himself to the Empress, and all the more strenuously on account of the risks he might have to run.

Every impulse of a really chivalrous nature was excited to a degree, when he recollected that he had not only an old friend to protect, but a sovereign to defend; a woman crushed beneath the weight of misfortunes to uphold, and a wife separated from her husband, as well as a mother isolated from her son, to console and re-unite to those belonging to her.

The Empress had remained standing as she addressed her request to the doctor.

'I beg your Majesty to be seated and to allow me a few moments for reflection,' he said. 'The responsibility that I am taking upon myself is considerable, and I want to nerve myself to justify the confidence which your Majesty has deigned to repose in me.'

He left the room, closing the door behind him, lest some inquisitive and indiscreet being might intrude upon and surprise the two fugitives.

'Here am I,' said the doctor to himself, 'associated in spite of myself with those by whom history is made. This unhappy woman, thrown aside by everybody, resigned to that wholesale desertion, being in consequence neither able nor willing to appeal to those who only yesterday called themselves her subjects, and having recourse to an American citizen in order to escape from France, places me in a singularly delicate situation. It is absolutely necessary that everything I do should be done before witnesses, who may in the future, should the necessity arise, bear witness to my loyalty and good faith.'

He then sent for his countryman and intimate friend, Dr Crane, told him what had happened, and begged him to be in readiness to start with him on the following morning.

The goal of the Empress' journey was England, and as she absolutely refused to go by train for fear of being recognised, and possibly insulted, it was too late to make the necessary arrangements for leaving that day.

The doctor, therefore, mentally arranged his plan of action, and returned to the Empress to inform her that she would have to remain under his roof for one night. The poor woman, physically worn out and morally over-excited, passed the night of the 4th of September in the bedroom of Mrs Evans, who was then staying at Deauville. A bed was improvised for Madame Lebreton at the foot of that of the Empress.

On the morning of the 5th of September, the Empress, who had slept and was consequently more herself, dressed herself as on the previous evening, except that as the little *capote* left her face quite exposed, she took a round hat belonging to Mrs Evans, and tied round it a thick veil, which rendered her recognition impossible.

The whole party took their places in the doctor's landau, a comfortable carriage painted brown. On the box were the coachman and the footman, in grey livery with black collar, in utter ignorance as to who were with their master.

The Empress sat with her face to the horses, on the right, with Madame Lebreton by her side, and the two American doctors occupied the opposite seat.

Passing through one of the gates opening on to the Avenue Malakoff, which was opened by the gardener, they set of at full speed for Deauville.

The great difficulty was getting out of Paris. The Maillot gate was obstructed by a barricade guarded by a detachment of the *Garde Nationale,* and that obstacle would have to be passed without the Empress being recognised.

As I had to do four months afterwards when I took Jules Favre to Versailles, Dr Evans leaned half way out of the right hand window to ask the sentry the way, and so the carriage passed the barriers slowly and without molestation.

They were safe.

The Empress behaved as any other woman in her place

would have behaved; instead of rejoicing she began to cry.

Saint Germain was reached. Then there was a halt for a few moments on the high road, and on they went again in spite of the Doctor's horses being thoroughly tired. When they arrived at Mantes they could go no further, and Dr Evans got out of the landau, leaving his travelling companions in charge of his colleague, and succeeded in procuring a berlin and two rather sorry horses. The landau was left behind and the journey resumed.

The difficulty in procuring relays was, in fact, the only serious risk encountered on the journey.

At a little village called La Commanderie, the village steeds had had enough of it and came to a dead stop, refusing to budge an inch even in answer to the whip. Dr Evans went on another voyage of discovery, and found under a shed a barouche which must have seen the Allies. A peasant offered to go into the fields in search of horses, and his offer having been accepted, two old screws were eventually harnessed to the antique carriage. The owner thought this equipage so exceedingly elegant that she said to the doctor,

'Such a handsome carriage as that is fit for a queen.'

The Empress shuddered and thought she was recognised, but there was nothing to fear. Chance alone had put this passing event, as the saying goes, into the mouth of the good old woman.

At Evreux the road lay right through the middle of the garrison, who were drawn up in the principal square, and surrounded by the entire population. The new Prefect, just arrived from Paris, and surrounded by the authorities and the Municipal Council, was in the act of proclaiming the Republic and making a speech. Dr Evans put a bold face on the matter, went up to him, and requested permission to pass on without waiting for the conclusion of this patriotic ceremony. Permission was granted, and thousands of eyes watched the progress of the old carriage, wherein was concealed the wife of Cæsar.

They left Paris at 5 a.m., and reached Deauville at 4 p.m.

During the journey the Empress remained sad, dejected, and downcast. Every now and then, however, she became drowsy and seemed to be asleep, but suddenly she would start up as if some ridiculous idea had crossed her mind, and would be lively and gay, talking much and laughing more. But the access of gaiety invariably ended in a flood of tears.

The poor woman had wept to such an extent that both her small handkerchiefs, like the one she left on the table at the Tuileries, were saturated with tears. She had also been suffering from a cold in her head since the 15th of August, so that the fine cambric was in a state more easily imagined than described. The doctor offered to wash and dry the handkerchiefs. The Empress refused at first, but at length consented, and the doctor set to work accordingly in a little ditch at the side of the road, hanging the handkerchiefs out of the window afterwards in order to dry them in the wind.

Throughout these two days the Empress had eaten nothing. She had merely nibbled a biscuit and swallowed a mouthful or two of coffee and of water. But her travelling companions were hungry, and she reproached them several times with spending their lives in eating. Deauville was reached at four o'clock in the afternoon, and the party alighted at the Hotel du Casino, where Mrs Evans was staying, and that lady at once assisted her husband to hide the Empress from all eyes until a vessel could be procured to convey her to the English coast.

While the doctor betook himself to the harbour, Mrs Evans was unremitting in her attentions to the Empress, whom she resembled in a striking degree. They might have been taken for twin sisters, one of whom, worn out by grief and fatigue, was being tenderly ministered to by the other. Mrs Evans packed up in a small bag such linen as the Empress might require, the latter repeating over and over again as she dried her eyes,

'Pocket handkerchiefs before anything else.'

The doctor found two yachts at anchor in the harbour, one the 'Gazelle,' belonging to Sir John Burgoyne, and the other, the larger of the two, to an American gentleman, Doctor Evans paid a visit to the latter first. The vessel did not seem to him particularly seaworthy, and before coming to terms with her owner, he went to Sir John Burgoyne and asked him if he would put to sea that night. He received a flat refusal from the noble Englishman, in whose honour the doctor thought he might confide. The safety of the Empress was at stake ; the Empress, who knew this gentleman, a personal friend of the Emperor.

Sir John Burgoyne persisted in his refusal. He was a foreigner, and did not wish to be mixed up in political questions. Besides, a storm was raging outside, the sea was rough, and the wind getting up : he would not consent to so imprudent an undertaking.

'Then I must have recourse to the American yacht,' said the doctor.

'I would not advise you to do so,' replied the Englishman, 'unless you are bent on going to the bottom. She is not a vessel, she is a tub, and would not stand the sea.'

Dr Evans made a last effort, and at length, towards

eleven o'clock at night, Sir John Burgoyne accepted the perilous but glorious mission of conducting the Empress to England. They were to put to sea on the Wednesday morning, the 7th of September, at six o'clock, but in order to avoid arousing suspicion, the passengers were to go on board the same evening between twelve and half-past.

This programme was carried out.

The 'Gazelle' was a sailing yacht, 45 feet long. The sides of her solitary cabin, where were installed the Empress, Madame Lebreton, the Doctor, and Sir John, measured only two yards and a half. In this hole three and twenty hours had to be spent in the midst of a regular hurricane, for the wind had not gone down. She was head to wind, that is to say standing out to sea, and could only make headway by tacking, the huge waves meanwhile rushing along her cockle-shell deck.

In the night the storm raged horribly, and Sir John Burgoyne, in a terrified state of mind, suddenly left the deck, and with haggard eyes full of tears went down into the cabin.

'We are lost,' he said.

And throwing the blame on the doctor, he added,

'It is all your fault.'

And then he disappeared, going up on deck as quickly as he had come down.

The passengers, astonished at this strange, unexpected, and hurried departure, looked at each other. The Empress could not help bursting out into a hearty laugh, so comical had been the appearance of this dismayed gentleman. What a strange nature is that of women! They tremble before an imaginary danger, they face a real one with a laugh. The Empress had nothing to fear in France, and she ran away. She was within an ace of shipwreck, and she laughed. A soldier of the *Garde Nationale* aroused her terror, the ocean in its wrath provoked her mirth.

At daybreak the wind and the sea fell, and the yacht made the harbour of Ryde. The party landed at once, and went to the Pier Hotel, the proprietor of which, at the sight of two drenched, shabby-looking, dishevelled women, accompanied by a man even more thoroughly drenched than they were, shut his door. They took refuge in the York Hotel, where they were received without any display of eagerness.

After having rested awhile the Empress proceeded to Hastings, and arrived in the afternoon at the Marine Hotel, where she remained about a fortnight. The first two persons from France to join her at this hotel were Miss Shaw, the Prince Imperial's English nurse, and my faithful Joseph, in charge of my first convoy of boxes.

There the Prince Imperial joined his mother. He threw himself into her arms, sobbing bitterly, and after the first embraces were over, the Empress, pointing out Dr Evans to the Prince, said to him,

'Embrace him, for he has saved me.'

Mrs Evans was also there with her husband, and gave the exile continued proofs of the most thorough and most disinterested devotion.

The doctor was also entrusted with the task of finding a suitable residence for the Imperial family. He decided upon Chislehurst, and hired Camden Place, which rented in his name during the first three years of their tenancy.

The Empress did not take the trouble to thank Sir John Burgoyne, and Lady Burgoyne had a year afterwards to give personal expression to her astonishment at the omission before it was rectified.

As for Dr Evans, he had nothing to expect from the Empress beyond a little frankness, and public testimony when an attempt was made to travesty the facts I have just narrated, and to represent him as having played a ridiculous part.

The Empress did not appreciate the fact that she lowered herself in appearing to regret and forget the strange circumstances of her flight from Paris, and the doctor has a right to be numbered among those people who, without any feeling of astonishment, experience the traditional ingratitude of all who have sat upon a throne, even though it may have been but for a moment.

CHAPTER VI

IN THE HOME OF THE EMPRESS

At the Prefecture of Police.—Secret Service Money.—The Chambermaid.—The Louvre invaded by the *Mobiles*.—Rochefort Preserves Order.—Return to the Camp of Saint-Maur.—In the Imperial Apartments.—The Toilettes of the Empress.—The Travelling Bag.—The Boxes.—Two Telegraphic Despatches.—The Faithful Joseph.—With Picard.—Good Advice.—Prince and Usher.—Epilogue of the Salvage.

ON the morning of the 4th of September, a commissionaire brought me the following letter,

'SIR,

'I do not know if this letter will ever reach you. I have entrusted it to a person who, I hope, will contrive that it shall do so. If there had been a reply it would have been addressed to you to my care. Thank God there are still some men of spirit, and you are one of them.

'VICOMTESSE AGUADO.'

I asked good-natured M. Pollet, the Commissary of
Police attached to the residence of the Governor, to procure
for me the addresses of one or two of the chambermaids of
the Empress, and I postponed until the following day the
task of furnishing myself with the necessary permits to
carry out my projected despatch of effects. It would have
been useless, and perhaps imprudent, to have mixed the
Governor up in the matter, and I preferred betaking
myself to the Civil Power, that is to say, the Prefecture of
Police, a convenient spot whither, in Paris, you go when
you do not quite know where you ought to go, and where
as a rule you find precisely what you want.

On the 5th of September, my turn of duty in attendance
on the Governor was over at 6 a.m., and I proceeded at
once to the Prefecture. There I found everybody in a
state of bewilderment. The *Sergents de Ville* were evidently
ill at ease. These admirable soldiers, recruited with so
much care under the Empire from among the non-commissioned officers, a thoroughly devoted and faithful body
of men, had come to the conclusion among themselves that
the revolutionists were in power. And it appeared very
strange to them to have to serve those people who, on the
previous evening, had been looked upon as the enemies of
the Empire, the Government, society, and order.

Insulted and abused by the mob, always stupid and
sometimes criminal, who in times of revolution lay violent
hands on public monuments and the representatives of
order, these poor devils literally did not know which way
to turn. On the previous evening, either in the Place de la
Concorde, or in the neighbourhood of the Palais-Bourbon,
or around the Hôtel de Ville, a goodly number of them had
had a narrow escape of being thrown into the Seine. They
had been insulted, struck, and their hats and swords had

been taken from them. Their clothes had been paraded as glorious trophies, and many of them, half-dead, their faces streaming with blood, and their uniforms in shreds, had only with great difficulty reached the Prefecture of Police. It is so pleasant and so easy to satisfy a petty personal spite, to avenge a writ or an arrest, while appearing to take part in a patriotic demonstration!

As happened on the previous evening at the Tuileries, I reached the office of the Prefect without anybody thinking of stopping me.

The Comte de Kératry had just taken possession of the Prefectoral Office. Standing behind a large Louis XV table, furnished with many drawers and littered with papers, he was looking over what his predecessor had left.

All the officers of the force, and the superior class of subordinates in black coats and white cravats, were drawn up in a respectful and solemn semi-circle opposite to the Prefect. An usher opened one drawer after another for him so that he might analyse their contents.

'What is this?' said M. de Kératry.

'The secret papers relating to the rioters of la Villette.'

'And this?'

'The belt belonging to your predecessor, sir.'

'Very well. Put it on one side with everything belonging to him, and see that they are carefully returned to him.'

One drawer resisted all the efforts of the usher, who tugged at it with all his might. It gave way suddenly and exposed to view piles of gold and silver.

'And what is all this?' exclaimed M. de Kératry.

One of the functionaries replied, with a low bow,

'That is the secret service money.'

'Secret service money! Take it away and count it. There will be nothing secret under my administration.'

And the whole body, absolutely dazed, stared at the Prefect in alarm.

The Comte de Kératry, to whose courtesy, tact, and impartiality I can pay no homage too great, for I was in a position to appreciate them during his very short sojourn at the Prefecture of Police, learnt very quickly that if bad faith is the soul of politics, money is the soul of the police.

I fancy the money then taken away was speedily restored to the secret service drawer, and that its total was replenished more than once during the siege.

The inspection over, and everybody having left the room, the Prefect made me sit down in the arm chair, while I unfolded my request.

'You are right,' said he, 'it would be disgraceful if the woman who has been the worshipped Sovereign of France for eighteen years, were to be obliged to buy a chemise that she might change her linen. See Picard as to the expense. You have my approval.'

Justified by this authority, purely moral by the way, I went in search of M. Ernest Picard, who gave a most cordial reception to the Orderly Officer of the Governor.

Short, stout, and with a good-tempered face, he seemed neither embarrassed nor surprised by the extraordinary chain of events which had just made a Finance Minister of him.

Our interview was conducted in a jocular strain. Amusing, but by no means trivial, he called me his dear friend at the end of ten minutes.

'Look here, my dear friend,' he said to me, 'in moments like these everybody has to do what he thinks he ought to do. Our consciences have to judge us. Go. Act for the best. We will put everything in due form later on.'

Before breakfast M. Pollet sent me the address of one of the chamber-maids of the Empress. I have forgotten her name, and only remember that she lived in the Rue des Bons-Enfants. I went to the house and found the whole family in tears. It was a simple household of the lower middle-class; but the chamber-maid had an elegance of air and manner which contrasted strongly with her surroundings. Women are gifted with the singular faculty of raising themselves easily, and almost without any appearance of transition, above the social condition in which they were born, from the moment that they come in contact with a superior class of society. And this young woman, who possibly had on her back an Imperial dress, resembled, in the midst of her family, a peacock strutting about in the centre of a fowl yard. The place was Bona-partist to the last degree, that was easily seen. The mantelpiece was crowded with portraits of the Emperor, the Empress, and the Prince Imperial at all ages and in every costume.

I appointed to meet the young woman in the evening, and I explained to her what I wanted to do.

A most extraordinary spectacle awaited me at the Louvre. The *Garde Mobile*, encamped at Saint-Maur under the command of General Berthaut, having become acquainted on the evening of the 4th of September with the fall of the Empire and the proclamation of the Republic, evinced a disposition to leave their camp, their huts, and their General *en masse*.

Once grant concessions to fellows of this sort, and there is no stopping; you must come to terms with them.

If a show of sternness had been made at Châlons, if a score of these brawlers and their ringleaders had been tried by court-martial and, if necessary, shot, the *Garde Mobile* would have been a far different *corps*. Intelligent and easily led, it would have rendered invaluable services.

But how could anybody expect energy and vigour from a Government which was falling to pieces, a Sovereign who no longer believed in his star, Generals not only defeated but ashamed of their defeats, and a world of flatterers and easy-going people, who had surrounded the Emperor for ever so long and were perpetually persuading him that everything was for the best under the best of Napoleons! Besides, all of them felt they were weak and had a presentiment of the fall that was inevitable.

The only concession which General Berthaut could obtain was that the *Garde Mobile* should content itself with electing delegates, who should go to Paris and find out if the Republic had actually been proclaimed and what was the complexion of the Government, and should then return and give an account of their very unmilitary proceedings to their comrades.

The individuals thus entrusted with an irregular mission were, however, joined by other *Mobiles* who looked upon their own free will as superior to any orders. The entire band in military uniform, increased by a large number of citizens picked up at the barriers and in the Faubourg Saint-Antoine, was several thousands strong by the time it reached the Head-quarters of General Trochu. The Rue de Rivoli was obstructed, the courtyard invaded, and the flower borders trampled under foot. The General, for whom there were vehement shouts, emerged from his office just as he was, bareheaded and in a jacket.

From the top of a flight of steps, which divided the

entrance to his apartments from the courtyard, he harangued the crowd.

Without the slightest respect either for his person or his office, the demonstrationists pushed and shoved each other until both the outer and inner staircases were invaded. And so compact was the crowd that the Governor had only to make a gesture to touch the nearest of his auditors.

On his right, three or four steps lower down, M. Garnier-Pagès, also bareheaded, with his long white hair parted in the middle and falling over his shoulders like an angel's, and his face enveloped, so to speak, in his gigantic and historical collar, like a bouquet in a sheet of paper, had come to the conclusion that, in virtue of his position as a member of the Government, he too ought to make a speech. Lastly, in the middle of the courtyard, Rochefort, with his severe head so full of character, Rochefort, whose features seemed to be carved out of wood, was surrounded, fêted, and thronged upon after a fashion calculated to take away his breath.

As a matter of fact nobody listened to the speakers, and everybody was talking at the same time. There was no reason why the scene of disorder should ever come to an end.

As I was passing under the archway, my arm was seized by M. Pollet, our Commissary of Police, who said to me,

'How are we going to get rid of these people?'

Being myself under the impression that the removal of this enthusiastic, revolutionary, and utterly useless demonstration to some other place would be rendering a real service to the Governor, I was endeavouring to make my way to him.

Carried rather than pushed along, I reached M. Garnier-Pagès. He was talking about 1848, Louis Philippe and Lamartine. A little more elbowing brought me at length to General Trochu, who was still speaking. In order not to put him out, I placed myself behind him, and interrupting him very unceremoniously, said to him in a low tone,

'I am one of your Orderly Officers, sir. Do you wish me to get this crowd away?'

He stopped short, thinking probably that what I was saying was worth more than what he had to say.

'Certainly,' he replied. 'But how?'

'You will see, sir.'

And I plunged once more into the midst of the crowd working my way towards the centre, where I succeeded in reaching Henri Rochefort.

'This demonstration,' I said to him, 'is absolutely purposeless. It is even injurious from a moral point of view, as for the most part it is composed of soldiers belonging to every branch of the service. Will you help me to disperse it and make the soldiers return to their duty?'

'I should like nothing better,' he replied.

On this, as on every other occasion when I was brought in contact with him, I can say nothing too strong in praise of the kindness, generosity of spirit, and disinterestedness of the famous pamphleteer.

Rochefort took my arm, I summoned four drummers with their instruments, who formed part of the group round him, and ordered them to beat a march. And placing at our head a shabby tricolor, which was about to be prostituted by a band of vicious-looking blackguards, we marched towards the gate. Two persons followed us, then four, then ten, and then the whole crowd went away as they had come, without knowing why. O sheep of Panurge!

'Where are we going?' asked Rochefort.

'I am going to escort you to the Hôtel de Ville, and after having asked you to do me one service I wish you to do me another. It will consist of saying a few words to the crowd in order to induce them to follow me. By this means I hope to get all the *Mobiles* back to the camp at Saint-Maur, for their presence in Paris, over-excited as they are, might bring about serious disturbances.'

This programme was carried out to the letter, and after a few words spoken by him amid a silence which astonished me, and which his prestige alone, immense at that time, could produce, Rochefort disappeared into the Hôtel de Ville, leaving me with the *Mobiles*.

A lieutenant, M. d'Orgeval, to whom was given the command of the delegates from the camp at Saint-Maur, rendered me a real service. One man cannot do much, but two, when united, multiply their material and moral force four-fold.

We organised our troop in military fashion; the sight-seers deserted us; the standard-bearer and the dozen men with him disappeared into a wine shop, and we were very soon left with a few hundred resigned and respectful *Mobiles*. They followed us without an unpleasant word to the camp at Saint-Maur, a tolerably long march, by the way.

At the Barrière du Trone, as every good action deserves its reward, I thought I would give them a proof of my satisfaction at seeing them so obedient and soldier-like. I gave the word of command, Halt! opposite a *café*. Two casks of wine were rolled out and broached without delay. Our men, in two files, went one after the other and buried their noses in the ruddy French liquid. They were pleased both with their refreshment and themselves, and the wine could do no harm. It was cold, and they had walked, talked and sung admirably.

An hour later, at the camp of Saint-Maur, I had the honour to report to General Berthaut the nature of the duty I had taken upon myself, and to restore to his command my little troop, who were drawn up in battle array close by, under the command of M. d'Orgeval.

I returned to Paris by rail and found the Governor awaiting me. He had given orders that he was to be informed of my return and that I was to be shown in to him at once. He laughed when he saw me, and thanked me for the promptitude with which I had rid him of the brawlers. For the first time off duty he spoke to me as man to man, and not as a General to his Orderly Officer. He was good enough to question me as to my past life and my family, and begged me to take the rest which he thought I needed. The ice was broken between us, and from that day the General showed me both confidence and kindness, which I always strove to deserve.

I wanted rest, truly. And the Empress' petticoats! I avow and confess—and all the Messieurs Prudhomme may preach morality to me if they will—it seemed to me that after having been with that dishevelled and brawling crowd, it would be pleasant to penetrate into a woman's dressing room, still impregnated and imbued with the presence of a pretty Empress. The smell of perspiration and wine made me long for the soft and delicate emanations of the iris. One cannot always be five-and-twenty!

True to her appointment, and with all the air of a well-to-do little *bourgeoise,* I found the Empress' chamber-maid in the Rue de Rivoli. I was accompanied by faithful Joseph, who was completely transformed and from the son of Albion that he really was, had become the orderly of a French officer, but still smarting from his misadventure in the camp at Châlons. I was furnished with a special passport and provided with every imaginable signature. I had, therefore, in order to gain admission into the private apartments, merely to follow the chamber-maid.

I should be exaggerating were I to say that disorder was at its height in the room. On all sides there were evidences of incomplete preparations for a hurried departure. Everything was in the state in which the Empress had left it at the moment of her flight, and it was difficult at the outset to throw off the depression one feels at the sight of a spot which has so recently been so full of life, and where that life has been abruptly broken off by an overwhelming disaster.

The large room used as a drawing-room and office by the Regent, her boudoir and her oratory, her bedroom and her dressing-room, formed a series of rooms overlooking and opening on to the gardens of the Tuileries.

The entire suite was furnished with all the refinement of modern luxury, and the luxury seemed out of place. It appeared to be quite out of harmony with the somewhat severe grandeur of the architecture. It was the drawing-room of Madame de Metternich transported to the Tuileries, but I am nevertheless quite certain that if the Ambassadress had inhabited the palace, her drawing-room would have been furnished in an entirely different style from the one before me.

We were still far removed from the moral and material sufferings brought upon us by the siege which was then about to commence, and which had for one of its results the imparting of a certain temporary tinge of austerity to the light, variable, and impassionable Parisian mind. But this luxury without style or character, this majestic mass of ornament, did not accord with the respect one ought to have, or with the ideas one naturally does have of royal grandeur. In a word, there was too much of the boudoir and too little of the palace.

I have never seen the private apartments of the Queen of England, or those of the Empress of Russia, but I would bet that they differ in a marked degree from those arranged by the Empress Eugénie at the Tuileries.

In the great drawing-room where the Regent worked and held receptions, there stood on the left a large Louis XV writing table, the bronzes of which had never been chased by Gouthière. On the right were large glass cases containing various objects and family relics, quite a royal museum on a small scale.

I noticed, but I did not linger over it, the hat pierced by three bullets which the Emperor wore on the day of the Orsini attempt, a hat with a broader brim than is worn now-a-days, and looking quite out of date. By its side were two Orsini bombs, a species of small shell, fourteen centimetres long, ornamented in every sense of the word with gun-nipples ready capped, and not unlike little hedge-hogs. When they are thrown, no matter on which side they fall, five or six percussion caps must be struck. One of them was intact. The other, burst into irregular pieces, was intended to have effected its murderous purpose.

There were also rich and curious snuff boxes; a very rare daguerrotype of the Empress as a young girl: a charming miniature of Queen Hortense, &c., &c.

On easels in the drawing-room were the portraits of the Emperor by Flandrin, and of the Princess Christine Bonaparte, *née* the Princess Ruspoli, an adorably beautiful woman. Besides these, there were bronzes, clocks, candelabra, rich curtains, puffs, cushions, low chairs, more puffs, *jardinières* filled with green plants, a profusion of embroidery, hanging ornaments, in short, the smart and over-elaborate luxury of the nineteenth century.

On the Empress-Regent's table was a large, open black morocco travelling bag which the unfortunate woman had not had time to take with her, and a small pocket handkerchief trimmed with lace. crumpled and still moist with tears. It was marked with an E surmounted by the imperial crown. In the bag were two linen chemises very simply made and without any embroidery. The only thing which distinguished them from those of any ordinary female, was the circumstance of their being marked in the middle of the breast with an E surmounted, as usual, by the imperial crown; two pairs of Scotch thread stockings, four handkerchiefs, a pair of shoes, two collars and two pairs of cuffs. One of the collars, turned down, had in it a horse-shoe in burnished silver, to be used as a brooch. Lastly, a very small Scotch plaid, one of those tartan shawls which are to be seen in any shop devoted to English goods.

All these things must have been hastily put together when flight was decided upon. In all probability the idea that a travelling bag might arouse the attention of passers-by, caused her to leave it behind at the last moment.

By the side of the bag was a bundle of telegrams. I was inquisitive enough to glance over them, and my attention was attracted by two of the number. The first, signed by Marshal Lebœuf, was addressed to the Regent and ran as follows :—

'The Intendance Department is doing very badly. The men are without shoes. LEBŒUF.'

The second, important in a very different way, was a copy of a telegram sent to the Emperor, a copy destined to be transcribed into a large register lying open on the left hand side of the table, where were entered all telegrams received and despatched. It will serve to explain the conduct of the Emperor, of the Empress, and also of General Trochu during the last days of the Empire. Here it is:

'To the Emperor,

'Do not think of returning here unless you wish to induce a fearful revolution. This is the advice of Rouher and Chevreau, whom I have seen this morning. People here would say that you were fleeing from danger.

'Do not forget that the departure of Prince Napoleon from the army in the Crimea has affected his whole life.

'Eugénie.'

I shall soon have occasion to revert to this telegram, and to comment on it, but I wish first of all to finish my work in the apartments of the Empress, even though, in doing so, I shall have to anticipate the course of events by a few days.

In the bedroom was a large modern bed, its head to the wall and its foot in the direction of the garden. On the right of the bed was a chest of drawers of exquisite shape and finish, the top drawer, which was open, being filled with about fifty sunshades of every shape and colour, some rich and some simple, one piled on the top of the other. The first to attract attention was of mauve silk, covered with black lace, and with a tortoiseshell handle in the shape of a hind's foot shod in gold. Another was of white silk trimmed with beautiful Valenciennes. On the ivory handle were minute bees, and it was in the shape of an Imperial crown, carved in openwork. A third was made of white lace with a solid gold handle, ornamented with turquoises. Lastly, there were a number of *chefs d'œuvre*, signed Gravel, Verdier, &c.

All the furniture in the room was covered with beautiful fabrics.

To the left of the door leading to the Emperor's rooms were three looking-glasses, such as one sees at a fashionable tailor's, framed in copper, and so placed as to allow of every part and position of the figure being seen.

At the side of the looking-glasses was a lift.

I had an expert guide to help me in my inspection, and I drew her out. Her explanation of the use of the lift was as follows.

Above the rooms of the Empress, and consequently on the second floor, was another corresponding suite. These, occupied by the waiting women, were furnished from top to bottom with large black oak wardrobes standing against the walls. In these wardrobes were put away all sorts of dresses, mantles, petticoats, supplies of linen, lace, materials in pieces, and a considerable stock of Chinese silks. There was a hat room, a boot room, and a fur room—in short, the well-stocked arsenal of a pretty woman and a Sovereign, who knew that beauty is a force to be reckoned upon, and that, as our forefathers sang, 'art embellishes beauty.'

In the room on the second floor communicating with the lift, that is to say, above the bedroom, were four upright lay figures of the exact height and size of her Majesty.

When the lady of the bedchamber had, through a speaking tube, transmitted the necessary orders for the Empress' toilette, the maids took the toilette in question out of the wardrobes, dressed one of the lay figures in it, and sent it down to the room below, where the Empress could inspect it and say, 'This is how I shall be dressed by and by.' And the lay figure returned to the second floor in its original nakedness.

I had to begin on the second floor, as I wanted boxes, and, besides, the furniture could wait. They were in the attics, so my companion told me. Joseph and I accordingly went on a tour of inspection aloft, and brought back fifteen large boxes.

We then, both of us, set to work on the most fantastic packing that can well be imagined. The chamber-maid emptied the wardrobes, and we bundled into the boxes, just as they were, the whole of the feminine belongings, which certainly had never previously been treated so unceremoniously and so rudely. Our fifteen boxes were crammed, and yet the wardrobes seemed as full as ever. We had another hunt in the attics, but in vain. I shall never forget that excursion under the roof of that immense palace. We did not know our way about in the least, and yet we were lords of all we surveyed, as by the flickering light of our candles we peered into what appeared to us to be unlimited and immeasurable space; catching a glimpse every now and then of a bit of star-lit sky or a ray of moonlight as we passed a window; speaking in whispers in spite of ourselves, and hearing amid the surrounding silence the sustained murmur of the populace without, a mighty buzzing, accentuated from time to time by the shouts of ' *Vive la République* ' shrieked by the street boys, or snatches of the *Marseillaise* wafted by the wind from the squares and quays.

We left the conclusion of our first batch until the following day, and went in search of rest, assuredly well deserved. When I say *we* went, I am doing Joseph an injustice, for he had to run about all night in search of a furniture van, which he would have to drive himself, and of other boxes, if any were to be had. He succeeded. A rumour was current that the Empress was in England. As a matter of fact she had made up her mind to go there, and had spoken about it to several of her friends, who had naturally repeated it everywhere. My orderly therefore took his departure for England, with orders to deliver his packages to the Empress direct.

Like every other railway station in Paris, that of the Nord at this time presented an extraordinary appearance. The fall of the Empire, the Revolution, peaceable as it had been, the departure of the Empress, the dread of the sufferings of the siege then on the eve of beginning, a dread, in fact, of the unknown, inspired so many people with the idea of running away with all they held precious, that every railway station was blocked to an extent beyond the power of any imagination to conceive. Trunks, bags, portmanteaus, boxes, were heaped up from one end of the station to the other in a mass at least two stories high. People who did not want to lose sight of their luggage were coming and going, protesting, imploring, weeping, or despairing. Others, happily careless, went their way, leaving to their servants the task of registering their luggage; they themselves quite comfortable, while their servants, by dint of fighting, disputing, and a hand to hand set-to with the luggage porters, managed to send everything safely away after a campaign and bivouack of four or five days' duration. As for those who went away and left the railway authorities to look after their effects, they received them two or three months after the end of the siege.

In such circumstances an official position is something

to boast of. The officer of the Governor had merely to show himself at the station, and his furniture van was taken direct to the platform, wheeled alongside a truck and unloaded in a few moments, without anybody suspecting whence came its contents or whither they were going.

I had given Joseph, the commander of the convoy, a few lines for the Empress, expressive of my desire to be of use to her, begging her to dispose of me, and to accept the homage of a Frenchman, to whom she was not only a Sovereign, but a woman in distress.

On the following day, man, luggage and letter all reached their destination, and on the day after that, I in my turn received the following note which Joseph had been careful enough to sew inside the lining of his British coat. Through an excess of precaution the letter was not signed, but it was in the handwriting of the Empress.

'MARINE HOTEL, HASTINGS.

'I thank you for the letter I have just received. It touches me profoundly. I am compelled to be brief here, but my heart does not feel the less. Believe, sir, that I shall be glad one day to tell you so myself.'

In order not to prolong this account of my proceedings in connection with the personal effects of the Imperial family, and in order also not to have to return to the subject, I must say that as my duty in attendance on the Government rendered my presence, by night as well as by day, more and more necessary at the Louvre, I had received an order to take up my quarters in the Palace itself. For some time I occupied the suite of the Duchess Stephanie Tascher de la Pagerie, grand mistress of the Palace, in the first block of buildings on the right as you enter from the

Rue de Rivoli. When that suite and the rooms surrounding it were converted into an ambulance depôt, I took
refuge opposite at the Grand Almonry in the Rue de Rivoli.

My presence at the Palace enabled me to accede to the
requests of the servants of the Imperial family who came,
one after the other, in search of their personal property.
Although I was not formally appointed to watch over the
material interests of the Imperial family at the Tuileries,
nothing left the palace without my order.

On the 13th of September I received the following
letter :

'SIR,

'I beg you to endeavour without delay to find in the
room of the Comtesse de Pierrefonds, a little frame containing a Virgin and an Infant Jesus. They are on a piece
of furniture near the bed. There is also an old ivory-
coloured sunshade, with the letters E. G. on the handle.
Also a prayer-book with an elastic band round it. These
are souvenirs highly prized by the Comtesse de Pierrefonds.
I think the sunshade will be found in a corner of the room
on a small piece of furniture.

'Allow me to thank you, sir, with all my heart.

'A. LEBRETON.

'Will you kindly send the things to the Prince de
    Metternich.'

At the same time I received a letter emanating from
the Prefecture of Police, together with the official authority
of the Minister of Finances, ordering me to take possession
of all the Imperial furs, which were in the hands of Valenciennes, furrier to the Crown, No. 21 Rue Vivienne.

H

This is the letter.

'OFFICE OF THE PREFECT OF POLICE.

'SIR,

'I have the honour to inform you that you are authorised to forward the furs belonging to the Empress according to the enclosed list, and to provide for their being safely delivered.

'I am, Sir, &c., &c.

'The Prefect of Police,

'COMTE DE KÉRATRY.

'To M. d'Herisson,

'c/o General Trochu, Governor of Paris.'

I think that a literal transcript of the list in question may be interesting; my feminine readers, if I have any, will be able to see what furs they require to be well dressed.

'SIR,

The furs belonging to the Empress were handed to me on the 22nd of April, 1870, as detailed herewith:

One Swansdown cloak, lined with Silver Fox.
One black velvet mantle, trimmed with Marten Sable.
One black velvet circular cloak, lined and trimmed with Chinchilla.
One velvet pelise, lined with Weasel, with Sable collar.
One Otter skin cloak.
One blue Cashmere opera cloak, lined with Swansdown.
One black Cashmere opera cloak, lined with Swansdown.
One hunting waistcoat, lined with Chinchilla.
One black silk boddice, lined with Chinchilla.
One grey silk boddice, lined with Chinchilla.
One Marabout muff.

One Sable muff.
One Silver Fox muff.
One Ermine muff.
One Chinchilla muff.
One Otter muff.
One Otter's head muff.
One Marten Sable boa.
One collar of Sable tails.
One collar of Marten Sable heads.
One pair of Chinchilla cuffs.
One pair of Silver Fox cuffs.
One green velvet wrap, lined with Canadian fur.
One carpet of Thibet Goat skin.
One white Sheepskin carpet.
One set of Otter trimming.
Two caracos of Spanish Lamb skin.
8¾ yards of Chinchilla trimming.
27 yards of Sable tail trimming.
One front and a piece of Black Fox.
Four strips, a wrist band, two pockets, two sleeves
    and one trimming of Black Fox.
Two Swansdown skins, in pieces.
Fourteen Silver Fox skins.
Six half skins of Silver Fox.
Twenty Silver Fox tails.
One Otter collar.
Three tails of Canadian fur.
Two Marabout collars.
Some odd pieces of Chinchilla.
Four large carpets of black Bear skin.
Two small carpets of black Bear skin.
One brown Bear, with head.
One stuffed Bear.

One white Fox rug.

One caraco, one petticoat, and one waistcoat of chestnut coloured plush, trimmed with Otter.

19¾ yards of Otter trimming.

Two Pheasants' skins

Three white Sheepskin stools.

One Sable dress trimming.

Three Sable skins.

Two squares of Chinchilla.

One Weasel tippet and two cuffs to match.

Two pieces Swansdown.

Two Pheasants' wings.

One stuffed Fox.

One pair of Otter gloves.

3½ yards of Skunk trimming.

Two court mantles bordered with Ermine.

Paris, September 13, 1870.

'VALENCIENNES.'

Authorised by the Minister of Finances.

ERNEST PICARD.

Authorised by the Prefect of Police.

KÉRATRY.

There were furs to the value of 600,000 francs!

I also received a little note with the crest of a swan with outstretched wings and a prince's crown. It ran as follows:

'DEAR FRIEND,

'The Empress would like to have the portrait of the Emperor, by Flandrin, which is at the Tuileries, and a glove box which will be found in a wardrobe in the room of Madame Pollet, her treasurer, at

Saint-Cloud. This box has on it the Empress' monogram. If you could send these things it would be very kind of you. It is doubtful whether a train will leave to-morrow, but if possible will you send your faithful servant to-morrow morning to see the man who will start from here.

'Yours sincerely,

'METTERNICH.'

I could not comply with the Prince's request in regard to the box. It contained some private papers belonging to the Empress, which were considered of sufficient interest, by those who found them, to be sent direct to the Prefect of Police.

I saw them in his office a few days after the investment.

Under any circumstances my intervention would have been of no avail. M. de Kératry thought himself bound in honour to have this box and its contents given into the hands of the Empress herself. He did this after the con-clusion of the siege.

I am not at all ashamed to confess that I took great interest in my new profession of furniture remover, and that the *rôle* of packer by conviction, was not in the least displeasing to me. I was under the impression that I had entirely cleared out the second floor, when I found myself confronted by a closed door, which I caused to be opened. Before me was the furniture of the room in which the Duchess of Alba died. As the Empress regarded every single thing as a holy relic of her sister, I enlarged my industry, if I may so express myself, in enlarging the extent of my convoys.

The successive convoys continued thus up to the investment. From the day when we were blockaded, there would have been no reason to be in a hurry if the efforts of the police had not warned us of a rising, and of the pillage by armed bands with which the Commune favoured us later on. As a matter of fact I redoubled my activity in order to finish my work and put all the valuables in a place of safety.

A number of people had visited the Imperial apartments since the 4th of September, and the Commission for the examination of papers had made a strict search which lasted several days. It was well known that the room contained important valuables—not merely in an artistic, but a material sense—and I was not at all easy in my mind.

I applied more and more frequently to the Minister of Finance, the gay and witty Picard, whose good spirits were' not in the least affected by the serious events taking place around him, and who kept me waiting for the necessary permits.

Each time my duty took me to him, I went into his office and was invariably received with a broad grin.

'Very well, very well. The Tuileries again, I suppose?'

One day when he had made me laugh inordinately, he said,

'Why the deuce do you take all this trouble? Do you think they will ever return? We have to get rid of two generations of Republicans at least before that. And again, if they did return, my friend, you must be very ignorant of the world if you imagine that they will bear you any good will for having helped them to move out of the Tuileries. Think for a moment; you are sending them their belongings, and your doing so is a proof that in your opinion they will not come back again directly, and that they will be away for a considerable time. Such a supposition is disrespectful and they will not forgive you for having entertained it.

If they do not come back, well—their gratitude will be precisely the same.'

In vain I posed as a courtly knight, as a philanthropist, in vain I told him how I thought it only just to look after the interests of a prisoner and a fugitive—the good-tempered sceptic merely shrugged his shoulders in a friendly sort of way and said nothing.

One day, however, when I went to the Ministry of Finance with special passports which the Governor had handed to me for distribution, I said laughingly to M. Picard,

'I shall only give you these in exchange for the permits for which I am being kept waiting.'

'Very good; give me mine and I will speak to the Prefect of Police this evening.'

The promise was kept, and at length I obtained the following papers:

'OFFICE OF THE PREFECT OF POLICE.

'I have the honour to forward you the enclosed letter. I am glad to be of further assistance to you, and I beg you to accept my very kind regards.

'JAY.

'M. d'Herisson, Aide-de-Camp to General Trochu.'

'PARIS, *October 1st*, 1870.
'To M. Vavin, Liquidator of the Civil List.
'SIR,

'I have the honour to request you to be good enough to cause all effects of the Imperial family which may still remain in the Tuileries to be packed up under your superintendence, and at the expense of whom they concern, and to deliver them to M. d'Herisson, who is authorised to receive them.

> 'I have the honour, etc., etc.,
>
> 'The Prefect of Police,
>
> 'Comte de Kératry.'

It is characteristic of human nature—and, as Beaumarchais says, one must make haste to laugh if one does not want to cry over it — that the Imperial family, who had spent millions around them, before whom all France had just been bowing the knee, and who had been cheered to the echo in the form of a *plébiscite* scarcely five months old, did not find a single person to advance the expenses of packing and transport. The modest purse of an insignificant captain had to provide for them.

When everything was ready I made an urgent appeal to the Liquidator of the Civil List, M. Vavin, that some steps should be taken to secure the preservation of the precious things still in the Tuileries. I most assuredly never imagined that the day would come when the only remains of this superb palace would be charred and burnt stones, and yet I was not without misgivings. Can any one tell what may happen? I said to myself. It was, consequently, a great relief to my mind to receive the following letter from a Captain of the Staff of the *Garde Nationale,* second in command in the Palace.

> 'Palace of the Tuileries, *November* 12, 1870.
>
> 'My dear Comrade,
>
> 'I have received an order from M. Vavin to allow the removal of the boxes in question. Will you, therefore, take them away at any time convenient to

yourself, but kindly give me a little notice, so that I may be present.

'Yours, etc.,
'PERSIN.'

I wrote at once to the Comte d'Uxkul, in temporary charge of the Austrian Embassy, to ask him to find room for the first boxes, and I received the following immediate reply.

'*November 15th, 1870.*

'SIR,

'You expressed a desire to deposit at this Embassy, twenty-three boxes containing the personal effects of Her Majesty the Empress. I have the honour to acknowledge the receipt of these boxes, which will remain closed and in security until you are pleased to remove them for the purpose of their being forwarded to their proper destination.

'I have the honour, &c., &c,
'COMTE ALFRED D'UXKUL.'

And now I have reached the epilogue of the salvage of three or four millions of valuables, and must recount the utter confusion of the insignificant Captain and the crushing revenge of the gay Picard.

After the war was over, I still remembered my boxes, and I sent Joseph to the Austrian Embassy to find them and convey them to the Empress.

The dear Prince de Metternich, who had addressed me in September as his dear friend, as large as life, took the trouble to have the following epistle sent to me.

'*June 20th, 1871.*

'SIR,

'His Highness the Prince de Metternich, after having perused the order given by you to your valet for the boxes deposited at the Austrian Embassy, directs me to say that, having received fresh instructions enjoining him to keep the said boxes until further orders, his Highness is not in a position to give them up.

'I have the honour, &c., &c,
'LEDRU, *Huissier.*'

This salutary notice sent by the usher of the Austrian Embassy spared Joseph another voyage, and me further anxieties.

But that is not all.

I expected, not a reimbursement of the expenses advanced out of my modest pay, but an acknowledgment, some souvenir of the Emperor or Empress. I waited ten years for this acknowledgment or souvenir. Then, after having expressed my astonishment, I sent in a memorandum of my disbursements. They were repaid. We are quits.

Moral—Do not grow sentimental over a half-packed travelling-bag, and always listen to the good advice of a Minister of Finance.

CHAPTER VII

THE EMPRESS AND THE GOVERNOR

A Despatch.—Trochu in Command—His Popularity.—Royal Ingratitude.—The Emperor's Promises.—Trochu in Paris.—Hostility of the Empress.—Breton, Catholic and Soldier.—M. Rouher.—The Emperor Removed from Paris.

THE despatch sent from Paris by the Empress to the Emperor, which, in my opinion, explains the respective conduct of the two sovereigns on the one hand, and of General Trochu on the other, has already appeared in these pages; but before commenting on it, I will ask permission to copy it a second time.

' To the Emperor.

' Do not think of returning here unless you wish to induce a fearful revolution. This is the advice of Rouher and Chevreau, whom I have seen this morning. People here would say that you were running away from danger.

Do not forget that the departure of Prince Napoleon from the army in the Crimea has affected his whole life.

'EUGÉNIE.'

When the Emperor—a phantom of a sovereign tossed about between his armies, a fatalist who no longer believed in his star, not daring to assume the command, roughly used by Bazaine, ill, and carrying in his bladder a calculus as big as a pigeon's egg, with the result that riding was fearful torture—when the Emperor arrived at the camp at Châlons on the evening of the 16th of August, General Trochu, as Commander-in-Chief of the 12th *Corps,* belonged to the Army of the Rhine. His independence, his consciousness of his own worth, his brilliant roll of service, the almost prophetic foresight which had influenced him to write a recent book on the army—a book full of truths and opinions confirmed by events as they succeeded each other— and his rather austeré manner—that of a hard worker—so little in accord with the habits of the Court Generals, had roused jealousy, rivalry, and enmity among the sycophants and courtiers who surrounded the Emperor.

The effect of this state of things was, on the one hand, to keep the General away from the Tuileries; and on the other, to gain for him the respect and esteem of all impartial men. In addition to this, the Opposition of all shades took pleasure in achieving popularity for a General so out of favour. And this popularity increased rapidly at the very time when the Empire was disappearing under the burden of its mistakes. Patriots relied on him as on a great general. The enemies of the Empire relied on him as one relies on the adversaries of those whom one detests.

The Emperor Napoleon III might have been a very brave man, the best man perhaps in his Empire, a most

steadfast and faithful friend; but he was none the less a
sovereign, and as such he was compelled by his very position to bring forward those about him.   The idea of turning
the popularity of the General to his own personal profit, and
of conquering this adversary, came quite naturally to him.
Things always do happen so.   Louis XII said that it would
be unworthy a King of France to remember the insults
of the Duc d'Orleans.   An admirable sentiment! a royal
sentiment! but a sentiment which, like all other things
here below, has its reverse side; and the reverse of forgetfulness of insult is forgetfulness of services rendered.
Louis XII should have added, 'It is impossible for the
King of France to remember services rendered to the Duc
d'Orleans.'   A pretender asks for devotion—a king forgets
it.   It is the human order, or, rather, disorder of things.
A statesman who had been in the service of the Empire
said to me naïvely one day, ' Always be in opposition.
The more you are feared the more desirous will they be of
buying you, and in spite of yourself, and against your will,
you will be laden with honours and dignities.'

Cæsar, who was not quite a fool, was made Emperor
by his creditors.   Did he pay them ?   That is another
matter.

Well, Napoleon III was worth more than the average
of monarchs.   He was borne aloft to power by a few
friends, and he had the rare merit of not forgetting them.
The highest praise that can be bestowed on a prince is to
say that he was not ungrateful.   That was no reason, moreover, why he should not have sought for support among
the Opposition; why he should neglect the popularity of
General Trochu, bound up with the Opposition as he was;
or why he should not have dreamt of returning to his good
city of Paris on the General's shoulders.

'Go, my dear General,' he said to him; 'you alone can contrive my return, and your popularity is the key by which the door of the Tuileries will be opened for me. Speak to the Empress. Concert with her. I have the greatest confidence in you.'

Kept at a distance from the Court during its splendour, the General had a right to refuse to be seduced by this romantic mission, or to be flattered at seeing himself summoned and caressed only when it was a question of upholding the monument which was crumbling to pieces on all sides. Moreover, he had only to look round him to find a striking example of national ingratitude. He had only to let his eyes rest on General de Palikao.

General de Palikao, after having conducted the most fantastic military adventure of modern times in a most wonderful manner, after an unexpected success, the importance and the difficulty of which can now be estimated by the light of events which are passing to-day in those fabulous countries, after having added a glorious page to our military annals, saw himself on his return, insulted, overwhelmed with jealousy, vilified, and basely calumniated by the impotents of the Tuileries. The Chamber, the servile servant of him who ruled it, refused the grant half-heartedly asked for by the Minister; and the Emperor, the accomplice, for the first time perhaps, of the universal cowardice, dared not give a bâton to his victorious General.

It was not until the cowardice to which he yielded had opened the way to the fall of the Empire that anybody thought of General de Montauban, of inflicting on him the portfolio of Minister of War, and of repairing the wrongs they had done him. The reparation was tardy and the devotion of no avail.

General Trochu, therefore, knew what he had to expect,

and could estimate in advance the amount of gratitude his
services were worth to him ; for a real sacrifice was asked
of him.

To give up his command, his fine little army, to go and
shut himself up in Paris with the Emperor, the *Mobiles*,
and the *Garde Nationale*, was a military operation which
had no temptation for him. The appeal was made not
only to his feelings as a soldier and a patriot, but also as a
Christian. He was told he had a dynasty to watch over,
a woman and a child to protect.

After much hesitation—and any man, were he a hero or
a martyr, would have hesitated in his place—the General
consented.

'Sire,' he said simply, 'I have your promise. It is
agreed that I go to prepare the way for your return, and
that I should not leave the army for any less important
motive.'

'Yes,' replied the Emperor, 'you have my promise. In
a little while I shall rejoin you. I only impose this sacrifice on you because it seems to me absolutely necessary.'

During this interview the *Mobiles* were defiling before
the Imperial Head-quarters, giving utterance to the filthy
insults I have already recorded.

As he left the Emperor, the General conceived the idea
of taking the *Garde Mobile* back to Paris. It was the first
act of his new part. It was the beginning of the execution
of the plan agreed upon which was to lead to the return of
Napoleon III to the Tuileries. It was a question of gaining
for the Emperor the gratitude of thousands of families
whose children would be restored to them.

What has not been said about the conduct of General
Trochu, and the secret reasons which induced him to bring
all these Parisians back to their homes! All that was

said was just as fair and just as loyal as was the conduct of the country towards the glorious soldier of Taku, Chang-Kia-Wang, and Palikao.

Such was the conduct of General Trochu at Châlons; let us see what he did in Paris.

He found the Empress hostile rather than distrustful. She affected before him a freedom of mind and a security which were very far from her heart. A Governor of Paris, paving the way for the return of the Emperor, a return which she neither approved nor desired, and General Trochu that Governor!

I will not insinuate for a moment that the Empress had thought of playing Jeanne d'Arc and of saving France herself, though perhaps it would have been pleasant to have restored a crown to him who had given her one.

And Trochu appeared on the scene to dispel this generous dream!

In vain did he protest his fidelity and devotion—it was made evident to him that not a word was believed.

'I am a Breton, a catholic, and a soldier!'—and they laughed.

Ah! bitter indeed must have been the cup which was held to his lips in that last fortnight of August, and at the bottom of it he found only disappointment, regret, and disgust.

When the Emperor received the famous telegram almost ordering him not to return, he must have been surprised, if indeed anything could then hâve surprised that great sceptic. But he resolved to pay no attention to it. He had promised General Trochu. He wanted to return all the same. And possibly the idea of a campaign with General Trochu was not altogether displeasing; for the Emperor, though subject to the influence of an *entourage* who execrated the General, both liked and appreciated the Commander of the 12th *Corps*.   One day, speaking of him to some friends at the Tuileries, he said laughingly,

'However that may be, Trochu is still the strongest of you all.'

Then it was that a man of immense talent, of a no less sense of honour, whose life was a model of that disinterestedness immortalised by antiquity, was sent to the Emperor to beg him not to return to Paris. I mean M. Rouher.

He had for the Emperor the same warm, personal, familiar affection, that General Fleury had, and he loved his country well enough to give his life for her, a life discounted in advance and worn out by the late hours, the struggles and labours of Parliament.

The selection of M. Rouher was all the more happy because he never would have taken such a step in connection with the Emperor if he had not personally been convinced, outside all the influences and the ambition of the Empress-Regent, that the presence of Napoleon III in Paris might bring about a catastrophe. It was not by chance that the Empress confided so delicate a mission to him. There is no advocate so good as he who is convinced of the excellence of his case.

The Emperor, shaken possibly to a certain extent by the telegram from the Empress, thought himself bound to yield to the persistence of his faithful servant. And thus was the promise given to General Trochu kept.

It is right, however, to say that at the last moment a despatch from Bazaine, summoning MacMahon to his aid, did away with all hesitation.

The Empress was informed at once that the Emperor had given way to reasons of State, and to her wishes expressed so categorically—I would say brutally if I were not speaking of a woman. Her attitude towards General Trochu immediately became more definite. From having been hostile she became offensive. Previously, she had shown no confidence in him ; now, every kind of refinement was called into play to give him evidence of an insulting distrust. So far was this carried that when he presented himself at the Tuileries, in the *salon* of the Empress, all conversation came to a dead stop as if by order. He might have been a spy breaking in upon a secret meeting of conspirators. All the faithful looked at each other in profound silence, and the unfortunate man, completely out of countenance, lost no time in beating a retreat, that is to say, retiring in good order, as he so often had to say when speaking of his troops during the siege. More than once, in fact, the Empress gave him to understand in so many words that his presence was tolerated because there was no help for it, but that it was in no way agreeable.

It would therefore be unjust to stigmatise as a crime the fact that General Trochu was chary of visiting the Tuileries, and that he left to the Minister of War the office, which the latter afterwards acknowledged, of providing for the safety of the Regent. If the Empress had been on terms with the General other than those she had established of her own free will, would not her first impulse have been to call him to her side and place herself under his protection? And God alone knows what would have happened if she had had the courage to take the step which she either dared not or would not take.

CHAPTER VIII

PARIS BLOCKADED

Return of Vinoy.—The Demonstrations.—Between Orderly Officers.—Merchants and Artists.—The Volunteers of '92·—A Review.—An Old Soldier and a Young Horse.—A Grand Officer of the Legion of Honour.—The Capitol and the Tarpeian Rock.—The Investment of Châtillon.—Ferrières.—Villejuif and l'Hay.—The Thrushes and the Little Foot Soldier.—Military Honour.

I HAVE already said more than once, and I repeat it, that I have no pretention to write the history of the siege of Paris, but that I limit myself to the narration of my own reminiscences.

I therefore pass over in silence the return of General Vinoy at the head of the little army he so successfully saved out of the clutches of the Prussians. The *Corps d'Armée,* commanded by Vinoy, was on the point of joining MacMahon at the very moment when the Prussians completed the manœuvre which resulted in the unfortunate Marshal being surrounded and enclosed in a circle of steel and fire. Vinoy arrived at the very instant when, from the Mezières side, the German regiments closed together like the formidable teeth of some monstrous animal. He had sent out a regiment of Hussars in advance along his extreme front, and the enemy took an officer and a few men, called the point of the vanguard, prisoners. The rest of the regiment fell back on the main body, and the *Corps d'Armée* returned to Paris. It was at that time the only regularly organised military force.

Neither will I allude to the fiery proclamations of M. Gambetta, nor the delirious demonstrations in the streets, nor the thunders of the newspapers. Everybody spoke in epic poetry, and they vied with one another in lyrical language. Unhappily, big words glibly took the place of lofty sentiments, and an inflated style stood substitute for energetic thought. In those feverish days we thought everything good, and we got drunk on phrases. Our brain was like the palace of certain drunkards, through which pure alcohol runs with no other effect than to produce a genial warmth. How, in the midst of a crowd vibrating like a torpedo, was it possible to avoid an electric shock in head or heart?

It often happened, nevertheless, that when we staff officers were by ourselves, and narrated all that we had seen on our daily rounds, we felt our enthusiasm depart, and despair succeed.

We did not mince matters in the green room, we passed judgment on men and things with king-like independence, and if the telephone had been invented, the Government by listening to our discussions would have been able to have availed itself of more lengthy information than was contained in the official reports.

One evening one of us was reading the circular issued by Jules Favre to our diplomatic representatives. When he reached the words, 'Not an inch of our territory, not a

stone of our fortresses,' he stopped. A positive thrill ran
through us.

'I suppose you call that beautiful,' said he to us. 'It is
beautiful, perhaps, but its beauty is transitory, for if we
give up, not an inch but whole leagues of territory, not
mere stones but entire fortresses, there will be no beauty in
it. And all of you who now look upon Jules Favre as a
great man, because he has indited this sonorous line, will be
ready to think him a fool.'

'And honour?' protested somebody. 'Does not that
take precedence of material interests?'

'I should be delighted,' replied the sceptic, 'to have it
proved to me that, when you are wounded in a duel,
honour obliges you to continue fighting at the risk of
being killed. I should be delighted to have it proved to
me that all the sovereigns and all the nations who have
made peace after disasters far less considerable than those
which have befallen us, were cowards and lubbers. If this
be so, I should like to know where I am to find any brave
people in Europe. Every nation has in turn been beaten
by us, and they one and all made peace when they found
themselves no longer able to fight on even terms. Was
Francis Joseph a coward to make peace after Solferino, or
Alexander II after the fall of Sebastopol, to say nothing of
many others both in recent and distant days? There is no
disgrace in being defeated, provided you have done your
duty, and the army which has defeated you has deserved
the victory by good fighting too. In regard to material
interests, my opinion is diametrically opposed to yours, my
dear opponent. Nations have governments in order that
their material interests may be looked after, and for a very
long time past, up to the present day, these governments
have executed their tasks here below, after a very miserable

fashion. What good did the Crimea bring us? None. Mexico? None. China? None. All the wars of Napoleon? None. So true is this that the English say of us, 'The French fight for the pleasure of conquering.' And they are right. When we are beaten, our territories and our millions pay the expenses. When we beat others, we let somebody else take the price of our blood. Look at England, and model yourselves after her, not altogether, but to a certain extent.'

'Then,' asked one of us, 'what ought we to have done according to you?'

'A very simple thing. We ought to have accepted the proposition of Palikao, an unconstitutional proposition which would have replaced the Imperial Government by a committee, and to have authorized this committee to say to the King of Prussia, "You have declared that you were making war, not against France, but against the Emperor. Very well. The Emperor is conquered and a prisoner, treat with him, arrange the matter between yourselves; it does not concern us." Napoleon and William would have worked out their little combinations. We should perhaps have lost something, but assuredly not all that we shall lose if we do not come victorious out of this impossible enterprise. There you have my opinion.'

'That would have been an invitation to proclaim the Republic.'

'Well?'

'Remember 1792!'

'Alas! We lack the non-commissioned officers of Louis XVI. The famous volunteers, whose existence has not otherwise been proved to me, would have done nothing if they had not been commanded by the old non-commissioned officers of the Monarchy. Sergeants were made generals, possibly, but at all events, that proves that there were sergeants in those days. Can you find any now ? They are all in Prussia or with Bazaine, that is to say, they are in all probability besieged in Metz as we are going to be in Paris.'

The speaker was one of the General's favourites, and I shuddered as I instinctively recognised the chief's thoughts in the officer's words, and understood that we were already confronted by that terrible antagonism — the complete history of the siege—between those who believed in victory, and those whose knowledge of warfare compelled them even now to foresee defeat.

There are times, nevertheless, when illusion is permissible—these are times when one need be of iron not to feel a thrill of hope. One of ·these was the 13th of September, when I was present at the finest review I have ever seen in my life.

The whole army, the *Garde Mobile*, the *Garde Nationale*, the Volunteers, the Free Corps, the Marines, the Artillery, and what little remained of the Cavalry, were drawn up several files deep in two immense lines, commencing at the Bastille, following the Boulevards, the Rue Royale, the Place de la Concorde, and the Champ-Elysées, and extending beyond the Barrière de l'Etoile.

The fully armed and equipped soldiers formed the front ranks. Behind them were those whose uniforms and arms were still incomplete.

Never was a more numerous and enthusiastic army drawn up before a more popular or more heartily cheered leader, or surrounded by a more thoroughly roused and demonstrative population.

The troops filled the whole of the road-way. The foot-paths seemed paved with human heads, others being ranged in rows, one above the other, in the windows, and over-flowing on to the roofs. It was a curious sight.

Mounted on a magnificent charger, the Governor rode in front of an imposing group of General Officers, followed by a squadron of aides-de-camp and officers of all arms, whose horses had not yet undergone any of the privations they shared with their riders during the siege.

Trumpets sounded, drums beat, and the soldiers presented arms, with shouts of ' *Vive Trochu!* ' or ' *Vive la République!* ' and the populace, waving their hats, caps, handkerchiefs, and sunshades, vied with the army in cheering vociferously.

I confess that when I looked at all the faces radiant with enthusiasm, and the glistening eyes, and when I heard the roar from every stalwart breast, I fully imagined that nothing could resist thât feverish multitude. Trochu, I knew, believed in the defence that day. I do not know how long his conviction lasted.

At the top of the Faubourg Poissonnière the Review was enlivened by an incident both comic and touching.

An old Admiral, with long whiskers and long white hair, was in command of the troops drawn up at that particular spot. He was mounted on a young and restive horse, which appeared to be causing him some anxiety by reason of the temper and impatience it exhibited at each blast of the trumpet, or roll of the drum.

He advanced to meet the Governor, who halted his escort in order to pay especial respect to one of the commanders of our best troops—the Marines.

When he was ten paces distant from the Governor, the Admiral reined up his kicking horse, and saluted with his sword. The animal, seeing the blade flash past his right eye, stood up on its hind legs, and went off at a gallop.

The Admiral, unwilling to compromise his reputation as

an intrepid horseman, a reputation coveted, from love of contrast, by all naval officers, mastered his steed, and brought him back after some forty plunges.

And he began to repeat his salute to the Governor, who, by this time, had advanced several yards at a walk.

At this moment the bugles of the battalion drawn up on the right of General Trochu sounded the general salute, and quick as lightning, and this time in real earnest, the Admiral's horse went off at full speed. The old soldier had lost his cap, and his trousers had run up to his calves; embarrassed by his naked sword and his reins, he was hanging on by the mane. We saw him disappear in the distance of the deserted road, pursued by a large dog which had got through the line of troops and was barking with all its might behind him.

Trochu, turning towards his suite, said, quietly and seriously :

' His doing that is very dangerous.'

A little further on we saw him stop and salute, with great respect, a simple *Garde National,* on whose breast glittered the star of a Grand Officer of the Legion of Honour. It was the Minister Duruy.

When we got back to the Louvre after this interminable review, Trochu, whom we were congratulating, replied,

' Yes, it has been very fine. But you cannot imagine how inconsistent these popular masses are. We have reached the Capitol—beware of the Tarpeian rock.'

Nevertheless, I knew that he was profoundly impressed, and· that if he was not quite overcome, he had several hours, perhaps days, of confidence and hope.

However, the investment began. Some of us, making use of our permits, which opened gates shut to the rest of the world, used to stroll along the roads to the south of

Paris, and were thus enabled to catch sight of the Uhlan patrols. One of the party got within reach of the infantry by dint of advancing under cover, and was honoured with a harmless volley. It was evident that the Prussians were beginning their envelopment of Paris from the south, and were marching on Versailles by way of Choisy-le-Roi. Their first plan was to interpose themselves between Paris and the still intact south of France. Manœuvering and fighting took place on the 17th, 18th, and 19th of September. The last of these days was the Châtillon affair. The Governor was not present at the engagement, which was by no means brilliant. The *Mobiles* and the Line killed each other by firing on each other in the confusion very natural tò young troops, and, wonderful to relate, the Zouaves gave the signal for the panic. When the red breeches were seen to recoil and take to flight, the helter-skelter became general. Half Paris, the left bank of the river, was thronged with soldiers, who had discarded both rifles and ammunition in order to run away the faster, and who already began to utter that sinister and cowardly phrase which was heard so often afterwards, 'We are betrayed!'

While these first engagements were going on, Jules Favre went to Ferrières. The honourable deputies who then governed France had such a confused notion of the traditions of government that the Minister took this step unknown to his colleagues. There is no need for me to record it, for all the world knows it. I recollect, however, the singular impression made upon us by reading the account of their interview, and of the diplomatic conversation between Jules Favre and Bismarck. The contrast between the two men was startling. Bismarck hammered out his sentences, relied absolutely on military necessities and the interest of the belligerent force, never put himself forward, and kept on saying, 'We—we want this—we must demand that.' Jules Favre spoke of his heart, his anguish, his emotions, his tears—his too famous tears. The report produced some such sensation as one would experience on seeing a poor old goat trembling between a lion's paws.

Our comrade, the sceptic, reassured his staff commentary by saying,

'If the old women meddle in our affairs, the thing will be complete.'

On the 23rd of September General de Maud'huy fought the battle of Villejuif, which gave us the Hautes-Bruyères redoubt, which we had to hold, and to a certain extent raised the tone of the army, completely discouraged by the Châtillon affair. Skirmishing went on up till the 30th. On that date the battle of Chevilly was fought. It was glorious, but useless. It gave us nothing, and cost us some brave lives, among them General Guilhem, who was killed when marching bravely at the head of his brigade.

On the next day but one after the Chevilly affair, General Schmitz went in person to the field of battle and then to the advanced posts of the Prussians, in order to demand the body of General Guilhem. I had the honour of accompanying the Chief of the Staff, and we were followed by a convoy of ambulance waggons with doctors and litter-bearers, so that we might rescue and bring back all the wounded we could find between the two armies.

The Prussian sentries mounted guard in pairs, each man being posted only a few paces from the next. While one of them went in search of the officer appointed to confer with us, I got off my horse and instituted a search in the neighbouring fields.

We were to the right of where the hottest part of the

battle had been fought.   There was not a tree that had not been hit.   The French *mitrailleuse* had mowed long lanes in the vines, cutting down plant and pole alike.   Nothing had been changed : nothing had yet been touched on the battle-field; and in certain places a sickening moisture marked the pools of blood with which the ground was reeking.   Here were helmets, there guns, and further on pouches, *képis*, sword-bayonets, belts, account-books, all sorts of soldiers' effects, and above all, a large number of cartridge-boxes.

I had an idea of bringing away a rifle, but a huge fair devil of a Prussian sentry, trying his best to make his porcelain blue eyes look ferocious, shouted out in German, 'Let go that rifle!'   I looked at him and he repeated, 'Let go that rifle!'   1 pretended not to understand him, and continued my walk, rifle in hand.   But as, when he called out for the third time, 'Let go that rifle,' I saw he was in a rage and was taking aim at me, I thought I had better not give him a chance, and I put down the rifle.   It was a *chassepot* and only remarkable because a Prussian bullet was imbedded in the butt.

I made a most minute examination of this corner because I wanted to note the effects of the terrific fire and the storm of shells I had heard and seen there during the battle, and I then regained the ambulance waggons.   As I passed through the vines I startled two thrushes which were quietly picking the forgotten grapes.   I experienced singular pleasure, as well as emotion, on hearing the cries of these two poor birds, for they must either have been on the spot during the bloody engagement, or must have courageously returned after the battle.   Close to the place where the two thrushes had got up I discovered a poor little infantry soldier, barely twenty-two, who had had both legs

smashed at the ankle joint by the bursting of a shell. One
of his feet was absolutely torn away—the other, the bones
of which were completely crushed, was still hanging by the
sinews and a strip of flesh. The poor little fellow had
dragged himself to where his foot was, about three paces
from where he himself fell, had seized hold of it in the
pool of clotted blood, and was pressing it close to him.
There he was, still alive after having been lying in the
vineyard for forty-eight hours—two days and two nights.
There was still a gleam of intelligence in his dull and glassy
eyes, and when he recognised my French uniform, he
mustered up strength enough to say in a low tone,
like a sick child, 'Something to drink.'

I leaned over him, took hold of both his arms, passed
them round my neck, and turning sharply, so as to put him
on my back, I carried him towards our waggons, without any
remonstrance this time from the German sentry. He
moaned slightly, and behind me I felt his remaining foot
swinging to and fro, knocking against my legs. I laid him
down on a litter and gave him a large glass of water, with
some rum in it. He drank and died.

During the first portion of the engagement our wounded
were, as a rule, hit on the legs, from the feet to the knees.
As the day wore on the enemy mended his aim. In the
evening all the wounds were either in the head or full in
the breast.

The body of General Guilhem, pierced by ten bullets,
was handed over to us. The Prussians gave it up with all
the solemnity possible under the circumstances. Eight
soldiers carried the bier, covered with flowers and foliage,
on Uhlan lances; and, as they passed onwards, the various
guards and isolated sentries presented arms, the officers
saluting with their swords. It was a more striking sight,

in the midst of the ravaged and desolated country, than the most gorgeous funeral procession that ever approached the gate of the Invalides.

On the 7th of October, that is to say, on the eve of the day when I was destined to spend such an unpleasant quarter-of-an-hour in the square in front of the Hôtel de Ville, I went to Creteil in order to conduct outside our lines Prince Wittgenstein, Military Attaché to the Russian Embassy, who was leaving Paris, furnished with all the necessary passports.

CHAPTER IX

AN AMATEUR DIPLOMATIST

In the Governor's Office.—An Unexpected Meeting.—General Burnside.—Armistice and Revictualling.—Governor and Interpreter.—Jules Favre.—Mr Washburne.—At the Advanced Posts.—How Parleying is carried on.—The Bridge of Sèvres.—The Facetious Adjutant.—Flags of Truce Attacked.—Volleys.

THE 2nd of October fell on a Sunday. Towards 1.30 A.M. I was sleeping soundly, when a loud knocking at my door roused me with a start.

' Who is there ? '

' I, Lunel.'

Commandant Lunel, who served through the Italian war, and was attached to the Head-quarters Staff of the General Commanding in Chief, was entrusted with the internal administration of Head-quarters. It was no sinecure. Ever ready to do anybody a service, full of amiability and always obliging, he was our providence, and we owe him innumerable horse steaks, with which he contrived to supply us constantly during the siege. He is now Military Commandant of the Palais de Justice.

'Get up.   The Governor is asking for you.'

I hastily put on the uniform I had just taken off, and went at once to General Trochu.

He was alone, seated in front of his desk, and dressed in the semi-civil, semi-military attire to which he was addicted—a lounging jacket and red trousers.   He wore a Greek cap, necessary by reason of his total baldness, which he never left off.   In his hand he held his large meerschaum pipe, which, as smokers say, was lovingly coloured.

'I am sorry, my dear fellow,' he said to me, 'to disturb you, but the arrival of an American General, who does not speak French, is announced at the advanced posts.   As I do not speak English, I wish you to act as interpreter. Sit down,' he added, as he pointed with his finger to one of those settees which are often found in high windows, 'sleep if you like. I will awake you when I want you.   I have work to do.'

I dared not lie down on the settee in the Governor's presence, and I slept as best I could in a posture as respectful as was possible.   Towards five o'clock the General roused me.

'You can go to bed again,' he said.   'The General will not come till later on.   Come back at eight.'

At nine o'clock the American General, preceded by a courier, entered the office of the Governor, who received him standing, in fine form, and surrounded by all his staff.

General Trochu bade me welcome the visitor, and was not a little astonished when he saw him suddenly come to me with both arms outstretched, and kiss me on both cheeks. I explained that six weeks previously I had made the acquaintance of the General on board the steamer which brought me from America, and had rapidly formed an intimacy with him during those eleven days of enforced confinement.

General Burnside was accompanied by the American Colonel Forbes. He informed the Governor, through my intermediation, that he had come to Europe, attracted by the grandeur of the military events which were taking place in France. He asked permission to visit Paris, as he had visited the Prussian army. He wished, after having studied the mechanism of the most colossal investment ever undertaken, to make himself equally well acquainted with the means of defence, and to contemplate the spectacle, so consoling to humanity, of a patriotism capable of giving birth to such mighty efforts.

General Burnside was no ordinary General. He is very popular in the United States, and played a considerable part during the war of the Secession.

Without being fully convinced that the General was attracted only by a feeling of military curiosity, the Governor hastened to say that he would do all in his power to make the investigations of his colleague easy and complete. The interview was a very cordial one. The American complimented the Frenchman on the martial and proud attitude of the city of Paris. General Trochu thanked him and replied that the population of Paris were undoubtedly resolved to hold out to their last mouthful of bread.

'I imagine,' he said, 'that the pleasantest thing I can do is to place your friend, M. d'Herisson, at your disposal. He will take you everywhere and show you everything.'

They shook hands cordially, and I took the American General as far as the Rue de Rivoli, appointing to meet him at one o'clock the same day.

The Governor had intimated that he wished to speak to me, and when I returned to his office, he honoured me with almost complete confidence in regard to the political situation then existing.

'It is necessary,' he said to me, 'that your relations with General Burnside should be profitable to the cause of our country. If he asks you, take him over the whole of the *enceinte* except the forts. Avoid taking him to those sections of the ramparts where the preparations for defence are not very brilliant. Without appearing to do so, take him to the most strongly fortified spots. He says he is not an emissary of M. de Bismarck, but treat him, all the same, as if the Chancellor had sent him. At this particular juncture, if we could obtain an armistice, a suspension of hostilities, in order to convoke an Assembly, on condition, of course, that we are permitted to revictual ourselves for the whole period of the armistice, it would be superb. M. de Bismarck may be willing, for we do not know what Bazaine is doing. But to obtain it we must seem as if we did not want it. Put on an air, therefore, of the greatest confidence, perfect security, and absolute tranquillity. Do not exaggerate. Be merely natural. Go.'

General Burnside, as a matter of fact, made a very superficial examination of our means of defence ; but I took him to Jules Favre, for whom M. de Bismarck had given him letters, among them a diplomatic communication in which he persisted in his resolve to forward only unsealed letters to foreign ministers resident in Paris, and as a matter of course to open any letters they might send to their Governments.

In Jules Favre's presence General Burnside protested that he was not sent by M. de Bismarck, and that he had not received any mission at the hands of the Chancellor But he nevertheless thought, he said, that he might say that the idea of an armistice would not be repelled at Versailles.

Jules Favre replied that from the moment the Chancellor admitted the possibility of an armistice he was at a loss to understand why he should have refused it when he, Jules Favre, went to Ferrières in person to ask for one, not to give the defence time to consolidate itself, as M. de Bismarck had alleged, but to consult the country on the possibility of coming to terms with Germany—a step of which the Government of the National Defence did not think they ought to assume the responsibility.

He added that the defence had been established subsequently to his visit to Ferrières—thanks to the efforts of the population of Paris. He further said that public opinion, having made up its mind that Paris was impregnable, and would succumb only to famine, called for the union of all energies to attack and fight the invaders of French territory to the bitter end. The city was well provisioned. If a capitulation was to be the end of the siege, it was far distant, and before it came to pass many things might happen.

If M. de Bismarck would consent to an armistice free from the impossible conditions suggested at Ferrières, and especially the military conditions which would place Paris under the Prussian guns, he was quite ready to sign it. The end he had in view, then as before, was to consult the nation, and if unofficial intermediaries chose to engage in the effort to bring the idea to a successful issue, he begged them in advance to receive the grateful thanks of the Government, and of France.

The American General and Colonel took their leave of the Minister, and returned to Versailles, after having requested permission, which was granted to them, to repeat the terms of the interview to the Chancellor. They only remained one day in Paris.

They returned on the 6th of October. They had seen M. de Bismarck, and came back bearing the following proposals. An armistice of forty-eight hours. The Prussian Head-quarters to grant all passports necessary to facilitate the departure of all citizens wishing to proceed to the departments to canvass the electors. Exception to be made in the case of Alsace and Lorraine, where no elections would take place. The elections over, and they would not affect, in any way, the military operations against Paris, a town in France to be named for the meeting of the assembly, which would have to pronounce in favour of peace or war.

The conference took place in a room adjoining the Minister's office in the Ministry of Foreign Affairs. There were present General Burnside, Colonel Forbes, Colonel Hoffmann, Mr Washburne, Minister of the United States, Jules Favre, General Trochu, and myself.

I acted as interpreter, and though Mr Washburne and Colonel Forbes understood and spoke French very well, I was none the less obliged to translate the conversation word for word. When I had translated an important sentence, which necessitated an effort both of memory and accuracy, Mr Washburne nodded his head in witness to the accuracy of the translation.

. On this occasion, which might well be called solemn, I saw, not for the first time, what slaves we are to our peculiarities. When General Trochu had to give his opinion, he made a speech. He went on and on, without troubling himself to ascertain if I was following him: I listened at first with the most profound attention, but at length the moment arrived when I felt that if he went on much longer, I should lose the beginning. I used then to interrupt him in order to translate all I could remember. It is very easy to understand that an interpreter cannot store up in his memory a speech extending over twenty minutes. The General never took that into consideration, and with him the same thing happened over and over again.

When the conference was over, Jules Favre and General Trochu requested permission to refer the matter to their colleagues, and I had time to turn the instructions of the Governor to account by showing my friend Burnside about. I played the part of guide in such a way as to give him the highest possible idea of our means of defence.

These interminable interviews were destined to be resultless. After having consulted his colleagues, Jules Favre in a last interview showed that the inconsistent and vague propositions of which General Burnside was the bearer, could not be accepted, that they would place the elections at the mercy of the enemy, and would not give the electors any means of expressing their real wishes. But, on the other hand, if the Chancellor would agree to an armistice of a fortnight, with proportionate revictualling, the French Government would gladly accept it.

The minister handed General Burnside a letter couched in these terms for M. de Bismarck, and after a desultory conversation on the events of the day, outside the scope of the political questions which had been under discussion, the conference broke up.

This visit of General Burnside brought me for the first time in contact with Jules Favre. On the conclusion of the interview, when he was obliged to go to Versailles to sue for peace, he asked General Trochu to let me have me as secretary. He knew that I had been educated in a German university, and thought that my knowledge of German might be of use to him in those sad negotiations.

In the course, also, of these interviews I discovered how hostile the Minister of the United States, Mr Washburne, was to us, and what harm he did us. The more General Burnside showed his sympathy with us, the more did the diplomatist appear to sympathise with our victorious enemies. Here we have another living instance of the truth that the Creator predestined the Frenchman to be a dupe. If it had not been for us, America would perhaps still belong to England. If it had not been for the ingenuous French nobility, the English would probably have got the upper hand of their subjects who revolted by reason of the tea and paper duties. We may say that we almost made America. At the time I am describing she remembered that fact only to applaud Prussia. Italy, that daughter to whom our blood gave life, furnished a still more repugnant example of ingratitude, seeing that the benefits conferred on her were more recent.

Mr Washburne discovered a thousand ways in which to show us his antipathy; one struck me particularly, as it was ingenious and almost Italian. He used to receive the American papers, and when he sent us any he took great pains to put an ink mark against what might interest us especially. After the war the Emperor William loaded him with favours and sent him his full length portrait.

He had not stolen either the favour or the portrait.

While I was re-conducting General Burnside to the advanced posts, he told me that he himself had taken the initiative in these negotiations and had made an urgent representation to M. de Bismarck in our favour, but that the Chancellor was in no way anxious that the interview should succeed, that it was a matter of absolute indifference to him, and that, moreover, whenever we might be obliged to treat, he whom the Germans call the 'Iron Chancellor' would cut out of the French cake the portion conquered by the Prussian victories. He told me, also, that on several occasions M. de Bismarck had expressed his absolute certainty that our internal divisions would complete the work of his master's armies.

At the advanced posts a rather curious incident happened, which was not important in itself, but as it gave rise to an interchange of notes between Paris and Versailles I will record it in detail.

When two armies come into collision, if there is a battle, and it follows its course until one of the two is beaten, retreats, or takes to flight, there is nothing more to be said. The victors bury their own dead and those of the conquered, who reform as best they can in some other position. But if after the battle, both remain face to face on the ground, if one of them, shut up in a fortress, is besieged by the other, if they still remain in contact, then whether they like it or not, their close proximity is bound to engender relations of some kind. Flags of truce come into operation in a multitude of cases; to make proposals; to impart news which one of the two thinks, from his point of view, would be useful for the other to know; sometimes for an exchange of prisoners, sometimes for the safe passage of neutrals, like General Burnside, or personages charged with diplomatic missions, like M. Thiers, from one camp to the other. Or there is a parley to obtain a suspension of hostilities for the purpose of burying the dead. In fact, there is an almost daily parley in the ordinary course of a siege.

Although nearly all the German officers spoke French it was natural enough that a French officer who spoke German should be chosen to communicate with them; and as that was my case, I was selected by the Governor as the habitual bearer of his flag of truce.

I, therefore, was regularly sent to parley with the enemy, and this was the course of proceedings. I went on horseback, furnished with either written or verbal instructions, according to circumstances, as far as the bridge of Sèvres, followed by a cavalry trumpeter who carried in his hand a flag of truce, a simple white napkin fixed on to the end of a stick.

At the end of the bridge of Sèvres which belonged to us, there was a little house half knocked to pieces by shells and riddled with bullets, which was called ' The House of the Flag of Truce.'

Up to this house everything went on smoothly, and the ride was not dangerous. We rode one behind the other on the lower side of the route, tolerably sheltered from the bullets by the trees planted along the road, as by a rampart. We had nothing to fear from the shells exchanged between the defence and the Prussian batteries. Their trajectory was so high that they passed well over our heads. It would have argued very bad luck, and great and very rare clumsiness on the part of the batteries in position, if a shell had fallen near either of us. It only happened once, when I happened to be in a *coupé* which formerly belonged to the Emperor. Shortly before I reached the Sèvres bridge a stray shell burst close to the carriage, and a fragment struck the body.

At our end of the bridge there was a barricade composed of all kinds of things. Before getting over it, we put our horses under cover and the trumpet sounded the 'cease firing.'

As soon as the trumpeter of the post on the other bank had sounded the German call corresponding to ours, we escaladed the barricade and waved our white flag.

The two calls could be heard a very long way off, for in those regions there reigned in the intervals of firing an extraordinary, solemn, mournful, and almost supernatural silence—the silence of death, that which on earth preceded the appearance of living beings. You might have heard a gnat fly between the advanced sentries posted on both banks, and you might have said that even the Seine, gliding slowly along the desolate landscape, had stilled the murmuring of its waters.

The Prussian officer bearing the flag of truce then advanced along the bridge from his side, as I did at the same time from mine. The middle arch of the bridge no longer existed, it had been blown up by dynamite. We halted on our respective sides of the yawning gulf and entered into conversation. I am bound to confess that my interlocutors were almost always young officers of distinguished bearing, of whom there are so many in the German Army. There are many drawing-rooms where conversation is carried on with less gracefulness than we displayed. We put on new gloves figuratively and in reality to converse.

When everything went on thus it was perfect, and I bore with a good grace the genial *badinage* to which I was treated by a sort of adjutant who commanded the advanced post of Sèvres, and who, as soon as he saw me, sent a mounted orderly to apprise the Prussian officer told off for the duty of parleying, whose quarters were away from the banks of the river.

These jokes lacked variety, and in the end they were reduced to one, always the same.

The animal took a few paces along the bridge and called out in German,

' Good morning, captain. You are thinner than you were when I saw you last.'

As I did not see any use in altering my formula so long as he did not change his, I invariably replied,

' I am in training and on strict diet.'

The fair idiot would reply,

'You have nothing to eat when you are hungry.'

To which I always answered,

'If you want anything do not distress yourself about it. You know the proverb—"Where there is enough for—"'

Frequently, however, once out of three times on an average, when we had mounted the barricade, we were saluted with a shot or two, and the bullets as they struck the ground at our feet, or lodged in the empty barrels which formed part of the barricade, made a strange noise. By degrees this mode of receiving us became too frequent to be borne; a complaint was necessary. One day, after the 'cease firing' had been sounded on my side and I had heard the corresponding call from the other bank, I advanced to the opening of the bridge without any officer coming to meet me, and the sentries aimed and fired at my trumpeter and myself. I saw them quietly adjusting their sights, for their aim had at first been hasty and ill directed, and if I had remained there I should certainly have been hit. I was obliged to retire and report the circumstances to the Chief of the Head-quarters Staff. A regular correspondence took place on the subject between Versailles and Paris, and there was very speedily a goodly pile of it on General Schmitz's table. The Germans asserted that they had never fired on a French flag of truce, but that on the other hand the French *always* fired on theirs. They may have been right except in the use of the word *always;* it is possible that some young and inexperienced soldier, some *franc-tireur*, may have fired on a Prussian flag of truce without hitting anybody. In any case the military notes which were interchanged were devoid of any sort of authority, and their despatch might have gone on for ever.

Things were in this state when I had to reconduct

General Burnside as far as the Sèvres bridge, to the little boat, moored on the French side, which was to transport him to the other side.

After the usual call had been answered by the enemy I gave my hand to the General to help him to mount the barricade. He had scarcely shown himself before four shots were heard, and the bullets, whistling about our ears, lodged with a startling noise in the staves of the casks.

I looked at Burnside, who did not stir. He was at a loss to understand it, and asked me what was the matter.

'They are firing on us,' I replied, with a laugh, 'and it is lucky that we escaped the clumsy fellows; and now, at all events, you who know all about this flag of truce affair have a proof that if the French have fired by mistake on a Prussian flag, the Germans fire with precision and conscientiously on ours, even after having answered our call.'

I had not finished speaking when two fresh bullets, whistling past the General's head, lodged, at about the height of a man, in the rough coating of a small wall adjoining the barricade.

The General, who had his doubts up to then, was convinced. I went to the wall, and, with the point of my knife, I extracted one of the two bullets, which was still warm.

'There,' I said as I handed it to him, 'if you want to cut short a matter of controversy in a peremptory manner, be good enough to give this projectile to M. de Bismarck. In your hands it will be an excellent argument to demonstrate the dangers which French, and even American flags of truce have to contend against.'

We embraced cordially. I took leave of him, and he was conducted by two *mobiles* to what was then called the Prussian bank.

A few moments afterwards he disappeared round a corner of one of the streets of Sèvres. His two *mobiles* returned, and silence reigned on the river, broken only by the distant roar of the cannon.

Do not imagine that the Germans were convinced, even after the evidence of a witness so important, so impartial, and so disinterested as General Burnside. Convinced, no doubt, that whoever has the last word is right, they reverted of their own accord to the incident. I do not think it would serve any useful purpose to copy here the correspondence which took place, and which Jules Favre has inserted in his book. Each remained convinced of the truth of his own story. So it always happens, even in war.

CHAPTER X

FROM THE CAPITOL TO THE TARPEIAN ROCK

The Major of the Rampart.—Flourens and Trochu.—A Demonstration on the Square of the Hôtel-de-Ville.—The Captain's Punishment.—Departure of MM. Ranc and de Kératry.—Bagneux.—An Audacious Spy.—Foreign Convoys.—La Jonchère.—Everyone in His Turn.—The Black Bird.

ON the 5th of October there was a demonstration outside and inside the Hôtel de Ville, under the leadership of a hot-headed fellow who played the inferior parts in the drama of the siege of Paris. His name was Flourens. Having been elected to the command of five battalions of Belleville, he refused to select any one of them, and asserted his right to command all. He had been appointed Major of the Rampart, but I have never discovered what that rank meant. He had roused the Belleville battalion to a pitch of fanaticism, and had persuaded them to demand municipal elections and the constitution of the Commune of Paris.

The *Garde Nationale* arrived under arms.   General

Trochu betook himself to the Hôtel de Ville, and was hissed and hooted. That was the beginning. General Tamisier, who commanded the *Garde Nationale*, was likewise hissed and hooted by these perfect soldiers. Flourens went into the Hôtel de Ville, and entered into negotiations with the Government, while the bands in the square played the *Marseillaise*. I was simple enough to believe that violent hands would be laid upon the Major of the Rampart, and that he would be cast into the deepest of dungeons until the end of the siege. The General preferred treating him in a parental sort of way, called him by his title of *Monsieur le Major* at full length, and asked him why he had deserted his post on the rampart. Under any other circumstances his irony would have been charming. Flourens did not understand it. ' I demand 10,000 *chassepots* and a sortie,' and he finally flung his resignation in the face of the Government. The most extraordinary part of the business was that the Government appeared to be alarmed by it, and General Trochu replied, 'Then I will resign too.' Flourens took his departure, and when he appeared again before his men their cheers made the windows shake. Then it rained, I think, and everybody went to dine.

A few days afterwards, on the 8th, a similar ceremony took place. Flourens was not in it. We received intelligence at the Louvre that the square of the Hôtel de Ville was black with people, that there was a great deal of noise and shouting, and much calling for Trochu.

The Governor simply shrugged his shoulders and said, ' These buffoons are determined to give me no peace.' He then called for his horse and rode off.

Commandant Bibesco and I were on duty behind him. He had no escort. We entered the square of the Hôtel de Ville from the Rue de Rivoli. Heads, nothing but heads.

It was like a huge tub covered with corks floating on the disturbed water. The compact mass, a very ill-disposed one, began to hoot us vigorously. We made our way into it. In a few minutes Bibesco and I were separated from the Governor, and I was very soon separated from Bibesco. I saw him ten paces from me; some men had rushed to his horse's head and had seized the animal by the bridle, heaping insults and abuse on him at the same time. Some others honoured me with similar attentions, and I then heard cries of ' *A bas les capitulards! A bas les traîtres!* ' I should have preferred being anywhere else. Afar off, above the crowd, I perceived the shining cranium of the Governor, who was saluting right and left, and, at a standstill like ourselves, was towering over the swarm of human ants from the top of his horse.

We were three lost men in the midst of that crowd of ten thousand. An impatient gesture, a movement of our horses, an imprudent word, or a momentary forgetfulness of the discipline which imposed silence on us, might have destroyed us, or caused us to be cut down, massacred, and reduced to fragments. We had to be careful, too, not to fall, for once on the ground there would have been an end of us. The crowd was like a mass of wild beasts, and keeping upright was our only safety.

It was, indeed, difficult to fall, for we were engulfed in human flesh. I felt my horse tremble under me, the poor beast could not move. I had not room to stretch my legs, and so as not to run my spurs into him I had to turn my toes inwards. Hands were on my holsters, on the cantle of my saddle, on my saddle-cloth, on my thighs; if I had had to draw my sword there was not room enough for my left hand to get at the hilt and carry it across to my right. There was nothing for it but to wait, to remain motionless, and to look attentively at my horse's ears.

At last a man made his way through the crowd towards Bibesco; I thought he was going to strike him. At this moment my attention was drawn away from him by another fanatic laying hold of me. He was tolerably well dressed and wore a long black overcoat reaching to his calves; he asked me to cry out, *Vive la Commune!* I looked at him as if I did not understand him, and naturally I did not open my mouth. My calmness completely exasperated him, he seized me by my epaulets, drew me violently to him, and spat in my face. Then he fell back.

For half-a-second I saw blood and it seemed to me as if the Hôtel de Ville was falling on my head. If I had been alone, if I could have set spurs to my horse and galloped on the heads of the crowd, I think I should have got my man. But the General was there. The glitter of a sword or a shout of anger might have caused him to be torn in pieces. I wiped my face. I felt I was damp, but not insulted.

At the same moment a small opening in the crowd enabled us three to get together again in front of the Hôtel de Ville. A battalion of the *Garde Nationale* was there. Jules Favre made a short speech, and spoke of the cannon which could be heard and should teach union.

And as I got off my horse, settled my uniform, and exchanged impressions in silence with Bibesco, I indulged in this reflection,

'Perhaps, my dear Captain, in a month's time they will be embracing your boots in the Place du Carrousel, two yards from here.'

Could the Prefect of Police, M. Kératry, have prevented these demonstrations? I do not think so, for we, with all the forces of the Capital at our disposal, were unable to repress them. His powerlessness gave him the idea of resigning, and even of proposing to the Government the suppression of the Prefecture of Police. It might certainly have been dispensed with, because, at all events for the time being, it was absolutely useless. M. de Kératry, as well as M. Ranc, left Paris in a balloon to join Gambetta in the provinces. M. de Kératry was succeeded in the Prefecture by M. Edmond Adam, and M. Ranc at the Town Hall in the Rue Drouot, by Gustave Chaudey.

A few days afterwards there was another engagement. Chevilly had cost us Guilhem, Bagneux cost us De Dampierre, who fell nobly at the head of the *Mobiles* of Aube at the entrance to the village. Thirty-three years of age, a glorious ancestry behind him, and a happy life before him !

All these engagements were barren of results. They were bound to be so. Fighting went on for four or five hours. Time was given to the Prussians to bring up fresh troops, and then we fell back ; and take note that if the blockade had unfortunately been forced, the victorious troops, without provisions, without convoys or ammunition, would have fallen to the last man in the fatal grasp of the Germans, who would have fallen back and surrounded them in the impassable and devastated zone they occupied round Paris.

On the eve of the battle of Bagneux we were informed that an officer of the line, who had come direct from the advanced posts, wished to speak to the Governor, to whom he brought a letter under cover of the utmost importance. He was a sub-lieutenant. We received him, and his letter was taken to the General. A few moments later an aide-de-camp of the Governor came to the messenger and asked him under what circumstances the despatch had been handed to him.

The sub-lieutenant stated that while on the main guard on the Châtillon side, quite close to the Prussians and concealed in a hut, he had seen an officer of the French Headquarters staff, who, with his back turned to Paris, appeared to be going to the enemy's camp.

Under the impression that the officer was making a fatal mistake, he sallied out from his hut, followed by several men, and attempted to induce the officer to change his course. The latter appeared somewhat surprised at being confronted by a guard, and, promptly taking out of his pocket a large envelope addressed to General Trochu, he said,

'I was looking for you. Take this despatch yourself to the Governor. It is important and urgent.'

And the sub-lieutenant, to his astonishment, saw him, after making a slight detour, continue on his way towards the Prussians.

When General Trochu opened the despatch, there was nothing in the envelope but a blank sheet of paper, folded in four.

A strict enquiry was instituted into the affair. The sub-lieutenant was punished for having left his post, and for having failed to recognise under the uniform of a French Staff Officer, a Prussian spy who had just paid a quiet visit to our lines.

A few days later, the exodus of the foreigners who did not wish to remain in Paris took place under the protection of the American Minister, Mr Washburne. There were several convoys. Eight or ten carriages, drawn by splendid horses, pairs worth 10,000 francs, which their owners naturally enough wished to save from the shambles, met at a gate settled beforehand; and I was entrusted with the duty of taking them as far as the Prussian lines. The passengers were huddled together inside and on the seats of these carriages, *coupés*, landaus, and victorias. More than once I noticed that the coachmen in livery appeared to be novices at their work, and I recognised under the cockaded hats of these charioteers faces I had often seen on the Boulevards.

I was all the more polite, I confess, towards the Americans, by reason of my distrust of the English, and my bearing resulted in my being continually asked for, by Mr Washburne, to conduct these little expeditions, as appears from the following letter—

'PARIS, *October* 23, 1870.

'MONSIEUR LE MINISTRE,

'I have the honour to inform you that the letter in which you requested me to provide for the departure of your countrymen at noon to-morrow reached me so late that it was impossible for me to give the needful orders.

'I will take the necessary steps to-morrow to secure their departure on Tuesday, the 25th inst., at the same hour, and I will place at your disposal my orderly officer, M. d'Herisson, in accordance with your expressed desire.

'I have the honour, &c., &c.,

'GENERAL TROCHU.'

I recollect that, one day when I was returning from one of these convoy expeditions, the first French sentinel whom I passed as I left the Prussians was a man of a certain age, with a soldier-like and energetic face, who wore on his long coat the cross of an officer of the Legion of Honour. I asked the officer in command of the main-guard who the individual was whose appearance had so struck me. He replied,

'It is Meissonier, the painter.'

He fought between his pictures.

On the day of the Bagneux engagement the shells from Mont-Valerien set fire to the Park of Saint Cloud, where one could see the perpetual movement of German officers; and from the bridge of Sèvres I saw all night long standing out in bold relief on the horizon, like a gigantic scenic effect, the black outline of the Imperial Castle, whence Napoleon III set out for the war, conspicuous amid an immense bouquet of flame which lighted up from below the clouds of smoke overhanging the *auto-da-fé*.

On the 21st was fought the battle of La Jonchère, one of the most bloody of all the siege, where Ducrot, who commanded, bore himself so valiantly as to win the enthusiasm of the Parisians, and at the same time to cause the Germans a few moments of fear in regard to the security of their Head-quarters at Versailles. There was it appears, a regular alarm at Versailles that day. M. de Moltke and the King of Prussia were present on the heights of Marly in order to encourage the fresh troops who defiled unceasingly before them down the hill towards La Jonchère and La Malmaison; these continued reinforcements ended by getting the better of our men, too few and too deficient of adequate reserves.

I do not know any pleasure from a military point of view more intoxicating than that of galloping over a field of battle where the troops are behaving well, to deliver an order or gain information. To the excitement of the moment is added the pleasure of seeing everything, instead of shivering behind a wall or at the bottom of a ditch, and receiving invisible bullets without moving an inch. You enjoy the feeling of responsibility without being borne down by the necessity of continually answering for men on whom you cannot always rely.

You see the machinery at work, and in a way affect the victory. Between the position of a staff-officer and an ordinary officer there is a difference to a certain extent analogous to that between a sailor, standing on the bridge and feeling the ship moving under his feet, and an engineer who is in the engine room, seeing nothing, not knowing if the enemy is being boarded or run down, or if the latter fate is happening to his own ship.

I galloped about during the whole of the day of the battle of La Jonchère, carrying orders, among the once joyous spots where I found, amid the noise and smoke of powder, fragments of my young days almost everywhere, and the reminiscences of the last year's gaiety.

On such days the Generals were like shepherds, the men like sheep, and the Staff-Officers like dogs running on the flanks of the flock to turn them this or that way, and even in front to turn them back. Nothing can be more interesting.

Three or four times I came across my brother, who was Orderly Officer to General Berthaut; he, too, had plenty to do, and had a somewhat singular adventure.

At the turn of a road he fell into the middle of half a score of Prussians, who seized his bridle, made him dismount, took him prisoner and led him away. A few paces farther on, the squad in the middle of which he was marching, came round the corner of a wall upon the *Zouaves* commanded by Jacquot.

My brother, who was educated in Germany and spoke German as well as French, turned round and said coolly to his conductors,

'Will you be good enough to give me back my horse, and since you made me prisoner allow me in my turn to make you the same.'

When night fell the retreat was sounded as usual, and in this retreat we lost ten guns, which did not prevent Paris—such was its desire to conquer—from looking upon this day as a victory.

Near La Jonchère I witnessed a curious episode.

Some soldiers who were rushing to the front called out as they passed me,

'The sergeant has killed the black bird. It was high time.'

A few paces further on I saw, writhing in agony, and for all the world like a circus clown walking on his hips, an individual, very carefully dressed in black velvet coat and knickerbockers, who had been hit full in the breast by a bullet fired, according to the soldiers, by their sergeant. One of them told me that for several days they had noticed this individual constantly on the watch for our sentries, and that he never lost an opportunity of giving them a bullet from his Snider carbine. He fired with extraordinary precision and rarely failed to hit his mark. They had nick-named him the black bird. He was an Englishman; an eccentric fanatic who made war on his own account as an amateur and an ally of the Prussians. He was despatched by a bayonet, and I am pretty sure that neither his watch nor his purse found their way to the English Embassy. At all events I had not time to find out, having business elsewhere.

CHAPTER XI

TROCHU AT HOME

The French and the Theatre.—The Staff of the Governor.—Madame Trochu.—The Governor at Table.—The Chief of the Head-quarters Staff.—Rehabilitation of Horse-flesh.—A Tale of Cheeses.—The Legion of Honour and the Military Medal.—The General's Pipes.—Father Olivaint.—Sainte Geneviève, Patron Saint of Paris.

FRENCH readers love to see great men, or well-known men, in their dressing-gowns—lovers of the stage, they not only have a taste for performances, but also the epicurism of the *coulisses.* The nearer the seats are to the curtain the more they pay for them. The regular subscriber to the opera prefers the corner where the drums deafen him, the double-basses groan in his ears, or the trombone cracks his tympanum, to the last row of the stalls, whence he can take in the whole scene with his eyes and the orchestra with his ears. In France only is the box of the Chief of the State placed close to the stage. Everywhere else it is in front—in the centre.

I am borrowing from the theatre, you see, a preamble for my description of poor General Trochu at home, though he certainly is not a theatre goer, and in all probability has never been behind the scenes. I am wrong, and I venture to say that though for all of us it is the height of enjoyment to see the artists in their box, my readers would not thank me to take them into the Trochu box, albeit a handsome one—in short, the Louvre.

The General appeared in his office regularly at half-past eight. He rose more than an hour earlier. He worked without cessation until the breakfast hour—eleven o'clock. At this meal, presided over by Madame Trochu, all the officers of the General's personal staff were present, except Commandant Prince Bibesco, who lived with his family in the Louvre above the Governor's suite of apartments. The Princess during the siege presented him with a little girl, who, like the grandson of Louis Philippe, received the name of Paris. I should have preferred Lutèce — much more poetical for a woman.

Here I think I ought to record the names of the officers who gravitated round this star of the first magnitude, whether as attached to the Personal Staff or the General Staff of the Government. They were Generals Schmitz and Foy, Colonel Usquin, Lieutenant-Colonel de Lemud ; Commandants Prince Bibesco, de Brou, Faivre, Vigneral, Lestrohan, Madelor, and Bidot ; Squadron Leaders Bourcart and Lunel ; Captains Brunet, Barrois, Thory, de Montebello, de Béarn, de Montesquioux, d'Hérisson, de Beaumont, Barthélemy, Delâtre, Brunet-Richard, and Lair ; and Lieutenants de Langle, d'Hendecourt, and Choppin d'Arnouville. M. Pollet, one of the most intelligent assistants in the Prefecture of Police, acted, as I have already said, as Special Commissary of Police, a civil Provost-Marshal.

Madame Trochu was a woman of very great merit, who commanded both respect and sympathy. Her countenance, calm, majestic, and sweet, was at this time framed in beautiful white hair, which made her look older than her husband. She divided her time between her household duties, to which she attended very closely, and frequent visits to the ambulances.

I remember her one day telling us at breakfast that she had been to pay a visit to the ambulance established in the Théâtre-Français, and that she had been struck by the simplicity, devotion, and quiet and composed bearing of the ladies of the house of Molière. She repeated what Mdlle. Favart, who was presented to her, had said.

' What, madame!' said the actress with a queenly gesture, ' you are the wife of our hero!'

And Trochu, modestly and slily, replied,

' The theatre never entirely loses its privileges!'

Besides his personal staff, the General entertained a few General Officers or distinguished personages every day. One day it would be Ducrot, an old comrade in arms, who chatted familiarly with him; another time it would be Krantz, also a friend and a schoolfellow as well, who afterwards organised the Exhibition of 1878.

General Schmitz occasionally came up to breakfast or dine with the Governor, but his appearances were few and far between. As a rule he took his meals on his desk by the side of his inkstand.

Never were human faculties, mental or physical, subjected to such a severe strain as that endured by General Schmitz.

The post of Chief of the Staff of a regularly organised

army is one which frightens many Generals, and which very few can fill efficiently ; but to be Chief of the Staff of an army which does not exist, but has to be collected and organised under fire, and which comprises and unites a turbulent and excited population; to add to these duties the functions of commissary-general and town-major, to see after arms and provisions, to confront the enemy without and within, to attend to Prussians and rioters—all this constitutes a very hell in which any other nature than that of General Schmitz would have become enervated.

Everything was done in a few days, and if the French did not then feel for the General all the admiration he deserved, the whole of military Europe did him justice by its astonishment.

Moreover, General Schmitz was no novice, and those who had seen him at work knew his capacity, not only as an organiser but as a soldier, a soldier in every acceptation of the word, a soldier attending to his colours alone, a soldier disdainful of politics, and willingly holding aloof from every party. In China we had seen him, under the command of Montauban, assure the success of an extraordinary and marvellous campaign, trace the plan of attack against a fort, bombard it, enter it through a breach, and plant the French flag with his own hands on the ruins, in sight of the wonder-struck English army.

The Germans, who know what Generals are, have in a classification of our commanders in order of merit, drawn up for their own edification, assigned him the second rank.

Together with the ordinary guests, the two officers in personal attendance on General Trochu were always at table. He had a horror of privileges, and with good cause, for he had suffered from them. He was the first to submit to being put on an allowance in regard to rations, and voluntarily placed himself on the same footing in regard to provisions, as other divisional commanders, instead of taking the higher scale to which he was entitled as Governor and supreme chief. The *menus* were, therefore, modest, and horse flesh was frequently the basis of our nourishment. And as a matter of fact it was not bad. Provided the beast is young and has not done too much work ; provided that the guest is like the beast, young, and especially if he, unlike it, has suffered a little, the two agree perfectly.

Towards the end of the siege, when the question of eatables became a capital and vital one, Trochu multiplied his invitations among the Officers of the Head-quarters Staff. In those hard times an egg cost three francs, and I fancy that the pay of the Governor at that particular time passed directly from the hands of the Paymaster-in-Chief of the army into those of the Head-quarters cook.

On one occasion a piece of good luck from an culinary point of view befell me, which brought me almost as much honour as a well conducted reconnaissance in front of an enemy would have done ; I was fortunate enough to supply the Head-quarters table. I was riding along past the central markets when my nostrils were pleasantly tickled by a strong odour of cheese. Naturally, my first thought was to find out the domicile of the maggots which revealed themselves so indiscreetly. I marked the odorous spot and made enquiries among the people of the neigh-bourhood. After much research I ended by discovering that not only were these blessed cheeses not for sale, but that, having been deposited in their present locality by some administration or other, they were probably forgotten, and were protesting in their way against the irksomeness of captivity. I went and made a circumstantial and detailed report to the Minister of Commerce and Agriculture, who knew nothing of the depôt in question. As every labourer is worthy of his hire, and the Agricultural Order of Merit had not then been invented, I claimed as the price of my discovery and exertions, a recompense in kind. On the following day I received the following document :

> ' MINISTRY OF AGRICULTURE AND COMMERCE.
> ' MONSIEUR LE CAPITAINE,
>   ' I have the honour to forward herewith, by order of the Minister, a gratuity of 10 kilogrammes of Dutch cheese. I regret that I was not in the office when you called. I would have handed you the gratuity on the spot.
>> ' For the Minister of Commerce.
>>> ' By Order,
>>>> ' CARMES.'

One day when we were at table, the General was informed that a functionary of the Legion of Honour wished to see him. He brought with him several water-colour drawings, showing the various changes which the Government proposed making in the insignia of the Legion of Honour and in the military medal.

' Here,' said the Governor to me, as he handed over the papers, 'you are the only wearer of this military medal. Choose the model which pleases you most.'

The designers had not brought much imagination to bear on their work. All the suggestions were horrible alike. I chose the model which appeared to me to be the least ugly, the ungraceful trophy which now surmounts the military medal.

' Why change ? ' said I timidly to the Governor.

' How do I know ? ' he replied. ' These gentlemen assert that it is necessary. As for me, I think nothing can possibly be in worse taste than these mutilations inflicted on an Order created by a sovereign.'

I dared not say how thoroughly I agreed with him. A nation, according to a saying as just as it is celebrated—and the conjunction of these two epithets is extraordinary in itself—having invariably the government it deserves, dishonours itself in seeking to dishonour those who have governed it.

One of two things—either the medal was a good institution, or it was a bad one. In the latter case it should have been suppressed. In the former, it should have been preserved as it was without being caricatured. With such narrow views as we unfortunately have ever with us, the head of Henri IV on the Legion of Honour created by Napoleon I would not excite any astonishment.

I myself have no words too strong wherein to protest against the stupid feeling which prompts the French nation, whenever there is a change of government, to attack the statues of fallen chiefs of the State or the emblems of departed *régimes*, even though these statues and emblems are works of art, and though the genius which fashioned them should render them sacred to all. As if a nation does not honour itself by having ever before its eyes material evidences of its past greatness or misfortunes! As if everything in the history of our ancestors does not form part of the national heritage, the common patrimony!

But I have gone a long way from Trochu. I will return to him.

The General was a smoker. The love he bore his pipe made him hurry his dessert, and he went down as soon as possible to his office where, enveloped in the clouds of his calumet, he set to work, interrupting himself only to receive such visitors as proved too strong to be kept in check by the

orderly officer in the first instance, and by General Schmitz
afterwards.   Regularly towards two o'clock he mounted his
horse, visited the forts, the ramparts, the various sections of
the fortifications, the arsenals and workshops, held
reviews and, in a word, did everything attaching to his
office and contributing to the defence of Paris.

On his return, between four and five o'clock, he worked
again until dinner.   After that with his pipe between his
teeth, he slept by the fireside until nine o'clock, that is
to say, until the time came for him to betake himself to the
Hôtel de Ville, where the members of the National Defence
met every night to consult under his presidency.

The room in which they met was on the first floor.   The
sittings were prolonged, three o'clock often striking before
they separated.

When he got back to the Louvre the Governor
returned once more to his office to work and smoke one or
two pipes, after which he went to bed, only to get up again
very soon and begin his daily round with a regularity
which was astonishing amid all the extraordinary and
irregular events that were passing around him.

The main features of General Trochu's character were
complete evenness of temper, imperturbable coolness, and
extreme kindness.   He was consequently a very agreeable
chief to serve under, and all the more so because his kindness was not carried to a ridiculous extent, and because he
estimated and looked after his officers solely in accordance
with their merit, their devotion, and the services they
rendered him.

From out the *habitués* of the Louvre and the familiar
friends of the General, one face, interesting and imposing alike, stood conspicuous.   It was that of Father
Olivaint, the Superior of the Jesuits of the Rue de Sèvres

who paid regular visits to the Governor. An old pupil of the Normal School, and a remarkable man in every way, this priest, who was destined very soon to merit a martyr's crown, had a sincere and frank affection for the General. There existed between them a sort of confraternity and devotion, and the priest, the man of religious duty, encouraged the soldier, the man of military duty. Their conversations were frequent, lengthy, and of the utmost cordiality.

By contact with this enthusiastic soul, the mystic soul of Trochu was aroused, his military doubts subsided, and he arrived at a belief in the possibility of a direct, miraculous, divine intervention to save France from the horror of invasion, and to drive back the hordes of the modern Atilla!

Attila! When these two men pronounced that name and called forth that reminiscence, there passed between them, poetical and sweet, the vision of the virgin of Nanterre, Geneviève, the young girl whose native village slept below, under the muzzles of the guns of Mont Valérien, and who, so runs the legend, with her distaff drove off the savage bands sent forth by Germany, the shaggy warriors whose descendants were once more encamped round Paris.

From their conversations, most probably, General Trochu conceived the idea of placing the city of Paris, afresh and with all due solemnity, under the direct protection of St Geneviève by an act of the Government, and of recurring to the ancient patronage of the heroine of the Gauls.

It was in the last days of the siege. The bombardment had just begun. He drew up a proclamation in this sense, and sent the manuscript to the Government Printing Office. It was set up as a placard to be posted all over Paris.

As usual, two proofs were sent to the Governor, to be by

him submitted for the approval of the members of the Government. When he had finished reading, a profound, icy silence prevailed round the council table. Everybody looked at everybody else. Not one of the astounded lawyers could believe his ears. Jules Favre sprang from his chair as if a shell had burst underneath him, and stood up, expressing his surprise and disapprobation with an amount of vivacity beyond the bonds of propriety.

He did not wish, he said with much gesticulation, to cover himself with ridicule in the eyes of his constituents. He would not join those who thought fit to call for the intervention of God and the saints in our affairs. It was against common sense. There was no need of God to thrash the Prussians. And then, in a vein of sarcasm, he added that the Prussians also believed in God and invoked his aid, and that it was not respectful to place that venerable personage in the sad predicament of having to despise Prussian adoration in favour of French genuflexion, or *vice versa.*

Once more General Trochu, defeated all along the line, retreated in good order. The proclamation was not posted up. I have kept a copy of this curious document, and here it is.

'PROCLAMATION.

'FRENCH REPUBLIC.

'The Governor of Paris.

'To the Defenders of Paris.

'To the Families of Paris.

'We have arrived at the fourth month of the siege, and this great effort has moved the country profoundly. It is in arms, and is everywhere valiantly contesting the territory against the enemy.

'I am a believer, and I have asked St Geneviève, the liberator of Paris in the days of the barbarians, to shield Paris once more with her protection. She has willed it so that at this very hour the prayer has been heard. She has providentially inspired in the enemy the thought of the bombardment which is dishonouring the German arms, which dishonours civilisation, and which brings out, in so brilliant and touching a manner, the firmness of the people of Paris.

'Women, children, sick and wounded, are perishing; but public opinion, which governs the world, is now and will remain wholly with us.

'When the enemy thinks that we are crushed by the bombardment, he will redouble his efforts. I am sure of repulsing him. Your hour will come.

'Prepare yourselves for desperate struggles. Be vigilant. Economise your resources. Place yourselves on regular rations. Let all those who have stocks of grain or flour hand them over to the Government of the Defence for the common need. Prolong the duration of the siege by every means that patriotism can inspire. In a word, continue the series of fruitful sacrifices of which you have given for so many days so noble an example. And, above all things, preserve to the latest hour your faith, which some seek to destroy, in the deliverance of your country.

'GENERAL TROCHU.

'PARIS, *January* 14, 1871.'

I trust I may be pardoned if I refrain from discussing the question whether Paris, when placed under the pro-

M

tection of St Geneviève, would have been saved, and if I do not dwell upon the somewhat ingenuous idea that God permitted the bombardment in order to make the justice of our cause clear, and to confound Prussia. It belongs to the category of unfortunate though necessary phrases which should only be re-read after victory.

But I have a right to think and say that when, in governing a great nation, one project is that of taking away from it all religious faith, and when, in order to realise that, the education of children is ordered to be carried on without respect for, or fear of, a Creator, it is necessary that something should be found to replace the faith which has given birth to so many miracles, so much devotion, and so much regeneration. Let us suppress God, if you will, but let us put something in His place. And supposing it to be impossible to discover a moral mechanism destined to replace the great mainspring which has ceased to please, it would be well to allow it to go on working, unless, indeed, it is considered preferable to stop the watch altogether.

And I am of opinion that a besieged Government which capitulates as ours did, after having disdained this moral weapon, is as culpable in the eyes of history, if not before a council of war, as the commandant of a fortress who surrenders it to the enemy without having once removed the leathern cover which protects the breech of his largest guns.

I will also willingly confess, however unimportant my confession may be, that it would be difficult to be more ill-advised than the author of this proclamation, entirely due to the pen of General Trochu. I will admit that this mode of representing the bombardment of Paris as an acquiescence of the holy patrons of the city in the prayers of the chief of its defenders, was a singular figure of rhetoric. I will allow that there existed six-and-thirty modes of qualifying the shells which destroyed several roofs on the left bank of the Seine before having done them the honour to give them notice—the results of a providential inspiration.

I will only ask if there were not at that moment in Paris men who, if they had possessed a pen and controlled a printing-office, would not have indited phrases even more ill-advised and ridiculous, and have been pardoned for them.

Let him among us who did not, either in public or in private, write nonsense during the siege, cast the first stone at the Governor of Paris.

CHAPTER XII

THE THIRTY-FIRST OF OCTOBER

Rise and Fall of an Idol.—The Three *Strata* of Paris.—Rochefort and Dorian.—
The New Popular Leaders.—The Capitulation of Metz.—With the Advanced
Posts.—Hypotheses.—Bourget.—Paris Waxes Wroth.—' *Vive la Commune.*'
' *A bas Trochu.*'—' *Pas d'Armistice.*'—Flourens.—On the Square of the Hôtel
de Ville.—Invasion.—At the Council Board of the Government. —A Night of
Anguish.—Picard, Adam, Ferry.—A Compact.—Deliverance.—The Engage-
ments of M. Ferry.

WHEN General Trochu arrived in Paris towards the middle
of August, invested with the title and functions of Governor, there were not ten people who would have refused to
acknowledge him as the first soldier of France, the saviour
of the country.

A month later a few men might be heard, timidly at
first, as if ashamed of their temerity, contesting his right to
be considered a practical General, if not his value as a
theorist, and mildly insinuating that the saviour would
possibly save nothing. These men belonged to the upper
and intelligent classes.

A fortnight later the *faubourgs* furnished a contingent some thousands strong to hiss and hoot him on the square of the Hôtel de Ville.

At the end of October he had against him the aristocratic quarter, the *faubourgs*, and the lower orders.

Paris contains two million inhabitants, but of this total there are, at the very most, only a few thousands who are capable of forming independent opinions—they are the upper crust. Instead of the word *croûte* I might have used *gratin* if it had not been monopolised by a few ridiculous fops and giddy women.

Below this is the main body, a thick *stratum* of people who live, eat, drink, sleep, and assimilate to themselves the ideas of other people—a *stratum* without any originality of its own, but not devoid of virtues.

Lower still, quite at the bottom, is one-tenth of the population, 200,000 individuals, devoid alike of originality and virtues, incapable of thinking, but quick to seize upon any idea, provided it is violent and subversive of order. Cowardly and ferocious alike, they are armed and ready to follow either rascals unconscious of their rascality, or deliberate villains clever enough to lead them. These are the dregs of Paris.

In quiet times the intermediate mass willingly submits to the influence and action of the intelligent, educated, and refined upper crust. In revolutionary times the dregs boil over as if under the action of an internal fire, invade the intermediate mass, penetrate it, drag it onwards, sully it, and upset it.

Trochu, then, at the end of October had lost the upper crust and the dregs of the Parisian population. But the upper crust did not say anything, and the dregs had **not** yet made any serious movement.

They were on the point of doing so.

The personages who surrounded Trochu were not calculated to excite enthusiasm or rouse applause. Nobody was tempted to worship them—they were merely accepted.

I make an exception in favour of two men, one in the Government, the other in the Ministry—Rochefort and Dorian. Rochefort from the commencement of the war had been, with Trochu, the most popular man. There was, however, a shadow of a difference; Trochu had all three *strata* with him, while Rochefort had but two; the upper crust held aloof from him. He was clever enough to leave the Government in time to preserve his popular favour intact. His resignation is dated the 29th of October.

As for Dorian, he, although a republican, rightly took up a non-political position, and, shut up inside the Ministry of public works, confined his thoughts and his action to the national defence, in which he was a marvellous worker, casting guns, manufacturing carriages, and producing ammunition. The masses, even the most stupid and violent among them, had preserved by some miraculous means, I know not what, sufficient good sense to appreciate this indefatigable worker, and to assign him in their devotion a place alongside their worst fanatics, with whom, by the way, his character was absolutely at variance.

The remainder had no prestige whatever, lawyers, philosophers, or old fashioned veterans.

Under the Empire they had personified the Opposition; on the 4th of September they seized upon the Government. The people looked upon the whole thing as natural and logical. They had never asked to be consulted, and the others accepted the silence of the populace as hearty consent, and indulgent public opinion as enthusiastic adhesion.

But they did not stand alone as guiding the adverse people

of Paris. Not unaided had they obtained the celebrated 1,400,000 *Non* of the *plébiscite*. They had instruments, men, under their orders. Like old and prudent generals, they had sent forth against the Imperial foe, young, impulsive, and impassioned colonels, and had promised them a share in the rich plunder. The enemy had succumbed, thanks to the rather powerful diversion effected by 800,000 Prussians. The rich plunder, considerably reduced, it must be confessed, by the invasion, had fallen into their power, and their auxiliaries in the rash struggle were ever at hand awaiting the division of the spoil, present at the cutting up of the quarry, but taking no part in it.

At the head of their faithful cohorts these young and impetuous colonels, such as Flourens, Millière, Grousset Rigaut, and so many others, waited idle and impatient. In order not to leave any stone unturned they had secured a few old idols, whom death had neglected, Blanqui, Félix Pyat, Ledru-Rollin, the shade of Barbès, quite an arsenal of ancestors, to bring into use. They were ready.

They asked, with inexorable, if not patriotic logic, why and by virtue of what rule, supreme power had devolved on the deputies for Paris, and not on themselves, the recognised chiefs of the popular troops; they considered it extraordinary that they should have been summoned at one and the same time to overthrow one master in order to put twelve others in his place; they compared their mandate with that of the Government, and saw no difference between them; they made capital out of the revolutionary appetites of certain battalions, and also utilised the irritation of some others who were vexed and humiliated by having shouted *à Berlin* so often, whereas, after all, they were caught in Paris as in a mouse-trap.

They were ready to act.   Opportunity and the word of command were alone lacking.

They found the word of command first.   Events and the clumsiness of the Government were preparing an opportunity.

On the 27th of October, the newspaper, *La Combat*, a blood-red organ, announced in precise terms that Marshal Baziane had sent an officer to treat with Prince Frederick Charles for the capitulation of Metz.

It was true, for the capitulation of Metz was signed that very day.   But nobody knew anything about it; nobody expected it, and the news fell like a bombshell in the middle of besieged Paris.

The Government were the first to be taken by surprise, and they denied it in a clumsy way, leaving themselves no opening for retreat in case the news should be confirmed, calling the Marshal, who had actually surrendered his army, the glorious Bazaine, and stigmatising the *Combat* as a Prussian organ.

How could this newspaper have been so well informed? Was it a mere chance assertion, or had hatred bestowed double sight upon its editors?   I do not think so, and I have a very simple explanation of the speedy propagation of the very serious news.

It was perfectly well known in the Prussian camp before Metz on the evening of the 24th, or, at all events on the morning of the 25th, that Bazaine was surrendering. On the same day detachments of troops left the Prussian camp by forced marches, on the urgent demand of the Versailles Staff, in order to reinforce the investing cordon round Paris, which was too weak in many places.

For we must not forget that, although, from a military point of view, it was impossible for troops sallying out of

Paris to break the line of Prussian battalions drawn up against them, we could on the next day, or the one following, have advanced at any spot against the enemy with forces numerically superior to theirs.

I am convinced that if, instead of General Trochu, Paris had been governed by a Pélissier, 200,000 of the *Garde Nationale* would have been killed before Paris. In all probability he would have had to surrender with the remainder, and he would have been accounted a butcher.

Consequently, on the 26th, there might have been outside Paris, especially at Saint-Denis, German soldiers from Metz, who knew that Bazaine was going to treat.

Now we have to take another circumstance into consideration. The French and German advanced posts did not spend all their time in killing each other. They nearly always kept well out of range. And frequently, when there was no fear of being caught by their officers, they approached each other, not exactly to fraternise, but to do each other some little service, or make some small exchange.

Not only did the Prussian sentries nearly always refrain from firing on the French marauders who sallied out to dig up the potatoes or onions forgotten in the devastated fields, but they occasionally compelled them to give up, or even to sell the produce of their perilous labour.

The advanced sentries came together sometimes to buy a pipe of tobacco. This may appear improbable, but it is, nevertheless, a fact. Or the German sentry, who is fond of bacon and had none, bartered his fresh meat for a bit of salt pork.

In a word I repeat, and I know what I am saying, that though individual intercourse was strictly and naturally forbidden, it was much commoner than might have been supposed.

Taking all this into consideration, it may very easily have happened that a German soldier, conversing with a French one, said to him,

'You know that some of our comrades have come from Metz. Bazaine is going to capitulate.'

The difference of language is no reason for rejecting this explanation, for there were thousands of men in the *Landwehr* who spoke French, who came from France, and even from Paris, to return thither *viâ* Mayence, Frankfort, or Berlin.

It is also said that a non-commissioned officer who was made prisoner at Saint-Denis announced the capitulation, and that he was never heard of again.

Again, it is stated that Prussia had in Paris, especially among the revolutionary press, spies who were never discovered, but who were in communication with Versailles, and that one of them brought, by order, the news to the *Combat*, which accepted it without any knowledge or suspicion of the connections of its reporter.

Finally, it was maintained that the revolutionary cohesion of the members of that school which recognises no frontiers, had silenced the hatred between the two nations, and that the Parisian socialists never ceased to correspond fraternally and secretly with the German socialists.

Of these four hypotheses mine is the best. I have cogent reasons for saying so, and if I keep them to myself, it is simply because the ascertained names of the bearers of the sinister news would not convey any information to anybody.

However this may be, the rumour that Bazaine was capitulating, or had capitulated, vibrated like the beating of the tocsin on the suddenly acute ears of Paris, and the counter statement of the Government relative to the 'glorious' Marshal did not in any way dissipate the anxieties or dispel the black clouds which overhung the minds of all.

On the following day, the 28th, at 3 A.M. General de Bellemare ordered a company of 300 *franc-tireurs* to take possession of Bourget. The order was executed, and the Prussian detachment occupying the village, which consisted of a double row of houses, one on either side of the main road, was surprised and driven out.

On the morning of the 29th the news of the capture of Bourget reached us at Head-quarters. General de Bellemare had acted without orders. The Governor and his Chief of the Staff considered the affair useless and irregular.

'This is increasing the death roll for nothing at all.' Such was the first reflection which greeted the despatch of General de Bellemare.

Situated on the north-east of Paris, rather more than three kilometres to the east of St Denis, Bourget, as General Trochu said formed no part of the general plan of defence.

The Prussians had been permitted to take up a position there from the 20th of September, and nobody had even thought of a sortie on that side.

Its capture could not compromise the situation of the investing army. It, however, compelled the Prussians to widen their circle and make a *détour*. It did not hurt them, but it inconvenienced them to a certain extent.

It is very certain that if the same action had been taken all round Paris, the German cordon, by reason of being extended, would in the end have been broken. But, as an isolated case, the attack and success were not of much account, and were not really worth the blood shed upon them.

Such was not the opinion of Paris. The papers and their readers looked upon the capture of Bourget as a veritable victory.

It would have been well if this view had penetrated into high places, however unreasonable and unmilitary it may have been.

General Trochu had repeated over and over again that his government was dependent on public opinion. He would, perhaps, have acted wisely, or at all events cleverly, if he had followed public opinion even in its folly, for, after all, it was not dangerous, and to fight for fighting's sake, if I may use the expression, is worth just as much in one place as another.

What ought to have been done then was to send battalion after battalion, battery after battery, to Bourget.

That is precisely what the Prussians did.

They probably attached no more importance to Bourget than we ourselves did. They had no more need of it than we had. But it did not suit them to lose any conquered ground whatever. Above all, it did not suit them to see any revival of spirit among the inhabitants of Paris, even though it was due to a success more apparent than real.

And so with admirable tenacity they did everything necessary to recover possession of Bourget. I believe that, if we had followed their example, the two armies would have spent their last man on this paltry position.

We did not imitate them.

As a matter of fact, General de Bellemare reinforced the handful of men who had got into Bourget. He brought up the numbers there to 3000, and asked for reinforcements and ammunition waggons.

The attack on Bourget took place by night. In the morning the Prussians returned the attack, and were repulsed. On the following day, the 29th, they bombarded the village from a distance. On the 30th they recommenced their artillery fire, and developed a movement to surround it. Half the defenders of Bourget, worn out by the preceding engagements, and demoralised by a night passed in the rain, took to flight. There remained in the village less than 1500 men, under the command of Baroche and Brasseur. They made a splendid defence. Baroche shot himself, and those who survived, about a thousand, were made prisoners.

Not until then was there any serious movement of reinforcements in Paris. Batteries marched along the Rue de la Fayette. It was too late. Everybody was in full retreat.

In order thoroughly to understand the disastrous effect produced upon public opinion by the loss of a position moral rather than strategic, it must be remembered that the very day we lost Bourget, the Prussians read in the *Officiel*, 1st, the announcement of the capitulation of Bazaine; 2nd, the news of the return of M. Thiers from his journey through Europe, and of his being the bearer of proposals for an armistice from the neutral powers.

The most expert of stage managers could not have more cleverly combined these three exciting incidents in an identical part of a drama—a defeat before Paris, the annihilation of our last and finest regular army, and the admission that our provincial forces had done nothing of any value, seeing that, at Paris as well as at Tours, there was an inclination to lay down arms.

The public spirit caught fire like a powder-train. The opportunity was a good one for the rioters.

As for the word of command, I have already said that it was ready to hand. It was, Commune.

The Parisian revolutionists demanded the election of municipal magistrates, and were bent on their being entrusted with the most ample powers, not only for the government of the city, but also for its defence. 'Paris is a town on the same footing as the rest,' they said. 'The members of the Government have proclaimed that a hundred times. The municipality of Paris ought to have the same prerogatives as the other municipalities.' They called that the Commune. The leaders were to have been elected as municipal magistrates, and to have thus formed a Government which was to put that of the National Defence in its pocket, to decree the sortie *en masse*, the diluvial sortie, to deliver France, and to hand over to her what Paris had conquered—communal autonomy. France thenceforward would no more be a republic than a monarchy. She would be a federation of 36,000 free and independent communes.

The idea was not so stupid as might have been supposed, seeing that it nearly succeeded. It was simply rather unripe. It needed ripening, and it was going to ripen.

To the accompaniment of cries of '*Vive la Commune,*' '*A bas Trochu,*' and '*Pas d'Armistice,*' the proceedings of the 31st October took place, and the insurrection was initiated which was destined to miscarry miserably, as everything miscarried at that cursed period—everything, even the revolution.

Some time before the end of October, we saw one evening from the Louvre a redness in the sky which covered half the horizon of Paris, and could proceed from nothing but a fire in the east.

'Go and see what it is,' said the Governor to me.

I got on my horse and rode along the Boulevards and the

Rue de la Fayette. The fire was at Buttes-Chaumont. When I arrived there I beheld a singular and magnificent spectacle. The lake in the park was on fire. It had been emptied and transformed into a warehouse for petroleum. One of the barrels had caught fire, the remainder burst, and when I arrived, the centre island seemed to be floating in a sea of fire.

From the top of a clump on some rising ground, a tall, handsome youth was giving hurried orders. His cuffs were covered with stripes, the number of which, as I afterwards learnt, were decided by his own sweet will. I went up to him to tell him that the Governor wished to know the cause of the disaster.

'It is nothing,' he said. 'Only a few barrels of petroleum which have caught fire. Tell M. Trochu that he need not be uneasy, that Flourens is here.'

In the gigantic aureole of a conflagration lighted by petroleum, in his own frame, I saw for the first time the Major of the Rampart, the man who was to play the principal part in the affair of the 31st of October.

The day was cold and gloomy; a cold, fine rain was falling, damping both clothes and dispositions. It was a great blessing for the Government of the National Defence that the insurgents had to suffer from stiffened fingers, muffled throats, and wet feet. If the weather had been fine and dry, the Government might very probably have been massacred amid the tumultuous, confused, and grotesque scenes that befell them during that day and a part of the following night.

From seven o'clock in the morning, men belonging to the *Garde Nationale* began to put in an appearance on the square of the Hôtel de Ville. Groups collected, and there were cries of '*Vive la Commune!*' and '*Pas d'Armistice!*'

The crowd increased, and at nine o'clock a column of a thousand men issued from the Avenue Victoria escorting a flag, on which were written these words, '*Levée en masse pas d'armistice.*' The *Mobiles* of Berry had reached the Hôtel de Ville to relieve the 115th battalion, and had been cheered.

Colonel Chevriot, who was in command of the Hôtel de Ville, had shut the door. Behind the gratings Arago, Mayor of Paris, in a voice like that of an angry bull, entreated the people to be calm. He then went upstairs to confer with the other Mayors of Paris, who had been summoned by him, and were deliberating about the opportuneness of proceeding at once to the municipal elections.

Meanwhile the Governor had received an intimation that things were going wrong. He resumed his uniform, took his sword, put on his epaulets, fastened on his breast the Cross of Grand Officer of the Legion of Honour, and, hoping to influence the people by the display of these brilliant emblems of his authority and his rank, he set out, followed by two Orderly Officers, one of them being Commandant Bibesco, to whom this cursed plan had already very nearly proved fatal.

He was greeted with shouts of '*A bas Trochu !*' '*Pas d'armistice !*' '*Vive la Commune !*' but he made his way without difficulty into the municipal palace.

Before leaving the Louvre he gave the Chief of the Staff a formal order not to move.

'It is of the utmost importance for us not to make a wrong move,' he said. 'Consequently, whether I come back or not, whether I be free or kept a prisoner, it is agreed that you do not move either a man or a gun without my personal order in writing brought by one of my officers. I rely on you to see that this order is strictly attended to.'

He went away and left us all deposited in the Louvre. The members of the Government, who were summoned by the telegraph which unites the Hôtel de Ville with the various Government offices and with the Prefecture of Police, arrived, one by one, and deliberated in the room set apart for their sittings, that is to say, the yellow room. The Prefect of Police, M. Edmond Adam, rejoined them, leaving his Prefecture protected by the *Garde Nationale*.

By degrees the numbers of the men of the *Garde Nationale* in the square increased and they became more menacing. The shouts of ' *Vive la Commune!*' redoubled. The most excited were already massed at the gates, and having, according to the usual sequence of events, chosen themselves as representatives of the rest, they demanded a hearing for a deputation of the People, who wished to speak to the Government.

It was one o'clock, one of the doors was half-opened, nobody knew by whom, a determined rush set it wide open and gave ingress to the so-called deputation accompanied by the first detachment of the populace. The door was, however, closed again.

The shouting crowd who invaded the large room numbered about a thousand.

The Government was not complete, the absentees being Jules Favre, of whom Ferry had gone in search to the Foreign Office, and Picard.

In the interval of waiting for these three personages, and in order to keep the people quiet, Arago left his mayors and entered the large room, followed by his assistants. Floquet, Brisson, Hérisson, Chaudey, and Tirard joined them.

Arago, mounted on a footstool, thundered away. He de-

N

manded patience, and asked for confidence, union and order in a voice which would have drowned the roar of a battery. The only answer he received was the shout, ' *La Commune !* ' *La Commune !* '

'Very well,' he said, 'I will convey your wishes to the Government.'

He went away. The persons with him took his place on the oratorical footstool, especially Brisson and Floquet.

'We too,' said they, 'want municipal elections, we too reject the armistice.'

They restored neither silence nor order. 'We want the Commune,' was the only reply. Once more they said, 'We want municipal elections.' And all of them persisted in their mulish obstinacy without there being a single man among them with sufficient sense to say, 'But, citizens, they are one and the same thing.'

The sensible man was, however, at hand.

The members of the Government begged Rochefort, the popular Rochefort, Rochefort their old colleague, who had come to them when he heard what was going on, to go and speak to the people, He went away for a moment, returned accompanied by Schœlcher, and said to his colleagues—

'They want municipal elections. Have you made up your minds to agree to them ? That is the knot you have to untie.'

'Yes,' was the reply from round the council board.

Rochefort returned to the large room, got up on a table, and declared, in the name of the Government, that the municipal elections would take place at once.

'No, no,' shouted these brutes, completely confused; 'we want the Commune.'

'But, citizens,' said Rochefort, shrugging his shoulders, ' it is the same thing,'

They did not understand. They called on him to get down. They took hold of his legs to pull him down. They shouted, ' *A bas Rochefort.*'

In the meanwhile Jules Favre, Jules Ferry, and Picard had arrived. Jules Favre, on his way to breakfast with M. Thiers, who had crossed the Prussian lines on the previous evening, and to give him instructions and power to treat with Prussia for an armistice, was informed by Ferry of what was going on. He placed M. Thiers in a carriage escorted by cavalry, and tried to reassure him in regard to the rising.

' We have often seen similar ones,' he said.

He then picked up Picard, who had come to the Foreign Office to say good-bye to M. Thiers, got into a carriage with him, found the quays blocked by the mob, turned off to the Prefecture of Police in search of information, learnt there that Adam was at the Hôtel de Ville, and contrived in the end to gain admittance through the private entrance, in spite of the entreaties of Picard, who wanted above all things to avoid putting his head in the lion's mouth.

By the time they arrived, General Trochu had made up his mind to put in an appearance in person. He went down to the large room, followed by Simon and de Pelletan. Ten minutes elapsed before he could obtain silence. At length the orator of the band, Joly by name, contrived to get a few words in and commence a speech.

He told the General, who listened to him with folded arms, that the loss of Bourget was an act of treason, that the armistice was treason, that the people of Paris wished to have done with this everlasting temporising, and that they wanted to appoint a municipal council to protect themselves, and so relieve the Government of half the burden which was too heavy for its shoulders.

Trochu replied, and as was his wont, without taking the slightest heed of ejaculations or interruptions, he began a speech as long as it was interesting.

It was not a question of capitulation, but of negotiation, and negotiation while Paris was being revictualled. Help had to be obtained from the departments, and the best way of obtaining this help was the appointment of an Assembly. He had made Paris impregnable. He answered for that. As for Bourget, its loss was of no importance, because it was not included in the general plan of the defence, and because it would have had to have been abandoned all the same. However, the Government was going to consider the news which had been submitted to them, and would take care to reconcile the wishes of the population with its own sacred and paramount duty, the defence of the Capital.

The General was noisily interrupted and even hissed at the conclusion of his speech. He lost his temper and hustled everybody on his way back, but the prestige of his uniform prevented the ferocious idiots from laying hands on him, and so he made his way into the Council room again, followed by his two officers, who placed themselves behind his chair.

The entire Government set to work to consider the question of the elections. On the same floor the Mayors were deliberating under the presidency of Arago, and underneath was the first batch of the invaders, still separated from the crowd which continued to vociferate and make a horrid din in the square of the Hôtel de Ville.

The Government forgot that some of its members had pledged themselves, in Rochefort's newspaper, to the elections, and the majority opposed them, maintaining, reasonably enough, that they meant anarchy, and that if the Commune was established, the Government of the National Defence would have nothing to do but make itself scarce. Arago presented himself once more to beg that the wishes of the Mayors should·be acceded to, and that the elections should be granted.

They replied that they were going to accede and put an end to everything in accordance with the wishes of the populace. The elections were agreed upon. Arago went to announce this good news to the Mayors.

It was half-past three, and Flourens had not yet appeared.

At this moment he arrived in the square at the head of his battalions, with their arms butt end uppermost, and made for the closed doors of the Hôtel de Ville.

Commandant Dauvergne evinced a disposition to resist this onslaught, and received a blow from a fist on his eye. He drew his sword and it was snatched from his grasp.

Some shots were fired at the lock of the principal door of the Hôtel de Ville, and it was battered with the butt ends of the rifles. In the end it gave way, and Flourens entered at the head of his men.

This time the invasion was wholesale. The immense square might be said to have emptied itself into the huge building.

The crowd invaded the great staircase, the offices, and the rooms, driving out before it the still deliberating Mayors, and finally, like a torrent, rushed into the room where the Government were seated round a table, and whither it was preceded by Arago, who continued his thunder, but had completely broken down, had laid aside his badge of office, and was altogether demoralised.

At this precise moment, like an eel that has come across a broken mesh in a net, Picard, ever cunning, the gay Picard disappeared through a little door in a passage, and left his colleagues still seated, to imitate at their ease the celebrated scene of the Roman Senate invaded by the Gauls. This practical and shrewd man had gone to fetch the guard.

To picture the Hôtel de Ville at this moment, from the ground floor to the roof, offices, passages, rooms, private apartments and all, no comparison is more apt than a basket full of frogs. From the bottom of the staircase to· the most hidden recesses there were nothing but men of the *Garde Nationale*, armed and unarmed, citizens of all ages and conditions, volunteers of every nationality. The mob brought with it its particular odour. The smell of its pipes and cigars alone contended with a stink as of wet dogs, and that reeking odour of oil on rifles and boots, and of dried sweat which exhales from a mass of troops, especially when those troops are dirty and have only been partially washed by the rain.

A damp atmosphere rose above the crowded and perspiring heads, caught you in the throat, and condensed itself on the window panes, looking glasses, and pictures.

Darkness came on gradually, lending a fantastic air to the scene, and making the actors look like ghosts.

Round the council table, behind the seated members of the Government, calm and silent, the men of the *Garde Nationale* were packed close one against the other, and were incessantly being jammed closer together by the arrival of fresh reinforcements.

Their leaders arrived, forced their way through the crowd, and as none of them were tall enough to tower above it, they scaled the council table. Flourens, Millière, Delescluze, Blanqui, Pyat, Mottu, &c., transformed the board of green cloth into a circus ring, and strode along the table, treading on the paper and blotting books, upsetting the inkstands and sand boxes, and crushing pens and pencils beneath their feet. They all shouted alike, and as their audience also shouted, nobody heard them.

Trochu, with his two officers still behind his chair, smoked his cigar, and watched the coming and going of these spurred or slip-shod heels on a level with his chest.

In the lamp-room the attendants in the Prefecture had, however, got ready the lamps, filled them with oil, trimmed the wicks, and cleaned the glasses. The administration, the immortal administration, found its last refuge there.

They brought the lamps and placed them on the invaded table, whence some of the leaders had jumped down for fear of being burnt from below by the lights of the Government.

The sudden light made the gilt epaulettes of Trochu and his silver star glitter into prominence. Instinctively he felt that he was too brilliant, too conspicuous in the midst of all these brute beasts, so he quietly took off his epaulettes and passed them to Bibesco, slowly divested himself of his star, and put it in the pocket of his tunic. Except for his kepi, he might have passed for a private in the *Garde Nationale*.

The arrival of the lamps brought about some slight show of order, and Flourens succeeded in making himself heard. He proposed to proclaim a government at whose head he modestly placed himself. Some laughed, some protested, and others ignored his propositions. Half-a-dozen rascals, delegated by themselves, went to deliberate in an adjoining room, and began to squabble at will.

Meanwhile Flourens went down to the square, mounted his horse, and passed through the midst of the battalions which were arriving and taking up their positions with their rifles butt-ends uppermost, neither knowing exactly what they wanted nor what was going on. They cheered him with the utmost confidence.

Side by side with the new government a committee was nominated to preside over the elections. Flourens was chosen president of this committee by acclamation, and with him were associated Victor Hugo, Félix Pyat, Delescluze, Ledru-Rollin, Schœlcher, Louis Blanc, Blanqui, and Millière. The formation of this committee, and the immediate elections for the Commune, were announced by means of *bulletins* thrown from the windows into the square. The *bulletins* were cheered. These people were possessed by a mania to cheer without cessation anybody or anything.

The unfortunate Dorian was painful to look at. Placed between his popularity and his duty, he wanted to retain the first and do the second. He went to the insurgents, who shouted, '*Vive Dorian!*' and to the Government, who said nothing, trying to temporize, to avoid compromising himself, and to conciliate.

Towards six o'clock Edmond Adam succeeded in escaping. He pretended to be ill, struggled, contrived to be hustled by policemen in disguise—for there were some even of them present—and disappeared to rejoin Picard.

At eight o'clock the tide set in strongly. The *Garde Nationale* in the yellow room were driven away by a stream of resolute men. The 106th battalion, commanded by M. Ibos, had appeared on the scene. They entered the room, surrounded Trochu, seized him, and carried him off. Behind him, in his wake, Ferry, Pelletan, and Arago succeeded in getting away.

The insurgent *Gardes* reformed in front of the other members of the Government, and drove them back into the room.

Favre, Simon, Garnier-Pagès, Leflô, and Tamisier, alone remained, and returned to their seats at the table.

While Dorian was hurrying to and fro, and making his futile efforts, the members of the Government protested. They requested to be made prisoners or to be set at liberty. Their resignations were demanded. They refused on the ground that they were not free agents. Finally they were made prisoners and consigned to the embrasure of a window. Some bread and horse-flesh afforded them refreshment, and they slept on chairs behind some of Flourens' volunteers who, half-drunk and more than half-asleep, were posted three deep to watch over them.

The confusion continued. By this time there were two or three governments, and five or six committees. Blanqui did not want Flourens. Delescluze did not want Pyat. A portion of the *Garde Nationale,* who had not derived sufficient nourishment from their own cheering, marched off to get something to eat.

The Hôtel de Ville stood out, black and damp in the darkness of the night, in front of the swarming square, and with its rows of illuminated windows behind which passed and repassed the outlines of the *Garde Nationale.*

Dorian was still parleying. He was joined by Delescluze who was put in the shade by the popularity of Flourens, Millière who found his colleague Flourens embarrassing, and Blanqui who began to be afraid.

Meanwhile, Picard, as soon as he was fairly out of the Hôtel de Ville, betook himself to the Louvre, where he found General Schmitz bent on carrying out the orders of the Governor, and resolved not to stir.

He next proceeded to his own office and took upon himself to order the assembly to be sounded for the concentration of the *Garde Nationale* on the boulevards. When Trochu arrived with the other members of the Government who had subsequently been set at liberty, they found the battalions which had stood firm falling in, and their officers talking to each other on the Bourse. Adam had joined his exertions to those of Picard. Trochu gave the necessary orders, and at five minutes before midnight the columns of the faithful *Garde Nationale* debouched on to the square of the Hôtel de Ville and by degrees surrounded the building.

At this moment there was an alarm.

As Jules Favre opened one of the windows of the yellow room to get some fresh air, a few shots were fired in the square, and were replied to by the defenders of the Hôtel de Ville. Fortunately the firing stopped there. The window was closed and Jules Favre resumed his seat.

Nevertheless, a feeling of uneasiness began to prevail within concerning what was going on without. The leaders said, 'We are surrounded,' and they became more supple and amenable to the exhortations of Dorian. Flourens mounted the table once more; he advised an agreement and departure.

Delescluze and Dorian agreed that the events of the day should be wiped out, and that the Hôtel de Ville should be evacuated on condition that no proceedings should be taken against anybody. Then came mutual salutes, and everybody went home saying,

'A simple misunderstanding. Good-morning.'

The insurgents accepted the situation, Delescluze and Dorian went out and conferred with Adam and Ferry. The latter pair, by no means satisfied as to the fate of their captive colleagues, and fearing lest by any act of theirs their friends should be massacred, and they themselves hurled out of the windows, agreed to the amnesty, and to bygones being bygones. All shook hands, and the two envoys from the Hôtel de Ville returned to the palace.

At this moment information reached Adam that the Indre *Mobiles* had been ordered to enter the Hôtel de Ville by a subterranean passage uniting that building to the Napoleon barracks, that they had carried out the order, and were entering the Hôtel.

M. Ferry declined to venture into the subterranean passage. Adam hastened thither, and emerged with the *Mobiles* into the yard of the palace.

He endeavoured to induce them to evacuate it, and succeeded in keeping the Breton *Mobiles* in check until the first batch of the *Garde Nationale* were clear away.

Ferry burst open one of the side doors of the building, and in his turn rushed into the Hôtel de Ville, and was lost in the crowd.

Finally, everybody walked off, arm in arm. Tamisier got hold of Blanqui to take him away, the Government was set at liberty, and the grotesque masquerade came to an end about 3 A.M.

No sooner were they out of the clutches of the riot, mild enough on this occasion, than the members of the Government met at the Louvre to consult with the Governor. Their exasperation knew no bounds, and it was a most comical sight to see these men, whom the revolution had made what they were, and who had profited by I do not know how many riots, superbly indignant at being hoist with their own petard.

It is always the same. There is no worse policeman than a converted rioter, no more supple chamberlain than a gilded jacobin, no harder master than an ex-workman.

They wanted to prosecute, arrest, and bring before councils of war, all the people they had recognised in the abortive movement, which, after all, was inferior to that of the 4th of September in one single particular—its want of success. And before they went to bed they had drawn up very long lists of persons to be arrested on the following day.

But when the following morning arrived the Prefect of Police appeared at the Foreign Office, where the Government were assembled, and absolutely refused to molest anybody in connection with the affair of the preceding day. He said that he had given his word to Dorian and Delescluze, who had stipulated, in the name of the insurgents, that the rising should not result in any prosecutions. He tendered his resignation. It was refused, and the meeting was adjourned to the same evening at the residence of the Governor.

At the adjourned council Picard urged the necessity of arresting the ringleaders of the 31st of October, and Adam insisted that the promise given should not be broken.

' Who promised ? ' exclaimed M. Ferry.

' You did yourself,' replied Adam.

. ' That is not true.'

Contradiction and provocation ensued. M. Ferry was pronounced by his colleagues to be in the wrong, so he apologised and held out his hand to the Prefect of Police.

As the Government persisted in ordering arrests to be made, Adam resigned and left the Prefecture of Police. As for Dorian, whose popularity had put the Government in the shade, but had nevertheless saved it, he was implored so urgently to remain in the ministry that he consented.

M. Cresson was appointed Prefect of Police.

Proceedings were commenced against the ringleaders of the 31st of October, but the supernumeraries only were arrested. The proceedings had no significance, and accorded with the armistice. Paris, which has already forgotten the 31st of October, neither understood nor was interested in the discussion. Those who were condemned to death did not die—at all events, not on this account. Those who were imprisoned did not remain there. The Commune' arrived in time to make both classes magistrates or generals.

Such is the history of the 31st of October.

Was Adam right to leave the Prefecture rather than break his word? Undoubtedly. No man is forced to give his word of honour so long as he has the alternative of death; but when once he has given it, be it to a murderer, a bandit, or a red Indian, he must keep it for his own sake, and for the sake of him to whom he has given it.

Turenne was one day robbed on the Pont-Neuf. He set great store by a watch which had been given him by the King. He offered to repurchase it from the thieves for a sum which he himself would pay them if they would call at his house for the money. He gave his word. The thieves took him at it. He kept it, and so far from having them arrested, he paid them to the uttermost farthing.

In the days I am describing there was unfortunately no lack of descendants of these thieves in Paris. The descendants of Turenne were the people conspicuous by their absence.

CHAPTER XIII

ELECTIONS AND NEGOTIATIONS

The Moderation of the Chancellor.—M. Thiers at Paris.—At Versailles.—The Negotiations.—Everything broken off.—A Lesson in Politeness.—Paris Resigned.—A Fresh Plébiscite.—Municipal Elections.—Universal Suffrage.

ONE of my colleagues went to Sèvres on the 30th of October to receive M. Thiers on his return from Europe and to Paris, after having crossed the Prussian lines and sojourned at Versailles, where he was received by M. de Moltke and interviewed M. de Bismarck, without, however, having any conversation with either of them on war or politics.

This same colleague escorted M. Thiers when he returned to Versailles on the afternoon of the 31st October armed this time with instructions and powers in due form, having a vague idea that a rising had taken place, but in ignorance of its importance and unable to learn its result.

It is known how he reached the Prussian Head-quarters

on the Monday evening, and spent Tuesday and Wednesday negotiating with M. Thiers, and, strange to relate, up to Thursday the Germans knew absolutely nothing about what had happened at the Hôtel de Ville on Monday.

If one could have believed three-fourths of the French publications relative to the war, the newspapers and public opinion foreshadowed by them—the Chancellor of Prussia, Count Bismarck, would have been, in regard to his master, not only a species of Richelieu beneath whose will everything bent, who commanded but accounted to no one for his conduct, a man of iron resolved upon achieving success and exhausting victory to the bitter end, who had prognosticated our fall and all that appertained to it, whom nothing stopped, who cared no more for the rest of Europe than for a cherry-stone, and who, in a word, knew exactly how far he could go and would not stop before he got there.

Nothing can be more erroneous than this conception.

First of all, the authority of the Chancellor was not without control, nor was it unlimited. He was continually obliged to explain his conduct, to discuss his actions, to convince the king, to fight against the counter-influence around him, against the counter-influence of the Prince Royal, against the counter-influence of Queen Augusta, against the counter-influence of the court *habitués* who had followed the king, and lastly, most powerful of all, against the military party.

The struggle between the Chancellor and the military party was incessant; it began with the Hohenzollern question, and only came to an end after the conclusion of peace.

To say that M. de Bismarck did not want war, would be silly. To say that he was resolved upon it and meant to carry it on to the bitter end, would be unjust.

When a gambler sits down at a baccarat table with a few thousand franc notes, and says to himself, 'I am going to break the bank,' he generally leaves the table without a franc.

When, on the contrary, he has sufficient command over himself to be bold methodically, and be ready to withdraw, he nearly always succeeds. To this latter class of gamblers M. de Bismarck belonged.

In the month of July, when Benedetti was discussing the question, all sorts of phases of opinion alternated at Ems just as in Paris. One day war was in every mouth, and old Moltke at once appeared to grow younger, his wrinkles disappeared, his face became more youthful, and his figure more upright. On the following day everybody said peace was assured, and once more Moltke became wrinkled, bent, and aged.

Count Bismarck would willingly have stopped after Sedan, and would probably have been content with Strasbourg as an indemnity. It was already in train. When in the presence of M. de Moltke, who was uneasy because he wanted to place his batteries round the edge of the basin at the bottom of which was our demoralised army, and he hoped to blow them in the air, when in his presence the Chancellor asked Napoleon III, 'Sire, are you surrendering your own sword, or that of France?' he expected the Emperor to reply, 'The sword of France.'

But instead of that, the Emperor said,

'I am personally your prisoner. As for peace, that rests with the Paris Government.'

And a smile of satisfaction stole over the ascetic and monkish face of the Chief of the Great Staff. The war would go on.

At Ferrières M. de Bismarck did not reject the proposals for peace; but his demands had increased, and Jules Favre considered them intolerable.

A fortnight later, in the early days of October, when General Burnside went to Paris, the success of his unofficial mission would not have been displeasing to the Chancellor. His luck continued. Count Bismarck had still tremendous power in reserve, but he would willingly have 'pocketed' the enormous gain already realised.

At the beginning of November, when confronted by M. Thiers, he was actuated by the same sentiments of prudence and comparative moderation. Gambetta made him uneasy, though he was not afraid of him. He did not exactly know how long Paris could hold out, and already on several occasions he had allowed signs of impatience to escape him.

'You will see,' he had said, 'we shall be here still when Spring comes.'

In order to imagine that at this period he would have been as exacting as he was three months later; to imagine that we should not have been more leniently treated, either from a territorial or a monetary point of view, or both, it would be necessary to prove that the surrender of Paris, the final annihilation of the provincial armies, south, east, west, and north, and the conclusion of the conventions which created the empire of Germany, were not weights in the scale; in other words, it would be necessary to prove an absurdity.

Consequently, when M. Thiers approached M. de Bismarck, he found a man disposed to come to terms, having wrung permission from his master to do so, and having, in order to wring that permission, fought and conquered the influence of the military party.

o

At the outset the negotiations proceeded favourably. The Chancellor consented to the armistice and the revictualling, the latter a capital question, for an armistice without revictualling is a voluntary blockade, a continuance of the siege without danger to the besieger and without hope for the besieged. He did not agree to legislative elections for Alsace and Lorraine, but he consented to a selection of notables to represent the population of those countries.

It must not be forgotten that these negotiations were set on foot, not for the conclusion of peace, but for a suspension of hostilities to allow of the election of an Assembly and the formation of a regular Government, and that consequently there was no obligation to give us any information about any definite claims on our territories or our money.

Things were in this state, and M. Thiers was sanguine of success, when on Wednesday night or Thursday, information was received at Head-quarters, first of all from the reports of the advanced posts and soon afterwards from the Paris newspapers—which were always to be had some days, occasionally only a few hours, old—of the events of the 31st of October.

The war party did not miss their turn to play.

Marshal Moltke urged the King to adopt his views. What! were they to stop when victory was within their grasp? What! were they going to declare peace with people who were tearing each other in pieces? What! were they going to renounce the glory of taking Paris, changing a Government of scarcely reasonable rioters for a Government of rioters even worse; and all this when the defence was on the eve of being paralysed, and the regular army of Paris probably occupied in fighting the *Garde Nationale*?

Were they going to negotiate, as they would with a great nation, with people who were killing each other, and of whom one-half would possibly ask the assistance of Germany against the other half? That was a grand idea, truly. They would be more than kind, they would be dupes, they would be fools to do anything of the sort!

On Thursday morning, M de Bismarck was summoned to the presence of the King. He argued the point to begin with, gave way in the end, and went back to his own quarters where M. Thiers met him.

There he spoke of the troubles inside Paris, of which M. Thiers was entirely ignorant. For the amateur governors who had come to terms with the rising had never even conceived the very elementary idea of sending an envoy to their representative to let him know that the rising was of no importance, and that they themselves were stronger than ever. That was far too simple a step for them to take.

Destitute of news, and not knowing whether they from whom he had received his instructions and authority were still living, M. Thiers fell an easy prey to the Chancellor, who had agreed to a continuance of the war. The latter had only to advance fresh arguments just as M. de Moltke sent forward fresh troops. He demanded military guarantees, a fort or two. It was precisely the same thing as demanding Paris itself.

M. Thiers could not refrain from saying, 'It is an insult. From that moment M. de Bismarck, quite imperturbable, continued the conversation in German until his visitor, completely put out of countenance, said to him with tears in his voice,

'But, Count, you know very well that I do not understand German.'

And the Chancellor, who knows and speaks French as

well as they do at the Academy, who knows the genius of our language as well as any professor of grammar, replied,

' I came back to my own language because only my ignorance of yours would have caused me to utter what you are pleased to call an insult.'

He himself has told this story and its lesson to his intimate friends.

There was only one thing left for M. Thiers to do— to return to the Sèvres bridge and confer with Jules Favre, for it did not suit him to re-enter Paris, where he did not consider himself safe, and which he was destined to leave so hurriedly on the 18th of March. M. Thiers had at this time already taken his precautions, and had committed his house and his old servants to the care of Edmond Adam, the Prefect of Police, who had undertaken to look after them.

M. Thiers was ambitious and very clever, a very well-informed writer, a very clear sighted popularity-monger; but he was never a thoroughly brave man, and a proof of this, if I may be pardoned for my levity, is that he was as clean-shaved as an actor or a priest. He loved to talk about war, but not to make it. He was fond of reviews, but did not relish powder and shot. Nobody is perfect, and taking into consideration his situation he was right. The object attained here below by those who kill each other is the building up of the fortunes of lawyers and orators. It is not the dog that gets the game. One cannot be dog and hunter at one and the same time.

M. Thiers returned to Sèvres, and saw Jules Favre. The Government deliberated, rejected the armistice with the additional burdens proposed by M. de Bismarck, and despatched M. Thiers into the Provinces again.

It must not be supposed that his mission, if it had

succeeded, would have displeased the middle classes of the capital, who were the most numerous, and the only people really interested. These classes were quite resigned to the idea of an honourable peace, and they began to discover that the siege was a very lengthy business, though they were perfectly ready to undergo, as they actually did, renewed distress and privation so long as they thought that honour commanded them to hold out, and that all was not lost.

The armistice would only have displeased a few military men who still deceived themselves, a few enthusiastic patriots, a few tenacious republicans who, after having admitted that the Empire was bound to be the ruin of France, could not admit that the Republic was powerless to save her, and lastly, the rabble of the 31st of October, who did not want peace because they were not fighting against the Prussians; they were being nourished on having nothing to do, and liked bearing arms because they hoped to make them implements wherewith to gain freedom, enjoyment, and idleness.

I had almost forgotten to mention the grocers who had not yet sold off their provisions, who were hiding them so as to realise better prices, and who, by the rumour of an armistice, were compelled to expose them for sale at a lower rate. Everything that remained unsold on the day when the armistice was rejected, disappeared into the cellars and came out again worth its weight in gold. These brave people were willing to be patriotic on condition that their patriotism did not interfere with their business.

How many men, alas! there are who think they are saying, 'I love my country,' while in reality they say 'I love myself.'

For this reason the best government is that which knows how to attach to the interests of its country the greatest number of personal and private interests.

When this is the case, men adore their country, in adoring themselves in her, to such an extent that they occasionally forget themselves, and sacrifice themselves for her.

It will be conceded, I imagine, that I do my best to be frank and to refrain from flattering anybody.

In all sincerity I ought to say that my conscientious belief is that the prospect of peace, of an honourable and lasting peace, preceded by the desired revictualling, counted for something in the vote of the 3rd November. People were not sorry to strengthen a government which was paving the way for peace, or to vote down the crowds who shouted, '*Pas d'Armistice!*'

It was a confused, singular, and fantastic vote.

On the 31st of October, it will be remembered, the prominent question was the carrying into effect the municipal elections, as the Government supporters called them; the Commune elections, as they were styled by their opponents. The Mayors assembled at the Hôtel de Ville had decided upon them, and the Government had consented. Placards in accordance with this arrangement were posted up, and immediately taken down.

On the following day the vote was to be taken on the question if the elections were to take place at once.

On the day after, the point at issue was changed, those who wished to continue the Government of the Defence in office were to vote Aye and the others No.

Aye and No. I recognised that. It was the plébiscite.

Yes, the plébiscite organised by its opponents. Aye

canvassed by the partisans of No. The boots of Bonaparte worn by the lawyers.

Nothing was wanting, not even the vote of the army.

In the month of May the Imperial plébiscite had been inconvenient enough to reveal to Germany, our rival, the number of our soldiers almost to a man. It was considered an absurd and dangerous proceeding.

In the month of November, that is to say six months later, day by day the Republican plébiscite revealed to our rival, now our besieger, the number of our defenders almost to a man. The Government, composed of men who had in May justly condemned the vote of the army as absurd and dangerous, in November considered this vote intelligent and without danger.

The voting took place on Thursday, the 3rd of November.

The army gave 236,623 Ayes, and 9,053 Noes. The population, 321,373 Ayes, and 53,585 Noes.

Like Napoleon III, the Government issued a proclamation expressing its satisfaction, and thanking the people for their confidence.

It was admirable.

On Saturday, the 5th, the nomination of the Mayors took place, and a certain Mottu, one of the leaders of the 31st of October, an out-and-out revolutionist and completely unknown, received the largest number of votes.

On the following day the Deputy Mayors were appointed. There were numerous abstentions, and the majority of these magistrates represented minorities.

I hope my readers have a sufficiently good opinion of me to know, without my telling them, that I took no part in these electoral fooleries. The expression is a strong one, but I am not afraid of it.

I fancy I see myself, an officer, going to deposit in an

urn a voting paper worth just as much as that of my General Commanding-in-Chief, or that of the soldier who cleaned my boots or groomed my horse; and no human power could have made me do a thing which I considered the most stupid and revolting of absurdities.

I am looking at the question from a purely military point of view.

If I had wished to look upon the question as a citizen, I should have done precisely the same. My brain absolutely refuses to understand a political mechanism which gives complete equivalence to the opinion of a doctor of laws and that of a man who can neither read nor write, to the opinion of M. Thiers and that of his hall-porter, to the opinion of Victor Hugo and that of his valet, to the opinion of the Archbishop of Paris and that of a town bully, to my opinion and that of my servant.

A nation whose existence depends upon that anti-seientific idea, on that barbarous mechanism, is an absurd nation, and in nature that which is absurd does not last. I am sorry for it, but so it is.

Paris, comforted by the news of the re-capture of Orleans, saw her dreams of armistice and peace fly away without any very excessive regret. The ordinary military and official routine recommenced after the stirring excitement of the 31st of October.

The Government made speeches and held sittings; the Governor worked and visited the arsenals; General Schmitz shut himself up and revelled in his infernal work; and we received visitors in the green room, listened to their complaints, and responded to their demands.

There were, however, several changes among the higher Government officials. Edmond Adam has resigned rather than break his word by participating in the arrest of the authors of the abortive rising which took place after the plébiscite. General Tamisier had played rather a pitiful part on the 31st of October. As a matter of fact, a portion of the *Garde Nationale* had mutinied. He commanded that corps and had not been able either to support it or to manage it. The result was that one half of the men deprived the other half of their arms. He resigned the command in favour of Clément Thomas, who seemed to be gifted with more firmness. His lot, too, was far different; he was not put aside by his soldiers: he was destined to be shot by them.

Blustering Arago no longer took any pleasure in associating with the Members of the Defence after he had begged them to decree the municpal elections, and after he had divested himself in their presence of his tricoloured scarf, the badge of his office.

These gentlemen never forgave him for not having succeeded in arranging for their safety in the Municipal Palace. He was replaced by Jules Ferry, who had the reputation of being very energetic, and whose bearing in opposition to Edmond Adam I have already described, as well as the military part he played on the 31st of October.

Marching companies of the *Garde Nationale* were organised, and several reconnaissances were made round Paris. Preparations were also made for the great Champigny affair.

Meanwhile Paris amused itself with its pigeons and their microscopic despatches, with its balloons, and with its clubs, where the orators were more violent and foolish than ever.

The moment has now arrived, I think, to give a sketch

of Paris in a state of siege, and to record the fresh forms which the inner life of Paris assumed during the closing days of November, when the siege may be said, without exaggeration, to have been at its height.

CHAPTER XIV

PARIS

Paris as an Individuality.—Everybody a Soldier.—Provisions.—Rationing Tails.—
Cats and Dogs.—The Animals in the Zoological Gardens.—Elephants'Trunks
and Feet.—Price of Provisions.—Gas and Balloons.—Carrier Pigeons.—
Restaurants.—Canteen and Ambulance Women.—A Friend.

THE Parisian no doubt exaggerates the importance of his town, and is apt to call up a smile when he talks of it as the centre of the universe, but he must nevertheless be credited with a serious, profound, and deep-rooted affection for the corner of the earth which he inhabits. If the former of these two sentiments stands in need of an excuse, the second requires no explanation, for Paris, I assert, possesses everything necessary to seduce, not merely the idler and the trifler, but the thinker and the artist.

Where can you find a town whose appearance is in itself so full of life and character? Or one possessing more individuality, or better calculated to tempt the pencil or the pen, to induce a dream or rouse curiosity?

Paris lives, Paris has a countenance, gestures, customs, vicious habits, manias. When you know Paris, she is not a town, she is an animated being, a natural person, who has her moments of fury, madness, stupidity, enthusiasm, honesty, and lucidity, just like a man who may sometimes be charming, and sometimes unbearable, but never indifferent.

She is loved and she is hated; she attracts or repels, but is never regarded coldly.

Nothing, therefore, could be more interesting and instructive than to depict, both in their entirety and in detail, the profound modifications brought by the siege into this colossal life and its outward appearances.

Unfortunately, for any such effort I should need the pen of a great writer, coupled with the pencil of a great artist, and I confess that personally I am utterly inadequate to the task, and that, moreover, it is outside the limits which I have set to this work.

I wish, however, to place on record here some of the pictures which struck me and roused my attention, for the simple reason that they in no way resembled anything I had hitherto seen.

The first thing that struck you in besieged Paris was the number of the uniforms. Everybody was a soldier, and the members of the Government were the only persons who did not wear at all events a kepi as a symbol of military costume. As soon, therefore, as any action was announced or in preparation, the streets and boulevards were filled solely by persons got up in clothes, the buttons of which, if not the cut, betokened uniform.

A stripe of red cloth sewn on a pair of trousers, a dozen white buttons on a jacket, a kepi costing thirty sous, and an absence of whisker denoted the soldier, the defender of his country. Individuals were met with their rifles on their way to fall in somewhere or other ; the omnibuses traversed the boulevards, bristling with barrels and resembling pincushions or porcupines.

In the cafés and restaurants the same military air prevailed. The squares and open places, as well as the ramparts, were utilised as drill grounds where improvised officers taught what they did not know to soldiers who knew even less.

Everybody, or nearly everybody, was a soldier. As for their being good soldiers, that is quite another matter. The middle classes, the shopkeepers, the *employés*, and the aristocracy, of whom the battalions of the centre consisted, did their duty steadily and seriously. But I should be uttering a falsehood were I to say that the battalions of the *faubourgs*, the popular battalions, were good troops ; and I am bold enough to state that they as a rule refrained from pushing themselves forward when the Prussians had to be fought, and only behaved themselves properly, from a military point of view, when they were confronted by the French army.

There were too many what we call *pratiques* in these battalions ; and when they are not kept in order by energetic officers and non-commissioned officers, one of them will suffice to disorganise the company to which he belongs, and to which he serves both as an amusement and a dissolvent.

Everybody did not fight every day, neither did everybody go on guard, but everybody had to eat ; and the question of provisions was not only the most important of all questions, but also that which, more than anything else, left its mark on the appearance of Paris.

During the period with which I am dealing, rationing was strictly carried out. It ought to have been put in effect the day after the investment; but at that time even those who were responsible for the government and issued the proclamation did not believe in the prolonged duration of the siege. The idea of holding out as long as possible was only indulged in later on, so as to compel as many Germans as possible to concentrate round Paris, and thus to second the action of the young dictator who, with a stamp of his foot, was making armies spring out of the ground.

Rationing was, therefore, put in force too late. If the step had been taken in time, Paris might have held out, perhaps, a month longer, for it is certain that at the beginning of the siege much flour was wasted.

Rationing obliged every individual, or every family, to attend in person at the shops of the butchers and bakers. Each household was furnished with a card issued by the municipalities and authorising it to receive so many grammes of meat or bread. The nurse, or the mother of the family, or the daughter, or the child, stood for hours outside the shop doors in rain and snow, with wet feet and shivering. God knows how many chest complaints, or how many cases of consumption and rheumatism were brought about in this way. The unhappy women bore these fatiguing expeditions, which were their sorties, without flinching or complaining. The women, throughout the siege, gave the men examples of courage, self-denial, and devotion, which the latter did not always sufficiently imitate.

It was a painful but touching sight to see these long lines of women, almost all dressed in black, huddled together at the tradesmen's doors, kept back by the soldiers on duty, with whom they began to joke until suffering and cold lulled gaiety to rest and occasionally substituted tears for it.

By degrees the shops became empty. The reserves

collected hastily before the siege, were exhausted, and while small children deprived of milk died in numbers, while others nourished on sweetened wine and bread became afflicted with rachitis, the adults set their wits to work to supplement the meagre ration allowed by the authorities.

The cat and dog butchers established themselves. Rat pies made their appearance. Stewed cat is not bad, and the poor beast had passed from the tiles to the saucepan long before the Prussians came. A young, plump dog is tolerable eating. As for the rat—the sewer rat—very fat and very large, except for a slight musky odour, he is twice as good, with plenty of pepper and nutmeg, as a duck in pastry.

The rats in Paris affect certain special localities, such as, for example, the neighbourhood of restaurants and hotels. One of their favourite haunts is the Jardin des Plantes, where they dispute with the rare animals or birds the food provided by the administration. Their sojourn in the Jardin des Plantes was very sad at this period, because the *employés* of the Museum slaughtered them in quantities and ate them.

The messmates of the rats—in other words, the animals in the menagerie, representing a considerable value, had, through the care of the executive under the direction of Milne-Edwards, been provided with sustenance enough to carry them through the privations of the siege. There was hay for the herbivorous, grain for the birds, and the carnivorous never lacked a succulent joint, seeing that, when Paris surrendered, there still remained more than 30,000 horses.

But if they had enough to live upon, they had no means of entertaining, and it happened that at the commencement of the siege, the animals of the Jardin d'Acclimatation, driven out of the Bois de Boulogne by the shells, went to their comrades for hospitality.

This could not last long, and from the middle of October it became necessary to sacrifice the new comers.

I give a list of the animals sold, killed, and eaten, which, I believe was never published.   At all events, I am sure that it is curious, and I owe it to the kindness of M. Geoffroy Saint-Hilaire, director of the Jardin d'Acclamatation.

DATE OF SALE.	PURCHASER.	NATURE OF ANIMAL.	PRICE. FRANCS.
Oct. 18, 1870	M. Courtier	1 Dwarf Zebra	350
,, 18 ,,	,,	2 Buffaloes	300
,, 23 ,,	M. Lacroix	2 Deer	500
,, 23 ,,	,,	12 Carp	150
,, 24 ,,	M. Deboos	2 Yaks	390
,, 25 ,,	M. Groszos	3 Geese	60
,, 27 ,,	M. Lacroix	1 Small Zebra	400
,, 28 ,,	M. Bignon	Lot Fowls, Ducks,&c.	862
,, 31 ,,	M. Deboos	1 Lot of Ducks	115
Nov. 3 ,,	M. X	11 Rabbits	100
,, 17 ,,	M. Deboos	2 Reindeer	800
,, 21 ,,	,,	2 Nilghaus	1,000
,, 22 ,,	M. Lacroix	1 Bengal Stag	300
,, 26 ,,	M. Deboos	2 Wapitis	2,500
Dec. 9 ,,	,,	1 Nilghau	650
,, 15 ,,	,,	2 Camels	4,000
,, 15 ,,	,,	1 Yak Calf	200
,, 20 ,,	,,	2 Camels	5,000
,, 29 ,,	,,	2 Elephants	27,000

I shall readily be believed when I say that in the slaughter-houses of Paris there existed no tradition relative to the slaughtering of elephants, and that, in consequence, there was some embarrassment in regard to transforming those two huge animals, Castor and Pollux, into butcher's meat.

M. Derisme, the gunsmith, came armed with a carbine and an explosive bullet, which was intended to overwhelm the brute.   Castor received the bullet in his body, and was not overwhelmed in the least. He merely bled profusely, but that might have gone on for a long time without causing death. The animal, accustomed to continual care, seemed convinced that the wound was due to an accident, and did everything his butchers told him with the greatest docility.

He next received a conical chassepot bullet, tipped with steel, in his head. Castor fell, but a third bullet was necessary to put an end to him.

Pollux did not offer so much resistance, and was killed by a bullet fired point blank behind his ear.

The elephants, as well as many other animals, were purchased, as has been seen from the list, by M. Deboos, the proprietor of the English butchery in the Avenue Friedland. This establishment became a sort of institution during the siege. It did an enormous business without seeking to make large profits. It remained to the very end hung round with strange appetising meats, and the ill-fed detachments of the *Garde Nationale,* when on their way to the ramparts, very frequently protested by shouting and hooting against the gastronomic riches displayed to view, and indeed, M. Carnot, Mayor of the district, and his deputy M. Denormandie, had to take measures for the safety of this establishment.

Elephants' flesh was sold at from 50 to 60 francs the kilogramme. The trunk fetched 80 francs the kilogramme. In fact the trunk and feet were pronounced by epicures to be delicious eating.

In the same house a litter of wolf cubs realized an average of 24 francs the kilogramme. The flesh was soft and flabby.

The animal for which M. Deboos paid dearest, was a little live lamb, weighing 25 lbs., which a *franc-tireur* had stolen from beyond the advance posts. It realized 500 francs.

Yak's flesh was unanimously preferred to all the others, and was acknowledged as being of quite exceptional quality.

The butchery did not sell horse flesh, but it procured some foals which it retailed as antelope meat. Those who ate it pronounced it succulent.

The cassowary flesh was bought by Baron de Rothschild, a good customer, and nearly all the parrots were eaten by Arsène Houssaye and Dr Ricord.

I append a few prices extracted from the books of M. Deboos:

	Francs
Paid for two small Wild Boars	1200
New Holland Cassowaries	200
Bears	500
2 Geese and 7 various Fowls	155
Paid for 2 Wolves and 1 Hind	570
2 Porcupines	100
1 Kangaroo	100
1 do.	150
1 Grand Cassowary	600

To return once more to the elephants, I have come across a letter from M. Geoffroy Saint Hilaire, to the great English butcher, of which the following is a copy,

'PARIS, *December 26th*, 1870

'MONSIEUR DEBOOS,

'In these days we do not know who is living or who is dying. Consequently we must not do business haphazard.

My responsibility to the Society which I represent will not permit of my handing over the elephants to you without having received the purchase money, or, at all events, without having some security in my hands. Will you, therefore, oblige me, if you take over my animals to-morrow or before I come off guard, by giving the keeper, Blondel a letter addressed to me, stating that you will pay the price of the two elephants, 27,000 francs, on Thursday morning the 29th of December. In this way, having security in our hands, my responsibility will be covered.

'Do not take this in bad part, I have entire confidence in you, but business is business.

'With cordial regards,

(*sig.*), GEOFFROY SAINT HILAIRE.'

Here is one more very exact list of the prices of provisions at the end of the siege :

		Francs
1 Kilogramme of Horse Flesh		20
1 do. Dogs do.		8
1 do. Ham		80
1 Cat		15
1 Rabbit		50
1 Turkey		150
1 Egg		5
1 Rat		2
1 Pigeon		15
1 Kilogramme of Butter		160
1 Litre of Haricot Beans		8
1 Bushel of Carrots		75
1 do. Potatoes		35
1 do. Onions		80
1 Cabbage		16
1 Leek		1
1 Head of Celery		2
1 Shallot		0.50
Green Wood, per 100 kil.		20

It will have been concluded from a perusal of the letter of M. Geoffroy Saint Hilaire, that no credit was given. That is true. Ready money was paid for everything. But, by way of compensation, a truce had been arranged between debtors and creditors. Landlords and tenants had signed a suspension of hostilities which was countersigned by the *concierges* themselves. And the bank clerks, instead of going from door to door with pocket-books whence issued notes to order, or where were engulphed bank notes, were under arms, like brave fellows that they nearly all are, in a splendid battalion which protected the Bank not only during the siege, but also during the Commune.

While the happy ones of the period, the wealthy, fed like Mohicans and discovered in Paris culinary resources which virgin forests reserve for the hardy trapper, I leave my readers to imagine what sort of food was eaten in the small restaurants, in the soup-kitchens and breakfast houses.

A few large restaurants alone had kept their aristocratic customers, the Café Anglais, Bignon, Voisin and Durand.

The Café Anglais was the place where the last piece of white bread was eaten. It was kneaded in the cellar. Voisin's was distinguished for the appetising way in which the nature of the food was concealed.

The stewards of the clubs rivalled each other in zeal and ingenuity. The tables of the clubs were a precious resource for a number of Parisians who had deposited their families in places of safety, and who had returned, as bachelors, to take part in the fatigues and excitement of the siege. The cost of these meals was only increased to an insignificant extent, and a man could appease his hunger without spending his wife's dowry in a week.

The candidates for admission into the large clubs were, consequently, numerous, very numerous, but generally unsuccessful, the old members not wishing to run the coffee-room fund too deeply into debt, or to exhaust the accumulation of provisions too rapidly.

There were, however, a tolerable number of admissions into the Jockey Club. It will, I think, be interesting to give a few details. In January, 1871, were admitted,

M.M. Prince de Clermont Tonnerre.

E. Blount.

Arthur O'Connor.

Baron Brunet.

Baron J. N. de Rothschild.

Comte de Kergariou.

Vicomte de la Londe.

Vicomte d'Haussonville.

Richard Wallace.

Comte de Quinsonas

Comte de Vigneral.

Vice-Admiral La Roncière le Noury.

Charles Haas.

Jules Bégé.

Edgar Passy.

Vicomte Edmond de La Panouse.

For the benefit of those who would like to know how the Jockey Club lived then, I give the *menu* of the 1st of January, 1871 :—

POTAGE AU PAIN.

1st Service.

Côte de bouf rôtie.

Poule au riz.

2nd Service.

Epinards au gris.

Glace groseille et vanille.

That was not so bad after a siege of three-months-and a-half, was it ? But it was meagre as compared with the ordinary *menus* of the Club. By way of comparison, here is an ordinary *menu :—*

Menu of January 1, 1884, at the Jockey Club.

Potage.

Consommé aux œuf pochés.

1st Service.

Soles â la Colbert.

Culotte de bœuf â la flamande.

Poulet sautés â la chasseur.

2nd Service.

Cuissot de chevreuil, sauce poivrade.

Pommes de terre â la créme.

Pannequets â l'abricot.

Dessert.

Poires, pommes.

Mendeauts, petits gateaux.

While I am on the subject of the Jockey Club, I trust I may be pardoned for displaying some confraternal pride, and may be allowed to put aside the cooking and the victuals in order to recall the fact that eight of the members of that large and aristocratic club lost their lives in battle. Here is the glorious list:— .

Comte Robert de Vogué, captain 1st Spahis. August 6. Battle of Reichshoffen.

Guy Dubessey de Contenson, colonel 5th Cuirassiers. August 30. Engagement of Mouzon.

François Fiévet, colonel 16th Artillery. September 1. Siege of Strasbourg.

Vicomte de Rafelis de Saint-Sauveur, captain 3rd

Zouaves. September 1. Mortally wounded at the Battle of Reichshoffen.

Louis Armand le Sergeant d'Hendecourt, captain on the Staff. September 1. Battle of Sedan.

André Picot, Comte de Dampierre, commandant 1st battalion *Mobiles* of Aube. October 13. Engagement of Bagneux.

Vicomte de Grancey, colonel, *Mobiles* of Côte-d'Or. December 2. Battle of Champigny.

Charles d'Albert, Duc de Luynes et de Chevreuse, captain and adjutant-major 1st battalion *Mobiles* of the Sarthe. December 2. Engagement of Ligny.

I ought perhaps, in obedience to the law of contrast, after having spoken of the still comfortable life of the rich citizen, to depict, in black colours and with bitter force, the existence of the poor, the workman without work, and the beggar. It would be difficult for me to do so for a very good reason. The siege of Paris was undoubtedly the precise period in our history when we had the fewest paupers. As a matter of fact, the State paid and fed every ablebodied man, his wife, and his children ; and the public fund —the State once more—took charge of the others.

By the force of circumstances, Paris at this time became a species of huge national workshop ; and I shall not easily be disabused of the idea that, if the national workshops of 1848 brought about the days of June, the forced and paid idleness of the siege had very much to do with the birth of the Commune.

And this is all the more true because wine and brandy were the only things which never had to be limited. The *Garde Nationale* took advantage of this, and all the world knows that the consumption of alcohol during this period was enormous. Add to this the continuous excitement of the clubs, and the fever engendered by absurd despatches and necessarily inflammatory proclamations, which fell from time to time into the midst of the population; the never-ceasing alternations of enthusiasm, anger, deception, and hope; the trouble wrought in the public mind by unaccustomed sights and panic succeeding to confidence; the brain disturbance caused during the last days of the siege by the continual roar of the bombarding ordnance; and perpetual anxiety—and you have the elements which made up what was called the obsidional madness.

Nevertheless, the Parisians of Paris, surrounded by neighbours knowing their districts, and sustained by the firmness of their mutual relations, got on pretty well; but what can be said as to those unfortunate beings who had fled before the invading armies, and were swallowed up in Paris without knowing a soul there? What can be said as to the poor devils who were driven out of their homes by the bombardment, and were hurled back towards the centre by the shells?

All unoccupied buildings were requisitioned for the people generally, some of them very luxuriously decorated, and inhabited in quiet times by aristocratic families. The refugees were encamped in elegant drawing-rooms. From walls lined with satin or from gilt mouldings were stretched cords, on which the washing or babies' swaddling clothes were hung to dry. Horse flesh was roasted at porphyry fireplaces. And these bewildered refugees, not knowing their way about the unfamiliar streets, remained indoors stupified, without thinking, and without knowing where they were or what was to become of them.

In the early days of December, Paris at night—and night falls quickly in December—was simply melancholy.

The Gas Company so cleverly managed by M. Camus,

had done everything that it could. At the outset it had laid in a considerable stock of combustibles, but what stock would have held out against the 800,000 gas burners which burned in the public thoroughfares of Paris, and against the millions of burners lighted in private localities ? The latter were the first to be deprived of light, and then gradually the lighted lamps in the streets became more and more rare. In some streets oil lamps were placed, in others, candles ; but the majority remained in darkness, leaving the immense blots of shadows which spread over the town to increase around them.

Paris without gas is fearful. When you are walking in the open country, if it is as dark as inside an oven, you have a feeling that everything is at rest and asleep around you. In Paris it is quite another thing. In the darkness and silence you feel that some huge, sinister thing is hissing and coiling itself round you. You become actually terrified. You might imagine yourself in a cavern full of suspicious rustling, of stifled groans, of open traps, until terror paralyses you and you feel your hair standing on end and changing colour.

The Gas Company, in proportion as it limited its lighting operations, converted its unoccupied workmen into a battalion, and then into two battalions organised, and wonderfully organised, by itself.

And it also husbanded its combustible resources to keep up with the requirements of the balloons, and to make head against the inevitable loss through leakage.

Everybody knows the history of the balloons during the siege. Their starting place was on the Place St Pierre, at Montmartre, and the first which ascended, on the 12th of September, was a captive balloon of 1200 cubic metres which was first of all used as a military observatory, and afterwards, on the 24th of September, was despatched with the first batch of letters.

In regard to making good the leakage in the pipes, that was a matter of paramount necessity for this reason. Everybody knows that gas for lighting purposes is combustible, but not explosive; it only becomes explosive when combined with air in a certain proportion.

To avoid this combination the pipes must always be kept full. That condition being observed, there was no need to anticipate, as was feared during the siege, the sight of an entire quarter of the town being sent into the air through the explosion of a gasometer.

First of all, a gasometer does not explode. The gas in it burns like a huge firework, if it is lighted, and that is all. We had an instance of this. A German shell burst in a gasometer. The gas caught fire and escaped in a few moments, like a gigantic and flaming meteor, through the opening made by the shell, and all was over. Another shell burst in another gasometer, and on this occasion the gas did not even catch fire. The Gas Company had in every one of its works sheet-iron plates, ready to be bolted on to the perforated parts. These measures of precaution were carried into effect, and repairs were executed under fire.

It would be unjust not to mention the organisation of our ambulance service, and the generous pecuniary sacrifices which the defence of the capital owes to the powerful Parisian company.

I have just mentioned balloons, and now I think of you poor little messengers—timid creatures—who have borne under your wings so many joys, sorrows, hopes and griefs, you carrier-pigeons, descended from the dove of the Ark, who, like her, left the Ark, of which Trochu was the Noah, and who never returned, alas! like her, with an olive branch in your beak to tell the wayfarers that the deluge was over, and that the waters were returning to their proper limits, that the German was returning to the country he had enlarged at our expense.

If you had lived in days of old, brave little carriers, altars would have been raised to you, or, at all events, as at Venice, a home would have been made for you. You were not only faithful, but you were heroic, for many a time have your little bodies been found frozen and prone at the foot of the trees wherein you had taken refuge in those terrible nights, when the cold sent the mercury down to twenty-five degrees below zero.

But we are as ungrateful as we are vain. France has treated you, O carrier pigeons! as she treats her great men. Not only did she forget you, but after the siege how many of you terminated your epic career in a saucepan, while your sons were dishonoured by the daily marketing of Versailles stupidities!

As far as I am concerned, I confess to being fanatic or foolish enough—whichever you please—not to have eaten a pigeon for the last fourteen years.

When a balloon went up, it carried, suspended to its cordage, baskets containing a number of couples of carrier-pigeons. When the balloon escaped the Germans, and when the pigeons consequently did not furnish a relish to sourkrout or sausages, they were carried to the seat of government, and were there entrusted with despatches in the following manner.

The tail of these birds is composed of nine large feathers, on the centre one was fixed a small quill in which was rolled the despatch, written on a scrap of thin paper, the writing being reduced as much as possible by means of photography.

The power of reduction was such that the four pages of the *Journal Officiel* of Tours or Bordeaux were contained on a piece of paper no larger than a postage stamp. A pigeon in this manner could carry as many as 20,000 private messages, or as many as would make a fair load for a carriage, if written in ordinary hand writing on ordinary paper.

The carrier-pigeon started, mounted upwards, flew near the wind, and made at once for Paris. Unless frozen by the way, or shot by the Prussian rifles, he arrived at Paris and entered his home by lifting up with his beak a little trap, which fell down behind him, and made him prisoner. Nothing now remained to be done but to detach the quill and take it to the Post Office.

The scrap of thin paper, by reason of the small characters on it, resembled a bit of grey paper. It was enclosed in an apparatus furnished with magnifying lenses and traversed by a jet of electric light, and the despatch was reflected on the wall, magnified immensely, and in the midst of a panel of light covering several square yards.

Seated at a table facing the wall twenty clerks then copied the despatches on to as many separate sheets as might be necessary, and the telegrams were sent off to the Government and private individuals on yellow paper, bearing at the top a small rectangular stamp bearing the words *Indication du Service*, and underneath, written by the clerks, the additional word, *Pigeon*.

The majority of the carrier-pigeons were supplied to the Government by M. Cassier, who, on the 27th of October, had himself taken a great number of these little messengers in a balloon, and had set them at liberty with his own hands.

In the month of July, 1871, that is to say, six months after the siege, I had the curiosity to ask him what had become of the pigeons. He replied that he had only four left. The remainder, more than two hundred in number, had succumbed under their fatigues.

From the letter he wrote me I extract the following—

'I append a list of the pigeons which have survived the fatigues of their flights, and have carried communications for the Government since the month of September last, when I offered them to General Trochu for the service of the National Defence.

> 1st. A red cock, taken from Paris by M. de Kératry. Returned in the middle of October (without a numbered despatch).
>
> 2nd. A red hen, left Tours, December 19, 1870, bearing official despatch series No. 36; arrived in Paris, December 20.
>
> 3rd. A blue hen, left Saint-Pierre-des-Cors, January 12 or 13, with despatch series No. 45.
>
> 4th. A mottled hen, left Saint Maur, January 18, in fearful weather, and arrived January 20. This pigeon, No. 4, closed the series of official despatches. It was the last to arrive in Paris during the siege.'

Paris, then, deprived of gas, went to bed early during this never-to-be-forgotten winter, and yet, from time to time it found means of going to the theatre, and the Gas Company still lighted, here and there, a few footlights in front of the actors.

The Comédie Française gave performances from its ordinary *repertoire* at least twice a week throughout the siege. The artists of the opera jointly gave several short performances.   Other theatres, especially the Porte Saint Martin, opened their doors for charitable performances. An ambulance had to be assisted, or a gun cast, or a battalion or a company containing artists had to be furnished with the means of doing a good work, and a comedy or a drama was played with interludes.

The *Châtiments* of Victor Hugo was an almost compulsory interlude.   I confess that I had no taste for these songs of hate bursting forth in the midst of Paris, darkened as she was, and in the grasp of the enemy's hand.   But everybody spouted their poetry, and just as, when I was a little boy, on every fine evening I invariably heard some girl or other warbling, '*Petite fleur des Champs*,' just as, later in life, I had to swallow the '*Feuilles Mortes*' millions of times; so when I went to the theatre or a concert, I was sure to come across some dismal individual who, rolling his ferocious eyes, would say,

'*L'enfant avait reçu deux balles dans la tête.*'

And everybody immediately made a face indicative of irritation and conviction.   While pity was being aroused by the two bullets which had strayed into the head of this hypothetical child, the German shells made mincemeat of real children at a range of some hundreds of yards.

I remember receiving the following expressively laconic circular letter—

'Monsieur and Madame Jules Leqendre regret to have to inform you of the death of their daughters, Alice, aged thirteen years and six months, and Clemence, aged eight years, killed by a Prussian shell.'

I have already said a word or two about the admirable women of the poorer classes who were to be found waiting at the doors of the butchers and the bakers.   And how about the others? you will say. They were all of them sublime or charming.

First of all, there were the ambulance women. I have no intention of giving a list of all the ambulances, public and private, or of taking my readers to the Palais d'Industrie, where the main depôt of linen was established—in itself a very strange and wonderful sight. I wish merely to record that the most distinguished ladies of Paris held it an honour to wear the white apron—actresses as well as women of the middle classes and the aristocracy. I dare not mention names lest I should forget any. I will make one exception, however, in favour of that amiable and very superior woman—Madame Adam. Whether as a private individual or, while her husband was Prefect of Police, as the wife of one of the foremost officials of the capital, she rendered herself universally revered by the ardour she brought to bear on everything, not only in ministering to the wounded, but in the struggle against want and in the charitable bazaars. She was, in a word, a compendium of every patriotic initiative.

And the *vivandieres*! What a treat for the eye when they marched boldly in rear of their battalions in red and black spencers, natty boots or morocco gaiters, kepis well on one side of their head, and the little casks on their hips.

Several actresses solicited this conspicuous mission. Dica Petit and Lina Munte were *cantinières* of the Rue de Bondy battalion; Berthe Legrand, of the Rue Drouot; Massin, of the Rue St Honoré, &c., &c. It was charming, and all the more so because if fighting did take place the gallant battalions would never have allowed the Germans to damage their pretty little *cantinières*, who looked as if they were made of china. Some pleasant moments were spent by us after all.

One other circumstance contributed to render the inconveniences of the situation more bearable; this was the pleasant relations, the exquisite cordiality established between people whose social standing varied considerably, but who stood shoulder to shoulder in the same rank, and were bound together by the holy brotherhood of the same danger incurred, the same death confronted together. I might cite thousands of cases of devotion which happened under my own eyes. Here is one among others.

On the 28th of November there were dining together at Bignon's, the Comte de Coriolis, Orderly Officer to General Mellinet; the Duc de Castries, sub-lieutenant of Cavalry; M. Arthur Meyer, and Captain de Neverlée.

There was to be a sortie and fighting on the following day, and the champagne was flowing.

Suddenly Neverlée, a fine, intelligent fellow whom I knew in China, said, raising his glass as if to drink a toast,

'This is my last glass of champagne. I shall be killed to-morrow.'

The others remonstrated with him.

'I shall be killed to-morrow,' he repeated, obstinately.

At this moment an American, Mr Hutton, who had been arrested as a Prussian spy at the beginning of the siege, but was subsequently released, made his appearance. He had been assigned a post in connection with the ambulances, and passed for a very well-informed man.

He held in his hand one of the first copies of the proclamation of Ducrot, which he had procured from that General's head-quarters.

'Dead or victorious,' he repeated.

On the next day but one, Neverlée was killed a few yards from a loop-holed wall. He and his horse had received thirty-eight bullets.

The Duc de Castries, who loved Neverlée as a brother, persuaded—at what cost I know not—a hackney driver to take him to the field of battle. He turned the dead over one after another, and at length under a heap of corpses he found the body of his friend, and brought it back with him in the carriage.

Was not that noble?

CHAPTER XV

VILLIERS CHAMPIGNY

The Grand Sortie.—Proclamation of Ducrot.—Dead or Victorious.—The Rise of the Marne.—The Engagements at Villiers.—Ladreyt de La Charrière.—Renault the Rear Guard.—A Tragical Meeting.—On the Field of Battle.—My Brother Wounded.—A Day's Respite.—At the Louvre.—The Despatch.—On a Mission.—Champigny.—The Ambulance Women.—A Priest.—The Ravens.—Under Shell Fire.—Trochu Exposes Himself.—Ducrot.—The Retreat.—The Second Affair of Bourget.—General Blaise.—New Year's Gifts.

THE logical and inevitable result of the proceedings of the 31st of October, of the plébiscite which succeeded it, of the rupture of negotiations, and of the good pleasure of the Parisians, was very clearly marked out. It was obligatory on the part of the Government to arrange for military action on a large scale against some point of the investing lines.

The Staff discussed the most advantageous direction from which to make the attempt to break through the iron circle. To go northwards led to nothing. From that quarter had come the torrent of helmeted men who had overrun the remainder of France.

Southwards it would be necessary to carry by assault the almost impregnable positions of Châtillon, lost by us at the very commencement of the siege.

There remained the west and the east.

To the west lay Normandy, a district adapted for an easy and abundant supply of provisions, of which we should do well to deprive the enemy so that we might make use of them ourselves. A sortie westwards was, therefore, taken into serious consideration, and we felt almost certain that on that side the German was weaker than elsewhere.

Meanwhile, the provincial armies were manœuvring round Orleans, resting on their right. To meet them and unite them to an army issuing out of Paris, to sew the Parisian strip, detached and cut off by the German army, on to the rest of the territory somehow or other was unquestionably the most reasonable movement. Provisions on this side were less abundant and less easy to acquire. But victory would have given greater military results, and would have produced an immense moral effect. It was decided to make the sortie by the east.

Pontoon bridges were prepared to span the Marne between Joinville le Pont and Nogent. Boats were requisitioned for the transport of the wounded and a portion of the warlike material. The Generals were told that their troops would be massed on the plain of Vincennes.

The movement commenced on the 28th of November. It was announced to the population by three simultaneous proclamations, the first signed by the members of the Government, the second by the Governor alone, and the third by General Ducrot, who was appointed to command the force to be employed.

The last mentioned proclamation was quite antique in style. It electrified the Parisians. It contained the famous words, 'I shall only return dead or victorious.' .

In connection with this celebrated sentence I am in a position to give what I believe to be a detail hitherto unknown. During the last days of November General Ducrot was in the habit of dining in the Rue de Miromesnil, frequented also by Ferdinand de Lesseps. While there the General received the proofs of his proclamation from the Imprimerie Nationale. He read it. De Lesseps, taking out his pencil, said to the General,

'You ought to add,—"As far as I am concerned, I am resolved that I will only return dead or victorious."'

'The devil,' said Ducrot. 'You strike hard!'

And after hesitating for a few seconds, he said,

'Very well, if you are bent upon it, " dead or victorious " it shall be.'

And so the famous sentence for which Ducrot was so severely reproached belongs to M. de Lesseps.

Two diversions had been ordered so as to mask the movement, distract the attention of the Germans, and draw away their troops from the point actually threatened. One was an attack on the peninsula of Gennevilliers. The other was an attack on Choisy le Roi, during which the marines carried the Gare-aux-Bœufs by assault with admirable bravery.

During the night of the 29th the troops took up their positions on the polygon of Vincennes, conveyed thither by trains following each other at a few hundred yards distance. The artillery rumbled with a sound like distant thunder along the roads hardened by the cold. The Marne was to be crossed at once. The bridges were ready, but the river had risen, and it was necessary to lengthen them. The Governor, who had retired to Vincennes for the night, chafed with impatience. There was nothing to be done but to wait until the Engineers had repaired the fault of the Marne.

On the 30th before daybreak the divisions moved forward against the enemy, who had had twenty-four hours to prepare for their reception.

The Faisanderie redoubt opened fire, and its shells, passing over the heads of our advancing infantry, reached the Prussian lines.

Three divisions took part in this first day's proceedings.

The Blanchard and Renault divisions, pushing straight on, drove the enemy back to the foot of the slopes of Champigny, while the Susbielle division attacked Mesly and Mont-Mesly on the right. It took possession of them, but was compelled to abandon them in consequence of the return of the Wurtembergers reinforced by fresh troops. It fell back on Créteil. The *Mobiles*, who were decimated, gave the signal of wavering, and dragged with them the troops of the line. There General Ladreyt de La Charrière fell ; this brave soldier died like a hero. From the spot where we were posted behind the governor, we saw the heads of the columns hesitate, then waver, and finally recoil before the Germans, who were really magnificent in battle, coming on in dark masses, and, at the moment of taking skirmishing order, raising their rifles above their heads as one man with deafening cheers, the result being that their battalions, like the grotesque figures in a circus, seemed to increase in size. The *Mobiles*, who had never seen anything like it, took fright. Ladreyt de la Charrière galloped towards them, and with the idea of drawing them on, he put his kepi on the top

of his sword and called out ' *En avant !* '   He was certainly
not fifty yards from the Prussians.   Suddenly the kepi and
the sword fell together—a bullet had smashed the General's
wrist.   Three minutes âfterwards he himself fell with a
bullet through his thigh.   He was carried to the rear.

This retreat left the right of the troops operating against
Champigny uncovered.   In the afternoon the *Mobiles* were
re-formed, and the Susbielle division was led on again to
the attack.

Its efforts expired at the foot of the crests of Villiers,
which the Prussians had fortified and garrisoned, and which
gave their name to this first engagement.

The sun was setting.   All was over for that day.

Before returning to Vincennes, the Governor sent me
with a despatch to the left wing, which had held its positions, and where Ducrot was.

In going and coming back, two very dramatic en-
counters befell me.   In going I passed General of Division
Renault, who was being carried to the rear with his leg
broken by the bursting of a shell.

Poor old Renault!   What a soldier!   In Africa he had
been nick-named ' Renault the Rear-Guard.'   He only
understood the bayonet, and if he had dared he would
never have allowed his soldiers to fire a shot.   Before each
action he had his sword sharpened, like a good workman
who is going to make use of a familiar tool.

He was carried home.   He lived for four days longer
without a suspicion that his leg had been amputated, obstinately bent on reading the papers to see the news, and
nearly always a prey to terrible delirium, in which he
never ceased to abuse poor General Trochu, who was his
bête noir, and to heap insults upon him.

On my return the encounter I had was not only dramatic, but it was distressing and in a way providential.

I must explain that towards the end of November, when any battle was vaguely announced and expected, the requests for permits, such as were issued to people desirous of searching among the wounded on the field of battle, multiplied until they assumed considerable proportions.

It had happened more than once that the arrival of these voluntary nurses with spring vans, hackney carriages, wagonettes and private carriages, on the field of battle had interfered with the movement of our troops, when, to use the time-honoured phrase, they were falling back in good order, and scenes of confusion were the result. The Governor, who had been an eyewitness of some of these scenes, gave an order putting a stop to the distribution of the permits, the issue of which was made by us personally during our turns of duty.

On the evening but one before the sortie, I was visited in the green room by two ladies, very well dressed, who came to request a permit to enable them to bring back one of the wounded and to take care of him at their own house.

I refused at first, and then one of them with tears in her eyes said,

'You see, sir, I have a nephew in the army of the Loire. And it seems to me that what I may be able to do for one of our poor soldiers here may prevent him from being abandoned on the field of battle, should he be unfortunate enough to be wounded.'

I replied that my orders were precise, and that I could not accede to the request.

They withdrew. Why I know not, but as soon as their backs were turned a feeling of regret crossed my mind, and seemed to strike my heart. I sent an orderly after them.

He overtook them in the courtyard, and asked them to come back.

'I am going,' I said to them, 'to abuse my position. As the Governor always ratifies the decisions arrived at by his officers, I am going to sign a permit for you and——I leave the rest to Providence.'

They thanked me with effusion, and I thought no more of the matter.

Well, on my way back from the left wing at nightfall, throwing the bridle on the neck of my tired horse, gazing on the rays of the setting sun, now red, now violet, with every outline of the neighbouring heights brought out in dark relief, and feeling sure that my horse, if left to himself, would never, even though his path was plunged in shadow, stumble against one of the wounded whom I heard groaning to the right and left of me in the bitter cold, which made their wounds smart and rendered them livid—I saw, some distance in front of me, an ordinary hackney carriage drawn by two horses at a walk. When I was close behind the carriage I saw a woman in black lean out of the window. She said to the driver,

'More quietly, please.'

I seemed to recognise one of my visitors at the Louvre, the aunt of the soldier of the army of the Loire. She had found her wounded man.

I rode up, the two poor ladies were there, seated on the front seat, and between them were stretched out the booted legs of an officer, lying down, rather than seated, in the bottom of the vehicle.

I leaned forward and saw epaulets on the uniform. The wounded man turned his head. It was my brother, the Secretary to the Embassy, Orderly Officer to General Berthaut. A fragment of a shell had struck him in the shoulder. He was delirious. He did not recognise me. I jumped off my horse, got inside the carriage, and kissed the hands of the astonished ladies.

I asked them for their address, which I had forgotten. I begged them to take care of the poor fellow, and promised, if my duty would permit, to spend the night by his side.

I rejoined the Governor at Vincennes.

The General, I do not know how, noticed my disturbed countenance.

'My poor d'Herisson,' he said, 'you have quite a funereal look about you. Reassure yourself we are not beaten. I am very well pleased with this first engagement. Unfortunately, we cannot recommence the struggle to-morrow. These young troops are so quickly disorganised when they have seen the enemy. One or two hours' fighting at close quarters and they are no better than a flock of sheep, in spite of their courage and their good will. We will arrange all that to-morrow. You will see.'

I told him of my sad adventure.

He sent me at once with despatches to General Schmitz, and told me to remain at the disposal of the Chief of the Staff.

The following day passed without any fighting, and was spent in the re-organisation of the troops, who had not only suffered during the battle, but also from the cold endured during the following night. The dead were buried. Ditches were dug. Champigny was fortified afresh. Soup was made, and everybody warmed himself as best he could. But blankets were wanting.

The Germans attacked on the following day, the 2nd of December, when the terrible battle of Champigny was fought.

I had not been placed under orders to follow the

Governor, and it was the first affair of any importance outside Paris which had taken place without my playing some small part in it. This went against the grain with me.

The Louvre was almost empty. General Trochu and all his Staff were on the field of battle; and, with the exception of the Administrative Officers and the clerks in the offices, throughout this deserted building and the large rooms as a rule so full of animation, but now so cold and void, there remained but General Schmitz and I.

The General sent an orderly for me, made me sit down, took an arm-chair near the fireplace himself, and said,

'I did not want to send you under fire to-day. It would be only fair that I should not do so, for you have done more than your share in that way. I should have liked to have left you out of this business, so that you might look after your brother. Berthaut has spoken of him to me, and I have been to see him. His mental condition is quite as serious as his physical state, and I quite understand that you are anxious in regard to the consequences of the wound he received the day before yesterday.'

Among military men one is least accustomed to such attentions, to such goodness, or to such almost paternal foresight and—why should I not confess it—the tears came into my eyes. The General continued,

'I am, nevertheless, compelled to ask you to rejoin General Trochu at once. Listen to me attentively. It is very important. A carrier-pigeon has arrived with serious despatches. Gambetta informs us that the army of the Loire is moving, and that he hopes on the 6th it will be encamped in the forest of Fontainebleau. Saddle your best horse and be off. It is of the greatest importance that the General should be warned of this as soon as possible, and that he should direct the day's operations with perfect knowledge of the cause—Do you understand?'

'Yes, sir.'

'Very well, repeat to me what I have just told you.— That is quite right. Once on the ground, make enquiries, and go immediately to wherever the General may be.'

I was going to take up a pencil from the table in order to make sure of my instructions by writing a line, lest my memory should fail me, although my commission was as simple as possible—Army of the Loire, December 6, Forest of Fontainebleau.

'Do not write anything,' said General Schmitz, stretching out his arm to stop me. 'If I had wanted you to write anything I should have simply given you a letter to deliver. Your mission is a verbal one entirely. Understand that if you were taken prisoner or killed before you reached General Trochu, the information found on you would be as important for the German Staff as it may be for us.'

'Allow me,' said I in my turn to the General, 'to do as I like. If I am killed or taken they will be clever fellows who can decipher my notes.'

And I wrote the few words I have already noted in pencil on my shirt cuff in Chinese characters.

Five minutes later I was galloping on the slippery pavement and the hard macadam which the frost had rendered sonorous.

At Joinville-le-Pont I came across the first troops. These were the infantry battalions of the *Garde Nationale*. They were in reserve, had piled arms, and with their ration bread stuck on their bayonets, they awaited the order to advance. The Faisanderie redoubt and the batteries placed in position on the banks of the Marne played continuously on the field of battle.

I crossed the bridges and went along the main road, bordered by trees, which leads directly to Champigny. On a lower side of the road was stationed a row of ambulance waggons.

On the right, in the fields, a sort of encampment of ambulance men and stretcher bearers had been formed. It looked like a lot of bee-hives. They were continually leaving empty and returning laden. Some went out to bring back the wounded, others carried them to the river, where they were taken on board little boats flying the white flag with the red cross. For many hundred yards the melancholy convoys followed one after another, and some of them were converted suddenly into funeral processions. The bearers in that case halted, laid the corpse on the ground, left it there, and went further afield to find another wounded man who might in his turn soon become a corpse. Do not imagine that the detachments of the *Garde Nationale* entrusted with this melancholy duty had a sorrowful air. In almost no time they became accustomed to it, and talked, laughed, and joked amid the dead and the wounded. There were also to be seen, making their way among the indescribable and bloody mass, many brave women of Paris belonging to every social class, and some of them to the very highest. All were dressed in black with white aprons and the Geneva armlet. They brought, or caused to be brought, with them portable stoves similar to those made use of by the proprietors of the coffee stalls outside the markets in the early morning. The majority were bareheaded and had their sleeves tucked up, and they came and went, active, gentle, devoted, tender, and lovely as ministering angels, carrying in their two hands cups of warm soup or smoking chocolate. It was a sight to break your heart. Ten degrees of frost!

O women! poor women! dear women! you were more worthy than the men. If they had shown half as much courage as you showed devotion, if they had shed their blood to half the extent that you shed your tears, I believe we should have been successful.

I was galloping all this time. A little further on, the road was encumbered with soldiers, and I was compelled to slacken speed for fear of riding over some of them. I rode down the slope on the right, and at the bottom came across a litter, surrounded by a group of persons, on which was lying an officer of the Geneva Cross. His horse was killed, and he himself had been hit by a fragment of a shell. He was a well-known Parisian, M. Ellissen, whom his ardour had tempted into the hottest of the firing.

I took care to enquire where I had the best chance of finding the Governor. A captain of *Mobiles*, slightly wounded in the left shoulder, told me that the General was in Champigny. I rode on and reached the first houses of the village, which had been attacked that morning by the Germans, taken by them, retaken by us, and subsequently put by us in a state of defence.

At this spot there was such an encumbrance of troops, massed one on top of the other that it would have been impossible for me to have got through if the non-commissioned officers, recognising my duties by my epaulets, had not ordered their soldiers to fall back to let me pass. I was obliged to walk my horse, and it was a good quarter-of-an-hour before I reached the last houses of Champigny.

I emerged at last right on to the field of battle.

Never in my life, not in any of the battles at which I have been present, have I heard such a fearful uproar. Shot succeeded shot without the interval of a second. Guns by hundreds, rifles by thousands, mitrailleuse by twenties hurled and vomited lead and steel. It was impossible to hear oneself speak.

I asked a colonel where the Governor was. Our two horses were touching and our legs also ; I put my mouth close to his ear to speak to him, and he put his mouth close to my ear to answer, and yet we were compelled, in order to make ourselves heard, to shout as if we were each of us on the top of a hill with a valley stretching out between us.

He had certainly seen General Trochu, but he had lost sight of him. He ought to be on the left of Champigny. While we were thus shouting with all our might in a most confidential attitude, two German shells fell behind us in the midst of the crowded troops. Neither of them burst ; the soft contact of the human body prevented them from striking the ground violently and from bursting by percussion. When they fell on the men they made the exact noise of a stone falling in the mud—flac ! One did not injure anybody, by what miracle I know not ; the other literally pounded two soldiers. Their comrades instinctively started aside and left, in an open space, the two poor devils beaten to a jelly, without human form, flattened and as it were spread out on the cold ground.

I left Champigny and bore to the left. A lieute ant, whose company was sheltered behind the wall of the last garden, ran quickly towards us, drew me to him, and said,

' Don't go that way, Captain. You cannot go ten yards beyond that house without you and your horse being blown to pieces.'

That was pleasant hearing, and I was nothing loth to make a slight detour. I was not anxious to be killed, and, at all events, I wanted to see the General before that accident happened. Nevertheless, in order to join him, it was necessary to cross the whole of the unoccupied portion of the field of battle, and the deserted, shell-ravaged fields where, only a short time ago, those troops had been drawn up who were now taking refuge in Champigny.

At last I discovered a somewhat less dangerous exit. Just as I set off at a gallop again a shell burst in one of the houses, and produced such a displacement of air that a number of soldiers were wounded—not by the fragments of the shell, but by the materials of the house, which were scattered in all directions.

I saw, flying over my head, a window with its shutters, which fell in a neighbouring garden, and played havoc with a clump of currant bushes. Chimneys toppled over ; there was a shower of tiles, beams, planks, rubble, and rubbish of all kinds, and clouds of dust rendering everybody and everything unrecognisable for several minutes.

I preferred not resting there, so I set spurs once more to my poor horse, who trembled under me, and was covered with sweat, notwithstanding the intense cold which froze my feet and put me up to my knees to the torture of the brodequin.

To the left of Champigny, looking at it with my back turned to Paris, I had caught a glimpse of a somewhat elevated roadway which led to the open country. I thought that this conformation of the ground would serve as a rampart, and I think I owe my life to it.

Consequently, instead of keeping to the roadway, over which passed and repassed a mass of metal objects calculated to impede and inconvenience circulation, I rode down into the fields. The roadway, which ran along the top of the embankment, was well over my head, and served as a shelter. I galloped thus for ten minutes, having nothing to fear except the French bullets which whistled not so very high above me. As for the German bullets, I was quite safe from them, and their shells had a trajectory which carried them far beyond me.

On this battlefield, which a short time before had been covered with living men, and where now the dead and dying seemed so numerous that they might have been taken for whole regiments lying down at the halt—alas! for the majority it was their great, their last halt—there was only one able-bodied man—a priest of the Foreign Mission.

Alone and isolated, without appearing to have an idea of the danger he was running, he was doing his duty and attending to his ministry ; he walked about beneath the shells and the bullets with a slow, gentle movement, as if he were crossing a dimly-lit church in the evening on his way to hear the confessions of the women on their knees under the sanctuary lamp.

When I saw him he was on his knees, in his large black robe, bending over a *Mobile*, whose pale, beardless face, wrinkled by suffering, gave him the appearance of a lad twelve years old. The priest placed his right arm under his head, and, with his ear to the soldier's mouth, he heard his confession. I approached him, he raised his eyes, gently laid the soldier's head on the ground, and came up to me.'

' Have you seen the Governor ? '

' Yes,' he replied, ' he is down there, five or six hundred yards from here—quite perpendicular to this road.'

' Thank you.'

And I set off again. When I had gone a few yards I turned in my saddle. He had raised the lad's head again, and was giving him the crucifix to kiss.

How foolish it is to wish to suppress this, to drive the chaplains away, and to have nothing better to offer to the wounded, instead of the prayers of yore, than a drink-stained *Marseillaise*.

Who can explain the mystery of the association of ideas? I suddenly thought, as I saw him thus half recumbent, with his arms away from his body, that he looked exactly like a raven, and the stupid *couâ* of the Paris street boy crossed my brain.

'Why not, after all?' I said to myself. 'It is not wide of the mark. These men are ravens, but divine ravens, who light on the battle fields, in the midst of the human carrion, to rifle souls.'

A few moments later I found the Governor; placing my horse close to his I repeated in his ear, word for word, the message of General Schmitz. It seemed to me that a flash of joy, springing from his eyes, illuminated his grave, severe countenance for a moment. It lasted only for a second, and then he turned his head slightly as a man does when he is not quite sure of anything.

'You are certain about the names?' he said.

I was all the more certain because I was reading them off my cuff.

'Very well,' he replied. 'You have had a long ride. Stay near me; I am going to send these gentlemen away.'

Calling to several Orderly Officers in succession, he sent them off one after the other with orders to different parts of the field.

General Trochu looked pleased, and his face, as a rule so wrinkled, was positively smoother than usual.

We went from one point to another, wherever fighting was going on and he deemed that his presence might give courage or dash to the troops.

At one moment two or three hundred *Mobiles* fell back in disorder upon us, all of them running with their backs turned to the enemy. The Staff deployed before them like a squadron of *gendarmerie*, and they halted, pitiful

R

enough, at the sight of the Governor, who at once addressed them.

This devil of a man, even under fire, knew how to string together charming, persuasive, noble, and correct sentences. He got them together and said a few kindly, affectionate words to them.

' Follow me,' were his final words.

Then, marching straight against the German sharp-shooters, he never stopped until the enemy's bullets whistled round us with that little strident noise one so quickly learns to know, and which indicates that the projectile is at its full speed. It is the proper range. The brave little *Mobiles*, thus encouraged, took up their position again, and fired away like men.

An Orderly Officer from Ducrot had just delivered a message to the General.

' Very well,' he said; ' wait for a moment with these gentlemen.'

We then turned to the left and rode up a little hill, from the top of which one of our batteries, placed in an amphi-theatre, was doing wonders. It was doing so well that the enemy seemed to have only one idea—to dismount it. Not a moment passed without a shell falling, now on the right, now on the left. Fortunately, only a few of them burst.

The General seemed to have chosen the exact spot where all these fearful projectiles had appointed to meet. We were all motionless under this iron hail; and the Governor quietly looked through his glasses at the enemy's positions, which were perfectly distinguishable by the naked eye. If we could see the Prussians moving, we were equally visible to them, and all the more so because we formed a compact and somewhat brilliant mass. Very soon we became the target of the German marksmen, and the number of shells redoubled around us.

The persistence shown by the General in remaining at this particular spot, without any special or particular reason for staying there, began to seem odd to us junior officers; and I heard the following whispered conversation going on about me.

'Do you not think that the General seems bent on being killed?'

'Precisely what I am saying to myself.'

'However, that is his look-out. But I do not see why he should necessarily have us killed too.'

'Bah! What does it matter?'

'That is just it,' said Ducrot's officer who was side by side with us. 'You should see Ducrot! He is absolutely mad. All to-day he has been riding a horse as white as snow, and he is continually galloping in front of the Prussians. I should like to have as many francs—not income but capital —as he has had shots, from rifles and ordnance, fired directly at him to-day. Would you believe that he charged the Saxons single handed? He cut one down with his small sword as if he had a regulation weapon in his hand. He is perfectly mad.'

And a young captain who was resting his elbows on his holsters, droned out the famous words, 'Dead or victorious.'

What was the object General Trochu had in view? Was he so accustomed to danger and did he despise it to such an extent that he paid no attention to it, and did not give it a thought; and had he taken up his position in this particular place just as he would have done anywhere else? Possibly. But I confess that for several moments I firmly believed that he was seeking death.

However, a projectile having fallen under his horse's

nose, there could be no doubt that to remain there any longer would have been suicidal. The Governor quieted his horse and slowly returned in the direction of Champigny. We then found ourselves between our reserves, who were advancing, and Ducrot's right which was thrown forward. The Orderly Officer of this latter General left us after having heard the Governor's orders.

We were making a general movement in advance.

The part of the battlefield which we were crossing was literally paved with the killed and wounded, and over it were scattered a dozen Christian priests, who were simply and heroically doing their duty. The General saluted them as he passed, and each large black hat was raised for an instant.

An infantry soldier, lying on the ground, whose left shoulder and arm had been smashed by a shell, raised himself on his right arm, and shouted,

'Are you General Trochu ? Well, *Vive la France !*'

The Governor, without stopping, returned the salute and replied,

'And we will save her, God helping us.'

A little farther on, two poor lank artillery horses, harnessed to the same ammunition waggon, had been wounded. Their traces had been cut, and they had been left there. One of them was standing motionless on three legs, the fourth being only a red stump. The other, with a hole in its flank large enough for a child to put its head in, was lying down, quietly nibbling the short but frozen, crackling, frost-covered grass, which nourished and refreshed him, and quenched his thirst. The poor beast was as quiet as if he were in the stable. He was at all events making a good meal before dying.

We had got out of the dangerous zone, and involuntarily we began to breathe more freely.

About five hundred yards in front of us, and consequently in a spot as sheltered and safe, one might suppose, as a lady's boudoir, the brilliant and unfortunate Commandant Franchetti, leader of a squadron of light cavalry raised by himself and admirably mounted, had just been wounded by a stray shell. Whence it came nobody knew. Ducrot had sent him to the rear to order the reserve artillery ammunition waggons to advance. The wound was mortal. Poor, poor fellow!

It was one of those chances which are called providential when they turn out well, and fatal when they end badly.

On the whole the affair had gone off well. We had fought the first day. We had spent the second day in our positions in recruiting ourselves and reforming our divisions. We had held our own on the third day under honourable conditions. Not only had we not fallen back, but our troops were encamped in positions once occupied by the enemy.

And then? Then—well nothing. Get out? Not one of the Generals had an idea of doing so, and the best proof of this is that the soldiers had not been ordered to bring their blankets with them for night work. As for the convoys of provisions necessary for an army on the march, they would have been useless because we were bound to re-enter Paris, bound to return whatever happened, even if the portion of the Prussian army in front of us had been annihilated or dispersed.

The *Garde Nationale* alone imagined that we were going to make our way out. Poor *Garde Nationale!* Their intelligence was subjected to rough proofs during the siege, and they did not understand much of what was going on. Not for one single day had they any conception of the possibilities and the necessities of the situation, and nobody had the courage to explain to them, nobody dared say to them, ' My good friends, your duty is to hold out as long as you can, and, by continual battles, to do as much harm as you can to the enemy, whom you force to remain around you, and from whom you thus set free the rest of France. But do not imagine for a moment that you can after any useful fashion pierce those investing lines—in other words, do not imagine that you can get out and join hands with the Provincial armies for a career of victory. Such a thing has never yet been seen, and never will be seen. The most complete victory at any one point could not restore you to liberty.'

But what was equally unintelligible to the *Garde Nationale* was the fact that the Prussians in front of them, who were 500 leagues from home, were well clothed, sufficiently fed, and always fresh, while our soldiers, who were at home, only an hour from the Capital, were perishing with cold. I confess that, in this instance, I was with the *Garde Nationale.*

At half-past four in December it is night. It was, therefore, in the twilight, illumined only by some isolated rifle firing on the lower ground, that we rode behind Trochu along the ranks of the troops who had just been fighting. Ducrot was not there. He had a slight wound in the neck caused by a fragment of a shell, and was taking a short repose.

When we returned to Vincennes, we saw behind us the plain before you reach Champigny, and the banks of the Marne which describe a curve in front of that plain, well-known to the Prussians, illumined by the flames of the huge fires lighted by the soldiers.

I have never been able to understand, by the way, why Trochu thought himself bound to give a theatrical account of his return to his quarters from the fort of Vincennes; why he considered himself obliged to announce to history that he was very tired; why in his proclamation he declared that the second battle was even more decisive than the first —neither the one nor the other was, or could have been, decisive—or why, lastly, the excellent members of the Government felt it incumbent on them to address a collective and public letter to him in order to congratulate him and inform him that they would have been glad to share his fatigues and his glory. They might have done so easily. There was plenty of work at Champigny for every-body, and if these lawyers objected to mingling with their fellow creatures in battle, on the score of being too old or too peaceable, they might have helped the women to tend the wounded. I am perfectly aware that any such pro-ceeding would have been useless and rather ridiculous, but in that case, why did they say that they desired what was useless and ridiculous ?

The Lord deliver us from literature in matters of Government! Amen!

It was necessary to take steps to prevent our young troops, disorganised by the enemy's fire and demoralised by the cold, from being left any longer face to face with the enemy, who were bringing up reinforcements every hour. The unfortunate soldiers were shivering in their coats, and two-thirds of them could scarcely stir.

During the night and on the following morning we carried orders to fall back everywhere, and the whole force returned to quarters.

We had three weeks' rest.

As for the rendezvous given by Gambetta for the 6th of December in the forest of Fontainebleau, we were not the only defaulters, for the army of the Loire lost Orleans and had to retreat, and on that very 6th of December I took to Sèvres a reply from the Governor to General de Moltke, who had the forethought to inform us of the success of his armies, and offered to allow the fact to be verified by a French officer sent from Paris for that purpose.

During these few days of idleness, Paris turned its attention to the question of food, and suddenly a rumour became current that provisions were running short. Panic reigned for a few days and the Government had to resist it. It did so by this declaration—'The consumption of bread will not be rationed.' And a few days afterwards the rationing began. In like manner, a month later, the capitulation came to pass very quickly after this other declaration, 'The Governor of Paris will not capitulate.' Be it remarked that all these enormous lies were told by the very men who justly reproached the Empire with continually lying. They borrowed that habit from it as well as the plébiscite.

For example, there was no lack of wine, brandy, or absinthe. There was too much of them, and their consumption was really extraordinary. Oncques never saw so many drunkards as during the siege. History wished to forget itself, they said, and to replace solids by liquids.

They substituted one for the other so willingly that old Clement Thomas, alarmed at the progress in the consumption of alcohol, thought he would make an example by calling public attention to a battalion which reached the advance posts at Créteil in zig-zag fashion. The commandant himself was reeling. The General declared that under such circumstances the *Garde Nationale*, of which he was the chief, constituted an additional danger. He was never pardoned for that piece of frankness. By it he signed his own death warrant, which was religiously carried into effect, as is well known, in a garden at Montmartre, on the 18th March, 1871.

The most peculiar feature in the case was that these drunkards, who were absolutely incapable of performing any duty whatever, were the most energetic in demanding sorties. They were as difficult to restrain in Paris as they were to maintain in front of the enemy. What a mob!

On the 21st of December fighting went on along the entire northern half of the perimeter of Paris, from Mont-Valérien to Nogent. The Prussians, who had learned to recognise the signs preliminary to the sorties, especially the closing of the gates which preceded them, were everywhere on their guard.

It was premature. To mass inexperienced and young troops, such as the French were, a very long time was necessary. The extemporised officers did not know much. The extemporised soldiers knew nothing. They were never ready. An immense amount of time was lost in getting them into line, man by man. And when the whole lot had fallen in in something like order, the columns got mixed up, the battalions overlapped, the convoys and batteries obstructed the route, and a fresh mess had to be disentangled.

In front of us three words sufficed for the Prussian leaders to manœuvre their battalions and companies without disorder, without any sudden halts, and without any confusion, just as children by a simple movement of their little hands can concentrate or disperse in skirmishing order the wooden figures fixed on a movable trellis-work.

The sailors fought like devils at Bourget, in that fatal town which had already cost us so dear, and which now found itself included in the general plan of defence. Six weeks previously, it did not form part of the plan. Why ? I do not know in the least.

The night was terrible ; I do not even remember having been so cold as I was during the rides I was obliged to take that night. The men were literally frozen in the ditches and hastily dug trenches, in the huts and houses open to every wind. The cold sent them to sleep, and very many of them never awoke again. For the first time I heard men say openly that night, ' We have had enough of this.'

I had a friend in the staff of General Blaise, and as I was passing close by Ville-Evrard, I shaped my course so as to shake him by the hand, for I knew that there I should find the General.

He was there, sure enough, with his officers round a large fire of beams and planks supplied from the *débris* of the houses blown up by our and the German shells. Seated astride a straw chair, with his steaming boots on the hearth, the General and his officers, cigar or pipe in mouth, were talking over the events of the day, and broke off every now and then to take a mouthful of old rum out of the common flask. I got off my horse and tied him to a tree. The greatest suffering a rider has to undergo is cold feet, and I was not sorry to warm mine at the bivouac fire. A place was made for me in the circle, and the conversation, stirred up afresh by a new arrival, became quite gay. There we were, roasted in front and frozen behind, turning ourselves round at irregular intervals as if we were on a gridiron, and surrounded by sentries, when a strange noise made us leap to our feet.

'It is a Prussian trumpet,' said the General. 'Where the devil can it come from?'

He had not finished his sentence when flames were seen coming up through the air-holes of the cellars of the surrounding houses, and I saw him fall with his face to the ground by the side of the fire.

I thought for a moment that we were all blown up, and that the fire from the hearth had reached the chamber of a mine. It was not likely.

The authors of the catastrophe were some Saxon soldiers who had taken refuge in the cellars of the houses. No search had been made in these cellars, thanks to the general carelessness in the midst of troops whom nobody knew, and to whom the ordinary regulations of discipline could not be applied. These Saxons hoped, no doubt, to escape by favour of the confusion which their discharge would cause in our ranks. They were surrounded and massacred.

We retired once more after this battle, and were compelled, a few days afterwards, to abandon the Plateau d'Avron, which the fire of some new batteries installed by the Prussians, and suddenly unmasked, rendered untenable.

This was the last military Parisian episode of the year 1870.

Her younger sister, 1871, rose mournfully enough. We left cards, however, and exchanged visits. A few exquisites procured, I know not whence, roses and violets for their beloved ones. The confectioners contrived to open a few bags of bonbons. But the favourite, the most refined and most intelligent New-Year's gifts, were eatables. Shouts of joy welcomed the man who arrived with a bouquet composed of a cabbage, surrounded with cut paper, or a bunch of carrots similarly adorned. A few nabobs went as far as a fowl. Ordinary folk exchanged pots of jam. There were midnight suppers; puddings were eaten, and pancakes were made as well as jokes.

I know Parisians—and they are the best sort—who, if they had lived at Pompeii, would have snapped their fingers at the lava, and would certainly have been discovered by the 17th century in an attitude ridiculous rather than Roman or classical.

It is not always necessary to be solemn, stiff, or whining, in order to do your duty, and more than your duty; and nobody, in France at all events, has laid it down as an axiom that heroism cannot march in front with gaiety.

At the time I write gaiety, I know, has taken to flight, or to borrow a familiar expression from the siege, has ' retreated in good order'; but I fear, alas! that heroism has gone before it in this ruin of old French sentiments.

CHAPTER XVI

BUZENVAL

Always the Commune.—A Fan.—A Magnificent Pedestal.—On the Roofs of Mont Valérien.—Across Country.—Forgotten!—By the Breach!—German Prisoners.—To the Bitter End.—A Council of War.—General Vinoy.—The Rising at the Hôtel de Ville.—Shooting.—A Fire in the Wine Market.

THE defeat of Bourget had irritated the *Garde Nationale*, and from that fact sprang the proceedings of the 31st of October.

The failure of the military operations of December roused the irritation afresh, and gave the rioters new hope. In order to calm the irritation and destroy the hope the Government thought another battle was necessary. It was more bloody and quite as useless as its predecessors, and brought about the proceedings of the 22nd of January.

The shocks of Paris never varied. As to defeat succeeded riot, so to riot succeeded defeat. Alternately daughter and mother, one to the other, riot and defeat shared the capital between them.

After Champigny, after the second engagement of

Bourget, after the evacuation of the Plateau d'Avron, the clubs resumed their thunder, and the sinister rascals who were going to organise the Commune began to agitate.

Their theme was always the same—the Government was incapabable.   Paris must take the defence of her destinies into her own hands.

And the *Garde Nationale* leagued together and commenced a series of manifestations.   And gradually there entered into the minds of the leaders that cruel, impious and yet logical idea, that the mob would not keep quiet until a certain amount of slaughter was allowed, and that, in order to cure Paris of her fever and reduce her excitement, some pints of blood must be taken from her.

'These rascals will not be content until we have proved to them *ad hominem* that they are incapable of extricating themselves out of the mess, and that the time has arrived to lay down our arms,' were the murmured remarks among the Staff.

Fearful, I admit.   But what was to be done ? How was anybody to prove to these men, incapable of understanding military matters, that the only thing left to them was to keep quiet, with piled arms,- patient beneath the shells which began to fall on Paris, (for the bombardment was the present, the New Year's Gift, of Prussia to the capital), until there remained just enough bread in the trough to allow of time to seek for more ?

Soldiers in these cases have a simple and practical method at hand—'You want to fight ?   Go.'

And they went to Buzenval.

This time it was not cold, but it had rained.   The ground was soaked, and the roads along which our poor cannons never ceased to roll, were completely broken up.

On the 18th of January, Paris was full of the sound of

arms. During the night of the 18th and 19th, the troops massed under Mont-Valérien.

The objective was Versailles, the commander-in-chief was Trochu in person, and the army was divided into three columns : the left wing, under Vinoy, attacked Montretout; the centre, under General de Bellemare, Buzenval; and the right wing, under Ducrot, extended as far as Celle Saint-Cloud.

This army, consequently, changed front to the left, the right on the move, and deployed like an immense fan, having Mont-Valérien and the Seine as a pivot.

The right wing had more ground to traverse in order to get into line. It was behind time, encumbered in its evolution by the convoys of artillery and the crowding of other columns on the roads.

The left and centre began the action, and at ten o'clock the Montretout redoubt as well as the Buzenval wall were carried by assault. So far so good.

On the terrace-like roofs of the highest portion of Mont-Valérien the Governor took up his position. It was a unique position, which permitted him to follow with eye and glass the movements of his army—a superb pedestal such as probably no commander-in-chief, no conqueror had ever had.

Surrounded by his entire Staff, he had only to give an order and the officer concerned saluted, went down the steps, found his horse at the postern gate, mounted, and, followed by the eye of the Governor as far as the spot indicated, directed the movement of the troops in sight of him who had just ordered the evolution. It was a marvellously grand sight.

We went on duty by turns. Each was entrusted with his mission, important or insignificant, according to his number on the roster. My turn came towards eleven o'clock. I had to go to Montretout, to the left, where the fighting was most severe, and convey an order for the troops to advance in the direction· of the Maison Zimmerman, where the *Mobiles* of the Loire-Inférieure, under the orders of their brave Commandant, the Baron de Lareinty, eventually entrenched themselves that same night, and bore themselves heroically.

Near the gate where our horses awaited us, a squadron of cavalry was posted to furnish orderlies to the officers, according to a roster similar to that which ruled the proceedings on the roof of Mont-Valérien. The very first feeling of every man who is about to risk his life is to have a good look at the comrade whom chance has bestowed upon him, and who may either save him or leave him to die. The cavalry man who followed me had a fair, honest, and sturdy soldier-like face, and he managed his horse in a most reassuring manner.

I had to remain until the movement ordered had produced its effect, and then to return at once to the fort to report to the Governor.

We trotted at first, but soon broke into a gallop. Behind us the batteries of Mont Valérien blazed away without interruption, and the direction of their fire indicated the route I had to follow. I made a slight bend in order to reach the open ground under the protection of the shells, and then I made across country. The farther I proceeded down the slope, the less distinctly I saw my goal, and paying no more attention to the fire of the heavy guns, I bent my course towards the crackling of the rifles.

Our horses sank up to their hocks in the muddy ground. A captain on the Staff, galloping as hard as we were, met me. But as he was ascending the slope I was descending, his horse, half buried, seemed to make no progress. When we were a few paces from each other there was a mutual recognition. It was Comte Delamare, one of my colleagues in the Jockey Club.

'Are you going there?' he shouted without stopping.

'As you see,' I replied.

'Good luck to you.'

We were already apart, both in a hurry, he to return and I to go on; and we were all the less disposed to chat on the way, seeing that he was at the end and I was at the beginning of the dangerous zone.

At this spot were the vehicles of the Foreign Ambulance. In the crowd of volunteer nurses the majority were absolutely devoted and sincere, but who could say that there were no traitors among them? After having had a close view of things in general, after having inspected documents, depositions, and papers of all kinds connected with the subsequent enquiries, many of us were convinced that in this particular department there were persons who were perfectly well disposed to give the enemy the benefit of any knowledge which they themselves possessed.

Having transmitted my orders and seen the movement executed, I turned my horse's head back towards Mont-Valérien, and hardly had I done so than a shell fell so close to me and the orderly who was following me, and whose scared horse closed instinctively on mine, that I was covered with earth and mud. At the same time I heard a concert of sharp whistling and deep humming, a mixture of sonorous and sweet notes, all the noises, in short, which are produced by fragments of shells, according to their forms and dimensions, as they are hurled through the air.

Just as I was struggling with my horse, which was peppered to such an extent that he wanted to bolt, my orderly galloped past me. He was still in his saddle. But one of the fragments of the shell had torn away the whole of the lower part of his stomach, and had carried away his intestines. The upper part of his body was only attached to the lower part by the spinal column, and there was an enormous red, gaping space from his sides to his thighs. He threw up his arms and fell, while his horse, hit in the withers, galloped off into space to the accompaniment of the clink of the empty stirrups. A cold shiver ran through me.

Three kilometres farther on, I was about to emerge from the dangerous zone, when I suddenly found myself in the midst of a battalion of *Mobiles*, deep in the mud and hidden from the enemy by a bit of rising ground.

'What are you doing there, Commandant?' I said to the chief of the battalion.

'We are waiting for orders.'

'But the whole army is in front. You are not numerous enough to constitute a reserve.'

'I believe we have been forgotten, for we have been here for the last seven hours.'

'Go forward then—Vinoy has just asked for reinforcements.'

'Possibly; but we are waiting for orders.'

'Very well, I give you the order to advance.'

'I can take no orders from you, Captain.'

'You are quite right, for you ought to have advanced of your own accord and have joined the main body as soon as you discovered that you were forgotten. I am Orderly Officer to the General-Commanding-in-Chief, and if you do not make your men fall in at once and execute the movement I have instructed you to make, somebody, other than myself, will come and convey the Governor's orders to you, most probably in terms very different from those which I have the honour to employ.'

He did not answer, but rallied his men and marched off after favouring me with a look which I did not forget for a long time.

As soon as I returned to the fort I had to set out again, this time to the right. At the extremity of the Park of Buzenval there was a wall which appeared to stop all movement on that side. I was sent to ask why guns were not brought to bear on it.

I reached the spot and this is what I discovered.

A regiment of the *Garde Nationale* had been there since morning, drawn up behind the wall and a little lower down.

In this wall there was a breach, and the Prussians from the other side covered this breach with bullets to prevent any one emerging from behind.

The drummer beat the charge; the Colonel gave the word of command, ' *En avant !* ' the regiment shouted, ' *Vive la République,*' and—nobody stirred. That went on for three hours—Ducrot appeared on the scene in person and shouted ' *En avant.*' He was answered by shouts, but nobody moved.

There were no guns at hand to batter down the wall. At this juncture a company of the Line appeared, commanded by a thin, grim looking Lieutenant. He was, I believe, Lieutenant Napoleon Ney.

He placed his men in front of the *Garde Nationale,* and commanded a sergeant to cross the breach at the head of his section. The sergeant started, heard the whistle of the bullets, and made a sign that it was impossible. The Lieutenant made a gesture as if to tear off his stripes. The sergeant repulsed him and marched straight to the breach. He fell, riddled with bullets. But behind him came the whole company ; they hesitated for a moment, and I saw the Lieutenant seize the soldiers by the body and literally push them into the breach. They got through it, deployed in skirmishing order, and dislodged the Prussians. The wall was passed.

I returned a second time to the fort. It fell once more to my turn to set out, for all my colleagues had been despatched with orders during my absence. On this occasion my mission was not dangerous. It was simply to convey to Paris about sixty German prisoners. They formed fours, and flanked right and left by *Mobiles*, marched off.

Under the conviction that none of us understood German, they interchanged on the march some quaint, amusing, and characteristic reflections.

'They say they kill their prisoners,' said one.

'That is not true,' replied another. 'But there cannot be anything to eat.'

'That is of no consequence,' said a third. 'I am only too glad that I have got off without a scratch, and, at all events, I shall see Paris.'

And their eyes sparkled at the word Paris—a veritable land of Canaan, which they despaired of entering, in spite of the promises of their leaders.

Thanks to this pacific decision, I avoided sharing with the Governor the greatest danger he had run during the siege.

Night was falling. In order to make one supreme effort before daylight disappeared, and knowing that this fight would be the last, General Trochu left the fort and went into the midst of the troops to encourage them by his presence. He passed between the various corps. Here were the infantry, rather worn out and disgusted; there the *Garde Nationale*, some battalions of which had done their duty heroically, but the majority had crowned their long and furious demands for a wholesale sortie by an equally wholesale desertion of their ranks. The Line twitted the *Garde Nationale*.

'Now,' shouted the former, 'you gentlemen of "war to the bitter end," now is the time to show yourselves. On you go.'

But the gentlemen of 'war to the bitter end,' did not show themselves.

On leaving the field of battle at night, after having recognised that he must once more abandon the positions he had taken and the heights he had crowned, seeing that they were menaced by fresh German reserves, the General, surrounded by his officers and followed by an escort, was crossing a field where a disorderly lot of men belonging to the *Garde Nationale* were marching on their return to Paris.

Suddenly a voice cried out, 'The Uhlans! The Uhlans! several shots were fired on the spot.

'It is I, Trochu,' shouted the General, riding forward. It was all of no avail. The firing went on in greater strength than before, and the Staff had to receive, almost point blank, the fire of a hundred men before the latter saw their mistake and recovered from their panic.

The darkness, fortunately, rendered their aim uncertain.

'We have got off very cheaply,' said the Governor, thinking that all his people were intact. As he spoke one of his Orderly Officers, Lieutenant de Langle, fell dead on his horse's neck. A chassepot bullet had hit him full in the chest and had gone right through him. His brother, a meritorious officer, was killed at the commencement of the war.

What a return to Paris must that have been for Trochu, after this final effort, this last battle, which rendered any fresh military action impossible, put a stop to the operations, and compelled the generals to hand matters over to the diplomatists.

If the generals had proved themselves more clever than lucky, the diplomatists were not to be any more clever than lucky.

And so it happened that the last words which the Governor heard from the lips of his army were contained in that sinister shout, 'The Uhlans!'

Despatch succeeded despatch, confident and reassuring, throughout the day, and Paris slept once more in hope.

On the following day appeared a final despatch from the Governor, announcing the retreat and expressing the cheering opinion that there would never be sufficient stretchers to bring away the wounded.

The Members of the Government were absolutely terrified when he came back to the Louvre. As for public opinion, it had energetically pronounced against him—not only the opinion of the violent section, for that had been known for a long time, but the opinion of moderate men, the middle classes, everybody.

A sort of Council of War was held immediately, at which were present the Government, all the Generals, and all the Mayors of Paris.

'There is nothing to be done,' said the Generals.

'Your position is no longer tenable,' said the Mayors to the Governor. 'Retire.'

'I will not tender my resignation. Revoke my appointment,' replied the General, and he made a long speech on the state of the army and the inconvenience of young troops, in which his desire to get rid of his military position was, nevertheless, evident.

'Revoke my appointment' is easily said, but who could do it in the case of General Trochu? His colleagues? He had as much authority as they had. The people? How and by what method of procedure?

At length, whether dismissed or having resigned, the Governor of Paris withdrew, retaining the Presidency of the Government. He could not act otherwise in face of the attitude, unanimous this time, of the population. It is needless, I imagine, to say that those very men who had shown themselves the quickest to fly at Buzenval, were not the slowest to rush against him. They could not forgive him for their own disgraceful conduct.

On the following day a Council of War was held, to which Generals, Colonels, and even Commandants were summoned. All bent before the inexorable necessity of laying down their arms.

Towards midnight of the same day the friends of Flourens invaded Mazas and brought forth their idol. On the following day, the 22nd of January, there was an attempt at a second edition of the 31st of October, but this time the Hôtel de Ville was not broken into. The Breton *Mobiles* garrisoned the Municipal Palace. The *Garde Nationale*, massed in the square, fired on them; they replied. There were both killed and wounded, and the red cross ambulances, after having collected the victims to duty who had fallen in the field of battle, now collected the victims of a riot who had fallen in the streets. Chandey, deputy of the Mayor of Paris, was at the Hôtel de Ville, and was accused of having ordered the firing. He was destined eventually to share the fate of Clément Thomas.

With the cessation of the command of General Trochu the duties of General Schmitz came to an end. The Chief of the Staff followed his leader in his retreat, and General Vinoy, who replaced General Troehn, chose as his assistant General de Valdan. Our mission was at an end.

General Trochu, the day after his fall, made use of an expression to us which has remained in my memory because it is instinct not only with mysticism, but also with simple, colossal, and almost blasphemous pride.

'I am,' he said to us, 'the Jesus Christ of the situation!'

Was the comparison in exquisite taste? I know not. But in any case it was somewhat groundless, for Jesus Christ died and Trochu lived; Jesus Christ saved humanity and Trochu saved nothing at all.

Shall I confess that I left the Louvre without regret? The part of a squirrel, always running inside its little wheel, and never advancing a step, began to tire me, and I longed for repose.

The last episode in my career by the side of the General was rather peculiar. A German shell, falling on one of the casemates of the wine market, had pierced the roof, and burst in the midst of a heap of barrels containing brandy, which caught fire. It was a gigantic bowl of punch, and its bluish flames, penetrating through the black branches of the trees on the quays, puzzled the Governor. I was sent to gain information. There was such a smell of alcohol in the neighbourhood, and its emanations were so suffocating, that I promptly succumbed to a mild intoxication, and having arrived on a horse I returned on a chair.

At the very moment when I was revelling in the prospect of lying in bed of a morning, a very excusable weakness on the part of a man who for a long time had not had a comfortable sleep, events laid hold of me again and forced me to be present at a spectacle which, if not as grand as that of a battle, was no less captivating, intoxicating, and harassing.

I allude to the negotiations relative to an armistice, the only things left to me to narrate.

CHAPTER XVII

AT VERSAILLES

The End.—Request for an Interview with M. de Bismarck.—As an Envoy.—On the Seine.—Dante's Inferno.—At Sèvres.—The first Interview at Versailles.—The Conditions of the Armistice.—I go to Versailles.—Two men, two Nations.—At Table.—What a memory.—My little Anecdotes.—The Jews.—Garibaldi.—The Chancellor's Cigar.—General d'Hautpoul.—General de Valdan.—M. de Moltke and Vincennes.—The Emperor at Home.—I walk with M. de Bismarck.—The end of the Bombardment.—Jules Ferry.—I treat all alone.—The Colours.—M. de Bismarck in a rage.—The first revictualling.—The Gratitude of Jules Favre.—A Piece of Practical Advice.

ON the following day, the 22nd of January, the populace were terrified by the following fearful state of things. French hands joined with German hands in shedding French blood; the chassepots worked with the Krupps; the *Garde Nationale,* harmless against the Prussians, was deadly against the French; and they were resigned to the prospect of peace. They had had enough.

On the 23rd of January I received a request from Jules Favre to present myself at the Ministry of Foreign Affairs. The Minister appeared to be a prey to the most lively and most demonstrative emotion. He took me by both hands, and requested me to convey a despatch to the address of M. de Bismarck on the following day before dawn.

I was not to show the despatch to anybody except the German outpost officers, into whose own hands I was to deliver it.

'Is it all over, then?' I asked Jules Favre.

'Yes,' he replied; 'we have only enough bread for a few days. God only knows what the Parisian populace will do to us when we are compelled to tell them the truth. It remains for us to guard against the possible disastrous consequences of the patriotic fanaticism which animates them. The Government will not withdraw from the responsibilities it has taken on itself, but its imperious duty is to secure food for the capital.

'The administrative service has made a mistake. We hoped to be able to resist for a few days longer. That last hope is now torn from us.

'Take this despatch and arrange for its transmission to M. de Bismarck as speedily as possible. Take every precaution necessary to that end. I need not tell you what confidence I must have in you to entrust you with such a mission and to tell you such a secret. Nobody, absolutely nobody, must know it. On that depends the tranquillity of Paris and the lives of the citizens, everything in short.'

From an excess of prudence the Minister would have wished me not to go to the bridge of Sèvres. I pointed out to him that since the business pressed, it would be better to select the spot ordinarily used for our military interviews. To choose another point in the line of investment was to hazard the possibility of having to wait a couple of days for the reply of the Chancellor, while, by way of Sèvres, we should have the answer in all probability on the same day.

In the end I relinquished the ordinary route, and, thanks to a special permit ordering all commanders of guards to lower the drawbridges for me by day or night, I reached Sèvres by the Bois de Boulogne, then entirely deserted. The despatch was to be delivered before daybreak, and without anybody, not even the advanced posts, having an idea that negotiations were going on.

In fact at daybreak on the following day, after having waited for an hour-and-a-quarter for the German officer, I handed him the enclosure of Jules Favre addressed to M. de Bismarck at a few minutes before 7 A.M. I informed the Minister of this by an express, and as I had nothing more to do then, and did not care about exposing myself under fire to no purpose, I went and asked, while waiting for the answer from Versailles, General Dumoulin, who was living at the villa of Baron de Rothschild at Boulogne, to ta'·e me in.

In what a pitiable state did I find that superb and charming residence! And how far distant, and yet actually so near, seemed the days when, after the Longchamp races, the *élite* of the aristocracy and the flower of European elegance used to assemble beneath its roof.

Towards half-past two a *Mobile* brought me a pencil note in the following terms :—

' Parley Guard, 2.15.

'To M. le Comte d'Herisson,

'The Prussian envoy has just arrived, and has begged me to say that he is the bearer of the reply of M. de Bismarck. He has also told me that the Minister is authorised to cross the Prussian lines. A carriage is at the disposal of the Minister.

'THE OFFICER OF THE GUARD,
'SAINTOIN.'

So the whole guard would know that Jules Favre was going to Versailles!

An hour later I entered the office of Jules Favre.

At the sight of the German despatch he was deeply moved, and had to recover himself several times before he was able to open it. His hands trembled.

He asked me if, as a matter of fact, it would be possible for him to present himself at Versailles that very day.

I replied that I had everything in readiness for him to leave Paris very early the next morning, as I had just done, but that when I discovered the indiscretion of the German officer, who had made the entire French guard cognizant of the instructions of M. de Bismarck, I had thought it best to request a cessation of firing at the bridge of Sèvres until 6 P.M. If he would start at once I undertook to conduct him safely to the bridge, provided he would allow me to regulate the route and pace of the carriage.

The reason for all this was that, though public opinion in Paris had almost resolved upon peace, as I have already said, there were still plenty of enthusiasts who would have looked upon the journey of Jules Favre as treasonable, and who, to intercept him, would have proceeded to any lengths, even to crime. It was, consequently, only necessary to find among any guard a few of these enthusiasts, to be unlucky enough to light upon those of them who were shrewd, suspicious, and alert, and the whole thing would miscarry.

It seemed to me, therefore, to be prudent to hurry matters before the rumour of the Minister's journey should get back to Paris with the return of the guard from the bridge of Sèvres.

In the court-yard of the Ministry of Foreign Affairs I had a *coupé* which had once belonged to the Emperor, which was driven by an old coachman of his, and drawn by two excellent post-horses from the Imperial stables.

By starting at once, although we had to reckon upon having to go out of our way in consequence of the barricades which obstructed the roads, we might yet reach Sèvres before the firing was resumed.

'Very well,' said Jules Favre, 'let us start.'

A few moments afterwards we were rolling in the direction of the Bois de Boulogne, the party consisting of the Minister, his son-in-law, M. Martinez del Rio, who insisted on accompanying him, and myself.

At the Bois de Boulogne guard, the Minister who was at the back between his son-in-law and me, hid himself behind us two. I leaned out of the right window, brandishing my pass, so as to obstruct the view on that side, and M. Martinez del Rio executed a similar manœuvre at the left window.

We entered the wood without having been recognised, without any opposition on the part of the *Garde Nationale* to the passage of the Minister—that was Jules Favre's great fear—and without having come across any Drouet preparing for us a second edition of the return of Varennes.

In the wood everything went off well, though every moment we were compelled to retrace our steps by a ditch cut across the road, or a barricade of freshly cut branches, and to make long *détours*. All these obstacles, which would have been nothing to anybody on horseback, were not easy of negotiation for a heavy carriage, half iron under its varnish, and laden with four persons. We were obliged to take them in flank.

On emerging from the wood nothing is easier in ordinary times than to get to Sèvres. But at this period things wont to be most simple were converted into insurmountable difficulties. · For instance, we could not follow the line of the quay alongside the river. Our horses would have been killed by the German riflemen on the other side of the stream before they had gone a hundred yards, and our carriage would have been riddled. We had to bear to the left. But on that side houses in ruins, and palisading torn from waste lands, completely obstructed the road.

Hoping to find an exit we drove down a private avenue, which turned out to be a labyrinth leading to nothing. At last by plunging through a carriage entrance and across some market gardens, smashing in our course an entire range of melon covers, we succeeded in gaining an open and practicable route which led us straight to the bridge. We had to wait rather a long time in the hut where I usually put up my horse—the House of the Flag of Truce. The German officer, not supposing that we should return the same day, had returned to his household gods, which, I believe, were located in the direction of Chaville.

We embarked on board the little boat which some weeks previously had conveyed Burnside and his fortunes. The Prussian sentries had pierced it with their bullets down to the water mark when empty, so that it resembled a skimmer. The weight of our bodies having caused this line to sink below the level of the river, the water rushed in on all sides by a hundred little natural sluices. It would have been just the thing for the preservation of fish. It was somewhat primitive as a means of transport for

Christians. We were really afraid of sinking. We began by stopping up the largest leaks with fragments of our torn handkerchiefs and pieces of paper. A tinned iron saucepan which we found at the bottom of the boat was transformed into a bailer, and with it I bailed out the water which came in through the smaller holes and the joints.

The Seine was drifting pieces of ice two or three yards square, which we had to avoid. That was easy, for the current at this spot is not rapid, and the ice made it slower still.

The night was black, and under the lowering sky the Seine would have seemed a river of ink if the conflagration at Saint-Cloud had not thrown ruddy gleams on the surface of the water. In places these had the appearance of blotches of blood rolling under a dome of smoke and fog. It was biblical, magnificent, what you please, but it was horrible.

With his high hat and badly-made legal black frock-coat, his countenance indented like a crescent of the waning moon, and his ministerial paper-case, Jules Favre was too modern to pose as Dante; while I, with my tunic, scarlet striped trousers, and kepi, could not have given a very accurate idea of Virgil. But if the appearance of the actors left something to be desired, the scene of Hell surrounded them, complete, sombre, mournful, and drawn by reality in proportions certainly more enormous than those of the visions of the immortal Italian poet.

On the German bank of the Seine—the war had given birth to this monstrous geographical expression—several Prussian officers awaited Jules Favre round an old closed berlin, lined with blue-flowered white chintz, and surrounded by an escort of Uhlans.

They approached with mutual salutations, and I saw that

the German officers, who had probably received their instructions, pretended to believe that the Minister was only crossing the Prussian lines in order to repair to London, to assist at a Conference then sitting there to consider the question of the North Sea.

Some days previously, M. Jules Favre had actually been invited to the Conference by the English Government, and had asked Count Bismarck for a pass. The latter at first consented to the journey. But he afterwards withdrew his consent fearing lest the diplomatic gathering should be made use of to implore the assistance of the neutral Powers, and declining to admit that Europe recognised the Republic by entering into relations with it before he, Count Bismarck, had made up his mind whether to treat with it or restore the Empire. Jules Favre, to whom the trip promised no pleasure, even wrote to M. de Bismarck and thanked him for his refusal, which, he said, had recalled him to a sense of his duties.

As the Minister did not request my attendance any further, I had no reason for offering him my society. I therefore left him setting out in the berlin surrounded by Uhlans. I saw the little *cortège* disappear round a corner of the road and I went to Sèvres to rest and wait for its return.

He did not return the same evening, nor did he reappear until late in the following afternoon.

His first words when he met me on the landing-place near the boat were,

'Ah! my dear fellow, I was wrong not to have taken you with me. My sufferings have been too great. If you do not mind, I will keep you by me until I return to Versailles.'

In conversation with Jules Favre at this period, and

even now when one reads his despatches, correspondence, reports and books, one sees that during the whole of the time he is playing the part of the character in some comedy or other, I forget which, who throughout the piece repeats continually—'How I suffer, my God, how I suffer! Oh! my head, my head!' It is very funny. But at this period he gave utterance to his complaints with such thorough conviction, he threw such an amount of sincerity into his lamentations, that the only feeling he excited was that of commiseration.

I replied that I was entirely at his disposal and, as we drove back in the Emperor's *coupé*, he recounted to me in detail his two interviews with the Chancellor. His account, which I wrote out the same evening, differs sensibly from that which, so he asserts in his book, he dictated on the following day and which he published.

He was conducted straight to the house of Madame Jessé, 22 Rue de Provence, Versailles, the very modest residence occupied by M. de Bismarck, the only advantage of which was its proximity to the Prefecture, where the King of Prussia, who for more than a week had been Emperor of Germany, was housed.

After the usual interchange of preliminary compliments, Jules Favre having remarked that he came to resume the negotiations of Ferrières, M. de Bismarck brusquely replied,

'The situation is no longer the same, and if you still maintain your Ferrières contention—'not an inch, not a stone'—further conversation is useless. My time is precious, and so is yours. I see no necessity for losing either.'

Then, changing the subject, and looking at his visitor, he added,

'You have grown whiter since Ferrières, M. le Ministre.'

Jules Favre pleaded the cares of Government and the bitterness of defeat; and the Chancellor, reverting once more to the object of the interview, hinted that the Minister had come too late, and announced that he was on the point of treating with an envoy of Napoleon III.

The scene took place in a little drawing-room on the first floor, and M. de Bismarck pointed to a door behind which the ambassador of the Emperor was supposed to be waiting.

He explained that nothing would be easier than for him to bring back the dethroned sovereign and impose him on France; that Napoleon III would easily find among the French prisoners detained in Germany a hundred thousand absolutely devoted men, who would be ample to support him when the Germans retired; and that, at the worst, there was still the resource of convoking a certain portion of the old *Corps Legislatif* and treating with it.

He became more animated as he went on speaking, and he continued almost in these words,

'As a matter of fact, why should I treat with you? Why should I give your Republic a semblance of legality by signing a convention with its representative? As a matter of fact you are merely a band of insurgents! Your Emperor, should he return, has a perfect right to have you all shot as traitors and rebels.'

'But if he returns,' exclaimed Jules Favre, in dismay, 'we shall have a civil war and anarchy.'

'Are you quite sure of that? And besides, in what way can a civil war injure us Germans?'

'Then you are not afraid of reducing us to despair? You are not afraid of driving our resistance to desperation?'

'Ah! you talk of your resistance,' said the Chancellor,

interrupting him quickly. 'Ah! you are proud of your resistance? Well, sir, let me tell you that if M. Trochu were a German General I would have him shot to-night. Nobody has a right, do you understand, nobody has any right, in the face of humanity, in the face of God, and for sheer military vain glory, to expose, as he is doing now, a town of more than two million souls to the horrors of famine. The lines of iron are cut everywhere. If we do not succeed in re-establishing them in two days, and that is by no means certain, a hundred thousand of you will die in Paris every day. Do not talk to me of your resistance. It is criminal!'

Jules Favre, thoroughly out of countenance, begged and implored that France, after all her disasters, should not be made to suffer the shame of having to put up with a Bonaparte. He then began to cry up the advantages of the Republic, an impersonal *régime* which alone could endure the hard and offensive conditions of the conqueror without absolute ruin, which alone was capable of giving adequate assurance to Germany that any treaty should be faithfully observed.

To make a long story short, before they separated, M. de Bismarck had promised Jules Favre to put in writing the conditions which seemed desirable to him and had been discussed by them. On the following morning, after having seen the Emperor and M. de Moltke, the Chancellor delivered to the Minister the plan of a Convention.

Armistice of twenty-one days—The army to be disarmed and to remain prisoners of war in Paris—The old battalions of the *Garde Nationale,* sixty in number, to remain armed for the preservation of order ; the remainder, with all free corps to be disbanded. The army to surrender arms *and colours*: the officers to retain their swords—The armistice to extend to the whole of France, and the respective positions of the armies to be marked out—Paris to pay a war indemnity and to surrender the forts to the Germans—The latter not to enter the *enceinte* during the Armistice—The guns mounted on the ramparts to be thrown into the ditches—Parliamentary elections to be held for the return of an assembly charged with pronouncing on a definite treaty of peace.

These were only the bases of the convention for an armistice, which was signed at Versailles on the 28th of January. Jules Favre hoped sincerely to be able to moderate its severity, and the negotiations between him and M. de Bismarck continued up to the very day of the signature. At intervals, on questions purely military, M. de Moltke and his officers, as well as two French Generals, took part in them.

In my capacity as Secretary and A.D.C. to the Minister, if I may use such a title, I was present at all these discussions except, as I have already said, the first one. It would be useless and wearisome to the reader to follow these negotiations step by step, and to report the successive conversations which all turned in the same circle. They, nevertheless, gave rise to certain salient, characteristic, and interesting incidents, which have fixed themselves on my memory, and which I think it useful to record.

On returning from his first interview with the Chancellor, the Minister gave me a *resumé* of the conversation I have quoted above. When he got back to Paris, he found his colleagues assembled at his office, and narrated to them the first results of his conference. They congratulated him, saying that, in the desperate situation in which they were placed, he had obtained all that they had any right to expect. The question of the war indemnity was taken into consideration, and Jules Favre was authorised to go as far as 500,000,000 francs if M. de Bismarck demanded that sum.

On the following morning, instead of remaining at Sèvres as on the preceding evening, I accompanied Jules Favre in the berlin, and entered the Jessé establishment behind him. M. de Bismarck, who was not habitually an early riser, speedily joined us in the drawing-room on the ground floor. There the Minister introduced me to the Chancellor, who looked at me for a couple of seconds as if he had seen me before, and asked us to walk up to the first floor.

The conversation began. We were all three seated at a round table. The Chancellor spoke ; Jules Favre replied. I took notes, and put on paper the arrangements made and the details agreed upon.

I was at the outset struck by the contrast between the two negotiators. Count Bismarck wore the uniform of the White Cuirassiers—white tunic, white cap, and yellow band. He looked like a giant. In his tight uniform, with his broad chest and square shoulders, and bursting with health and strength, his proximity overwhelmed the stooping, thin, tall, miserable-looking lawyer, with his frock-coat wrinkled all over, and his white hair falling over his collar. A look, alas ! at the pair was sufficient to distinguish between the conqueror and the conquered, the strong and the weak.

Jules Favre on this occasion insisted especially on the necessity of allowing the whole of the *Garde Nationale* to retain their arms. He had given way in regard to the *Mobile* and the regular army, one division of the latter, however, being allowed to retain their arms in order that they might be attached to the troops reserved for police duties, and the firemen. But he was obstinate in regard to the *Garde Nationale.* He showed that it would be impossible to disarm them, that they would revolt, that blood would flow, and that to allow them to retain their arms was the only way of making them endure the armistice.

This lasted a long time, because when General Trochu was not present to extinguish him, Jules Favre was very long-winded.

At last Count Bismarck consented, but I remember that he made a prophetic remark to Jules Favre:

'So be it, but believe me, you are making a blunder. And sooner or later there will be a heavy reckoning for you with the rifles you are imprudently leaving in the hands of these enthusiasts.'

The war indemnity was again discussed, and the Chancellor said with a smile that Paris was such a fine lady and so rich a personage, that it would be an insult to ask less than a milliard.

We shall never be able to pay it, your Excellency,' said Jules Favre. 'The war has completely ruined Paris. We should have great trouble in getting together a hundred millions.'

The amount was eventually fixed, as it is well known, at two hundred millions.

The dinner hour having struck, the Chancellor invited us to dine with him. Jules Favre, who wished to put into proper order the notes taken by me, begged to be excused, and asked that his dinner might be sent up to him. I, therefore, was the only one to follow the Chancellor into the dining-room on the ground floor, where a dozen officers and officials of the Chancellor's department awaited us, all in full uniform.

The Chancellor, who occupied the centre of the table, placed me on his right hand.

I remember that the table, otherwise very well set out, and ornamented with massive silver for campaign use, was lighted only by two candles, stuck in the necks of empty bottles; that was the only detail, calculated perhaps, that reminded one of a camp.

We had scarcely taken our seats before the Chancellor set to work to eat with a good appetite, talking the whole time, and drinking goodly bumpers of beer and champagne alternately out of a large silver drinking cup which bore his monogram.

The conversation was carried on in French.

Suddenly, to my profound astonishment, M. de Bismarck said to me,

'Monsieur d'Herisson, this is not the first time I have had the pleasure of meeting you.'

'It is true, your Excellency; but I cannot imagine that an incident, as insignificant for you as it was remarkable for me, can have retained a place in your memory, side by side with such great interests, such vast designs, and such stupendous successes.'

'Wait a moment,' he continued. 'It was in 1866, at Baden, on the steps of the Mesmer residence, where the King of Prussia was staying, you were introduced to me by the Princess Menschihoff.'

It was quite true, and I willingly joined in chorus with the officers present, who fluttered with admiration and exclaimed,

'What a memory! It is prodigious! What an astonishing man! There is no one like him!'

Was this the cause of the fleeting relations already suggested between us? Did the Chancellor, who for six months had never seen any but captive or humiliated French officers, and had never spoken to civilians except to impose sacrifices on them, or reject their requests, did he experience an involuntary moral relaxation when confronted with a free minded officer whom, when seated at his table, he could neither treat as an enemy or a slave? Did my attitude of careless unconstraint contrast with the behaviour of Jules Favre, who, on the previous evening, remained throughout the repast as if he had fainted in the chair on which I was sitting; who, buried in his long hair, appeared, when he was addressed, to rouse himself from a nightmare, and who, from time to time, dried his eyes with his table napkin — was the contrast pleasing to the Chancellor? Himself a hearty eater and drinker, did he like to see my youthful appetite, for the privations of the siege having left a void within me, I emptied my glass and left nothing on my plate.

I do not know. But I soon found out, from imperceptible signs, that I was not disagreeable to Count Bismarck. He stirred me up, gave me my cue, and incited me to speak. He might have been the mistress of a house wishing to show off one of her guests to the best advantage.

When, to use the familiar expression, I saw how the land lay, I let myself go and began to chaff these gentlemen in true Paris fashion.

'Do not believe,' I said to them, 'among other stupid tales, that we are as hungry as all that. And besides, among us there is so much elasticity that what overwhelms other people makes us laugh and joke. For instance at the beginning of the siege, there was a very strong feeling against the *Sergens de Ville*. They wanted to drown them all, neither more nor less. Then they cut off their moustaches and sent them off by threes to render assistance wherever it was needed. Now nobody pays any attention to them and they go about by twos. It is said that this is a necessity because the two who remain have eaten the third.'

And Count Bismarck's admirers, whose formulas were rather lacking in variety, exclaimed,

'What gaiety! It is prodigious! These Parisians are astonishing! There are no people like them!'

I next gave them a history of the China campaign and told them stories of the other world.

It was better to talk thus, it seemed to me, than to discuss politics which I did not understand, or the war just when it was a saddening subject so far as I was concerned.

The part I had to play possessed neither the importance nor the character of that of Jules Favre, and I am even persuaded that the small concessions which I personally succeeded in obtaining, as will be seen in due course, from M. de Bismarck, were due to my high spirits, to the persistent gaiety of my character, and a freedom of mind which I continually cultivated.

M. de Bismarck is totally unlike our statesmen. He is not in the least degree solemn. He is downright gay, and in the middle of the most serious questions he voluntarily makes some little joke, some humorous remark, under which, however, the powerful lion's claw can be felt.

Moreover, my anecdotes must have pleased him, for I read in a book written by Dr Moritz Busch, his secretary, and called, *Count von Bismarck and his suite during the War in France.*

'In exchange for these and other anecdotes, the chief told d'Herisson various things that could not then have been known in the clubs and salons of Paris, but would be heard there with pleasure. For example, the conduct of Rothschild at Ferrières, and the metamorphosis by which grandfather Amschel from a little Jew became a great one, thanks to the Elector of Hesse. He several times called him the *Court Jew,* and used the same expression in regard to the Jews among the Polish nobility.'

M. de Bismarck, indeed, told me that the reception of the Germans at Ferrières afforded much ground of complaint. According to him it was the steward of Baron Rothschild rather than the Baron himself who was to blame. · 'But,' he added, 'like master like man.'

And he then went on to tell me how the Jews were detested and despised in Germany, and how the best society held aloof from them.

Frankly, it was impossible for me to follow him on this ground, and I confessed that in France, for the moment at all events, we had not the same repugnance. Besides, he must have thoroughly understood that I could not share his sentiments, and that, as a French officer, I was all the more disposed to admire the courage of Baron Rothschild, seeing that in displaying this courage the Baron risked more than many others did. It is very possible that Grandfather Amschel was too fond of money; but, even to-day, when years have elapsed since the conversation, I must state that his grand-children, although they may love their money, know how to spend it not only royally, but intelligently and artistically.

I cannot forget that, not very long ago, when I wished to undertake some scientific explorations and archæological researches which were more honourable to the nations concerned than profitable to those who contributed towards the expenses, I found four-fifths of the necessary funds in the highest Jewish society.

I hastened, therefore, to turn the conversation from the anti-semitic ground where M. de Bismarck had placed it.

and I told him some sporting anecdotes On that score he is inexhaustible.

When we went upstairs to rejoin Jules Favre, who was still writing, the ice was broken, and the French Plenipotentiary appeared quite astonished at the familiar terms employed by the Chancellor in terminating the conversation he commenced with me at the dinner-table.

The same evening, like some practised coquette who likes to show herself under every aspect, M. de Bismarck, after having astonished me with sparkling evidences of his charming, if somewhat rough, good humour, allowed me to witness an explosion of his formidable anger. To make use of a metaphor more appropriate to this truly great man, I had heard the lion in repose, purring like a cat when she is caressed, and I was going to hear him roar furiously, erect, with his tail stretched out and his mane on end.

In the course of these long and laborious negotiations, I remember having seen the Chancellor of the Empire seriously angry on three occasions. I am going to narrate the first outburst; the second arose in connection with the defence of Saint Quentin, M. de Bismarck, in his capacity as a German leader, being furious at having seen an open town offer such an unexpected resistance, that it had forced a German army to retire, and covered the retreat of a French army. He could not forgive the courage and patriotism of a simple lieutenant, whom the force of circumstances had placed in command, for having surprised the great German Head-Quarters Staff and upset its calculations. This lieutenant was my friend, M. Xavier Feuillant.

Lastly, I had the honour of personally rousing the third outburst of this magnificent anger under circumstances which I will recount shortly, and where I was more fortunate than prudent—*felicior quam prudentior*—as Lhomond's syntax has it.

Well, this evening Garibaldi was under discussion.

On going up to his room, the Chancellor had a white saucer containing three superb Havannah cigars placed on the round table at which we were sitting. His admirers sent him numbers of boxes, which were piled upon the sideboard. In fact, the enthusiasm of the nation allowed him to want for nothing during the campaign, and the Jessé establishment received within its portals the most exquisite products of German gastronomy, the finest wines, and the most perfect beer ever brewed on the other side of the Rhine.

He often said to his intimates, 'If they want me to work well they must feed me well.' And he said to the Prince Royal, whom he had invited to dinner, and who was going into ecstacies over the good things on the table, 'You see, your Highness, that the inhabitants of the Northern Confederation absolutely insist on having a fat Chancellor.' These good inhabitants saw their dream fulfilled, seeing that later on, when he returned to Germany, he must have been obliged to reduce himself. If he worked well at Versailles, he most assuredly fed well; and I may add, in passing, that he fed his guests well also.

When the interview was on the point of commencing, the Chancellor took the saucer with the three cigars, and handing it to Jules Favre, he said,

'Do you smoke?'

Jules Favre bowed and replied that he never smoked.

'You are wrong,' said the diplomatist cuirassier abruptly. 'When an interview has to be undergone which may occasionally lead to discussion or give rise to violent language, it is always better to smoke while you are talking.   When you smoke, you see,' he continued, as he lighted his cigar, ' the cigar you hold in your hand, put between your lips, and do not like to let go, has the effect of slightly paralys- ing your physical movements.   Morally, without depriving us in any way of our brain power, it soothes us gently. The cigar is a diversion ; and the blue smoke which mounts up in wreaths and is followed by your eyes in spite of yourself, charms you and renders you more conciliatory. You are happy, your sight is occupied, your hand engaged, and your sense of smell satisfied.   You are disposed to make mutual concessions, and our work—the work of us diplomatists—is made up of reciprocal and never-ceasing concessions.   You, who do not smoke, have one advantage over me, who do smoke—you are more wide awake ; and a disadvantage—you are more inclined to be carried away and to yield to a first impulse,' he continued, with a sus- picion of raillery.   ' At all events, I am sure the Captain smokes.'

And he pushed the saucer towards me.   I confess, though from a less elevated point of view than that selected by the Chancellor, that a good cigar always tempts me.   I thought it proper, nevertheless, to decline.   I wished to be all ears—to have nothing to distract me—and, besides, I felt myself too inferior in position to these two men to allow myself to place myself on the equal footing of persons who smoke together.

The negotiation began seriously and quietly.   The Chancellor said simply and sincerely what he wanted, with astonishing frankness and admirable logic.   He went straight at the mark, and at every turn he disconcerted Jules Favre, who was accustomed to legal quibbles and diplomatic jobbery, and did not in the least understand the perfect loyalty of his opponent, or his superb fashion of treating questions, so different from the beaten track.

The Chancellor expressed .himself in French with a facility I have never met with except among the Russians, who adapt themselves to our language so rapidly and so happily, the difficulties of their own language rendering the study of foreign idioms mere child's play. He made use of expressions at once elegant and vigorous, finding the proper word to describe an idea or define a situation without effort or hesitation.

While taking from the ministerial portfolio the documents as they were required, and writing notes from dictation, I enjoyed this unexpected lesson in rhetoric and conversation.

When the point arose in connection with Garibaldi and the army of the Dijon, the Chancellor's eyes sparkled, and suddenly assumed an expression of savage anger. It was evident that he could scarcely express his frank but violent ill-will.

' I understood,' he said to Jules Favre, ' that we were to leave him and his army outside the conditions of our armistice. He is not one of you. You can well leave him to me. He has in front of him a small *Corps d'Armée* whose strength is equal to his own or nearly so. Let them fight it out together. Do not let us bother about them.'

Jules Favre replied that that was quite impossible. It was true that Garibaldi had not been asked for his assistance. The first time he offered his services to the Government of the National Defence in a telegram sent to Rochefort on the morning of the 5th September, his assistance and that of his two sons were refused. But circumstances having converted the Italian free-lance into the General of a French *Corps d'Armée*, it would be cowardly for him, the representative of France, to abandon Garibaldi, and exclude not only him, but also his *Corps d'Armée* composed almost exclusively of Frenchmen, from an armistice which ought to profit all alike.

Moreover, the Province by accepting Garibaldi's offers of service, which Paris had thought proper to decline, had enveloped the foreigner in the folds of the national flag, and it was impossible to abandon him.

During this address, very much longer and certainly more eloquent than the colourless abridgment of it which I have given, and whilst Jules Favre was proving that the honour of the country was involved in such a question as this, Count Bismarck's anger had increased.

He fidgeted in his chair; he even laid down his half smoked and still smoking cigar on the edge of the saucer, and tapping the table very sharply with his forefinger, he exclaimed,

'I must have him, nevertheless, for I mean to parade him through Berlin with a placard on his back with these words on it; 'This is the gratitude of Italy.' 'What! After all we have done for those people! It is infamous!'

At this juncture I made a somewhat bold venture, but one which, with a man of Count Bismarck's distinction and education, might have a chance of success. It actually succeeded.

I took up the saucer with the cigars, and, half smiling, half bowing, in an attitude of respect and entreaty, I handed it to him.

He remained for a few seconds without seeing what I meant, and then the fire in his eyes suddenly went out.

'You are right, Captain, he said. 'It is no use getting angry. It leads to nothing—on the contrary!'

And the conversation resumed its natural and moderate

tone. The army of Garibaldi, and Garibaldi himself were included in the Armistice.

Nevertheless MM. de Bismarck and Jules Favre could not bring matters to a conclusion by themselves. There were certain technical questions to settle, for which the intervention of military men was necessary, and it was agreed that Paris should nominate a General, furnished with the ῾full authority of the Commander-in-Chief, who was to attend on the following day to confer first of all with M. de Bismarck, and afterwards with M. de Moltke.

On the same evening, after our return to Paris, it was decided that General de Beaufort d'Hautpoul should be entrusted with this disagreeable mission, and I was̄ directed to take a despatch to the General, ordering him to accompany the Minister to Versailles as military negotiator.

This brave and worthy soldier, who lived in the Avenue Neuilly, when he had made himself acquainted with the contents of the despatch, showed the greatest surprise and anger. He walked up and down the room, gesticulating and exclaiming,

῾They cannot possibly ask me to do·such a thing! They have no right to dishonour the career of an old soldier by compelling him to put his name to such a capitulation. Am I responsible? Am I Commander-in-Chief? I will never do it. I would rather die.'

And he began to cry like a child. The tears ran down his weather-beaten cheeks, and ran drop by drop along his white moustaches. It was a harrowing sight. He continually came back to the same idea.

῾Why have they chosen me? Why me more than anybody else?'

It will be readily understood that I had not set out

U

without knowing beforehand that I should have to reply
to his objections, which had been absolutely foreseen by
the Government and the Staff. I remarked, therefore, to
the General that he was the Senior Divisional General
in Paris.

'Not at all,' he replied quickly; 'there are other Divisional Generals in Paris who were promoted on the same
day that I was.'

I replied that that was true, but that, among all these
Divisional Generals, he had been the Senior Brigadier.

He had nothing more to say. The task he had to perform was horrible and repulsive: it certainly was a blow
to his honour as an old soldier, but this same honour made
him accept the sacrifice he was asked to make, and showed
him that duty compelled him to submit and obey.

A few hours afterwards we were all once more at
Versailles, sitting round the table with M. de Bismarck.
Poor General d'Hautpoul bore on his face the traces of the
terrible struggle that had taken place between his pride
and his duty. His features were absolutely distorted, and
he had aged ten years during the journey. Brusque,
sombre and taciturn, he sat with his table-napkin on his
knees, scarcely touching the dishes that were set before
him, with choking throat, and only replying in monosyllables to the questions addressed to him by the
Chancellor in tones of courteous sympathy and deference.

He drank glass after glass of cold water, and after some
observation or other made by a German officer, he suddenly
broke out, as if an explosion had taken place within him,
and replied hotly,

'Ah! it is a very lucky thing for you that we have
come here to treat with you, for our troops are animated
with excellent feelings. My *Mobiles* and my *Gardes*

Nationaux have become perfect soldiers, and if it had depended on me, instead of dining here at your ease as you are doing at this moment, you would be far away, you and your dinner too.'

When a profound silence at a dinner-table succeeds an animated conversation, some people say, 'An angel is passing,' others say that 'A chill has been cast.' There certainly was a great chill, but I prefer the former metaphor—an angel passed by. It was the angel of patriotism soaring above our heads.

The end of the repast was most painful. On getting up from the table I placed myself behind Jules Favre. M. de Bismarck motioned his guests to the door of the room. They understood the silent order of their chief, and disappeared. The Chancellor then rejoined us, and, pointing over his shoulder to General d'Hautpoul, who was feverishly drumming on a window at the other end of the room, he said to the Minister.

'If you intend to bring that gentleman here again, you may as well say at once that you do not wish to continue the negotiations, and we can break them off from this moment.'

Jules Favre apologised. He explained that the General had come much against his will, and solely to obey, to accomplish a very painful duty. He promised the Chancellor that on the following day he would be accompanied by another military plenipotentiary.

The Germans have sought to explain this unexpected scene by saying that the General had drunk too much, and was intoxicated. Poor, brave man! He had only drunk three glasses of water. In this instance they have given proof of almost as much good faith as when they confidently affirmed that they never fired on a flag of truce·

The same day, on my arrival at Versailles, I discharged a commission entrusted to me on the previous evening by General Trochu. Deprived of all military power, he was restricted to his functions as President of the Government, and had lost almost all his prestige and all his influence over his colleagues. He called me to him, and said,

' My dear Captain, as you go every day to Versailles, do me a service. I know Prince Wittgenstein, aide-de-camp to the Emperor, personally. I should like you to give this letter into his own hands.'

I held out my hand.

' Wait a moment,' he added. ' I have no idea of transforming you, now that I have no more military despatches for you to carry, into a postman; and if, outside the negotiations carried on at Versailles by the Minister of Foreign Affairs, I address a letter to Versailles, I wish you to know its contents.'

I was about to protest from motives of politeness, when I very opportunely remembered a remark once made to me by General de Montauban. It was in the Straits Settlements, and we had to drive across Singapore in a carriage. The General asked me to get in first, and I persisted in declining what I thought was too much honour. I had, nevertheless, to give way, and when we were fairly seated in the carriage, the General said to me,

' I made you get in first because, just now, you are on the side of the carriage where you ought to be as interpreter. I am not at all angry with you for having wished to give way to me, but remember that among soldiers the first politeness is obedience.'

I was mortified, and the lesson was graven on my memory. I listened, therefore, without protest to the letter of the General to Prince Wittgenstein. It was a miniature masterpiece in style and sentiment. The ex-Governor addressed himself to the heart of his old comrade —to his feelings of honour and equity—and without humbling himself in any way, he begged him, so far as might be in his power, to influence the mind of the Emperor, whose friend and aide-de-camp he was, so that conquered Paris should be respected as she deserved to be.

After reading the letter, the General added,

'It shall never be said that I did not do everything I could in the interests of the town I was charged to defend.'

I sealed the letter myself and took it with me.

The Emperor resided in the Prefecture—in the same building which was very soon to serve as a palace for M. Thiers. Prince Wittgenstein was on duty in attendance on him. I betook myself to the Imperial residence, and at the door a sentry received me with his bayonet at the charge; the brave Saxon could not understand an armed French soldier having the audacity to endeavour to enter the Sovereign's house. The officer of the guard did not share the scruples of the sentry, but sent an orderly to conduct me to the rooms occupied by the Prince.

I record this somewhat insignificant incident because the spectacle then presented by the Salle des Pas-Perdus, which served as a vestibule or waiting-room to the imperial apartments, struck me and moved me profoundly.

In the Salle there was a veritable army of generals, officers of all grades, of every age and branch of the service, all in brand new full-dress uniforms, and all adorned with embroidery, large ribbons and decorations of every kind. Helmets glittered, spur-rowels jingled, and swords clattered on the marble flags. And what athletic and haughty figures they had, how full of joy and pride they looked! What tranquil and easy assurance was theirs.

Everything breathed of success, health, opulence, and strength.

Just as I arrived the Emperor was going out. The grenadiers presented arms, from the court yard came the noise of the horses' hoofs of the troop falling in, the pawing and whinnying of a lot of frisky horses awaiting their masters, a few short words of command from the officers, and in the midst of the living hedges of bowing officers, and above the rounded backs crossed by many coloured ribbons, I saw, from the corner where I was hurriedly shut in and concealed, the modern Charlemagne, proclaimed only a week previously, pass along the grand glass gallery of the palace of Louis XIV, the sovereign master who held us all beneath his knee, calm, smiling, and with his helmet in his hand allowing us to see his aged head and his rough, fatherly countenance.

And when in thought and with the rapidity of lightning I traversed the route which was the scene of so many of my journeyings, and when I saw our generals, sad, sombre, unattended, flying in a way from the troops they had commanded, their uniforms soiled and themselves worn out by the labours of the siege, and when I thought of the poor tattered soldiers—the harrowing contrast which was before me day by day in my little room in the Rue de Provence, I mean the contrast between the Ministers of the two nations, Bismarck the colossal and Jules Favre the lachrymalwin, stood out in bolder relief and assumed enormous proportions.

I bit my lips till they bled to repress the sob called forth by that involuntary resurrection in my brain of our misfortunes and our shame confronted by all this glory and prosperity.

The same day I heard a curious interchange of impressions and opinions between M. de Bismarck and Jules Favre, for it must not be imagined that they conversed all the time solely on the object of their mission. The conversation, guided as a rule by the Chancellor, frequently wandered, and capriciously touched upon every possible subject.

Jules Favre had been speaking of the love of France for liberty, her taste for a republic, and her republican sentiments.

'Are you quite sure,' replied the Chancellor, 'that France is as republican as you make her out to be?'

'Certainly,' said Jules Favre.

'Well, I do not agree with you. Before we entered into negotiations with you, we did not neglect, as you may well suppose, to study the moral state of your country and to get at an exact account of it. In spite of this war which has been so disastrous to you, imposed, by the way, on Napoleon III by the French nation rather than desired by him, as I have already told you—and it was this consideration which allowed us, after having overthrown the Empire, to fight France, our old and real enemy—in spite of the disasters and defeats of your army, nothing would be easier, believe me, than to re-establish the Empire. I will not maintain against you that it would have been received with acclamation in Paris, but it would certainly have been accepted or submitted to in the country. A plébiscite would have done the rest.

'No; if we have not treated with the Bonapartes, it is simply because we have found it more advantageous to treat with you. As for the pretended love of France for the Republic, it would have disappeared with marvellous facility.

'You have not been long in power. Wait: when you

have had the management of men for some years, from the liberal you are now you will become authoritative, from republican, monarchist,   Believe me, you cannot lead a great nation, nor can you render it prosperous, outside the principle of authority, in other words, monarchy.

As Jules Favre protested, the Chancellor continued,

'You will come to it. It will be in spite of you, I admit thoroughly, but you will come to it all the same. You are too clear-sighted not to recognise it speedily, and too patriotic to persist in that case in your error.   Look at me.   How did I begin ?   I was a liberal, and it is only by sheer force of reasoning, by the evidence of facts and the experience of men that, loving my country and longing for her good and her greatness, I became a conservative— ultra-conservative if you prefer it.   The Emperor con- verted me.   My gratitude to him and my respectful affection date from that far-off time—that difficult period when he had such confidence in me that he supported me alone before and against everybody.   If to-day I am the man whom you see, if I have rendered some service to my country, I owe it all to the Emperor, and I am no more tired of saying that than I am of loving my Sovereign.'

Jules Favre did not reply to this profession of faith, but I imagine that, later on, when he asked pardon of God and men, the distant echo of the Chancellor's words must have vibrated in his poor tired brain.

I have explained how the military mission of General d'Hautpoul came to an end on the very day that it began. The Chief of the Staff of the new Governor, General de Valdan, who succeeded General Schmitz, was directed to discuss the terms of the military portion of the armistice convention.   This discussion was not under the direction of Count Bismarck. It took place in the house occupied by Marshal **von** Moltke.

There were present the Marshal, a German General Officer, and two Colonels on the Staff; M. de Bismarck Jules Favre, General de Valdan, and myself.

After the various clauses of the military convention had been discussed, Marshal von Moltke dictated them, and the text was written in duplicate by a German Colonel and me.

We were installed in a rather large room with two windows. The Marshal, with his back to the light, presided, having on his left General de Valdan, and on his right M. de Bismarck; by the side of M. de Bismarck sat Jules Favre, separated from the remainder of the German colonels by a table at which the German Colonel, who acted as secretary, and I wrote.

With his clean-shaven face, which bore evidence of suffering, and was, as it were, crackled with an infinity of small wrinkles, M. de Moltke did not in the least resemble a soldier such as we love to portray them in France. He rather resembled a Benedictine monk, or an ascetic, or an old actor.

Each one of his words, clear, sharp, and precise, seemed to be produced by the vibration of a steel tongue. You could feel instinctively that he thoroughly enjoyed having under his hand the humble plenipotentiaries of humiliated France and conquered Paris.

Dressed in a very simple uniform, he wore the ribbon of the Iron Cross knotted in his button-hole and not sewn on his breast. The majority of the German officers wore the same decoration, just as the Russian officers wear their principal military order—the Cross of St George. He had at his neck a cross in blue enamel resembling a Maltese cross.

In his white tunic, at once simple and imposing, and despite the propinquity of the conqueror of all our armies, Count Bismarck, amid this small staff, nevertheless resembled a monarch surrounded by his court.

General de Valdan was in undress uniform with epaulettes, and Jules Favre naturally wore his everlasting frock-coat, which, when he was sitting down, gave his chest the appearance of the bellows of an accordion. Both General and Minister had a sad and downcast air, as may easily be understood.

When the discussion turned on the various points round Paris which were to be occupied by the Prussian army, and the enumeration of the forts which were to be handed over to them, General de Valdan said that he was desirous of sparing the Parisians the humiliation of surrendering the fort of Vincennes.

'It represents to us,' he added 'a remarkable historical reminiscence. At the time of the invasion it was gloriously saved by General Daumesnil.'

Marshal von Moltke replied very quickly and very drily, that he regretted it very much, but that they had not met to discuss questions of sentiment or history, and that, considering the situation of the fort, completely surrounded by trees, it was of the highest strategic importance that it should be occupied by the German armies.

General de Valdan replied that he did not know that the position was of such importance, and that if he made a point of exempting it from the Prussian occupation, it was solely—he begged pardon of the Marshal—in order to give a semblance of patriotic and moral satisfaction to the Parisians, a satisfaction which in its way was a political question interesting to both nations, and calculated to facilitate their mutual relations.

The Marshal persisted, and we were about to pass on, when I thought I might interpose a timid observation.

'I beg your Excellency ten thousand pardons,' I said, 'but I believe you are mistaken.'

'How?' replied M. de Moltke, who looked at me with blinking eyes, as if he wanted to see something in the far-off distance.

'Because the fort of Vincennes is not surrounded by trees. It certainly is at the side of the forest of Vincennes, but it cannot be said that a fort near a forest is surrounded by trees.'

'I beg your pardon in my turn, Captain,' replied the Marshal; 'the fort is completely surrounded by trees. However, it is easy to ascertain that.'

And taking a map which one of the officers had hastened to pass to him, he spread it out on the table where we were writing.

The map was coloured, and on it appeared the fort of Vincennes completely surrounded by a green tint.

'This map is not correct,' I exclaimed at once. 'There is no wood on this side; and again, here on the right there is no indication of the camp of St Maur.'

'Are you sure?' said the Marshal, surprised by the confident assurance of my assertions.

'Perfectly sure, your Excellency, and there is no great merit in it. My brother, Orderly Officer to General Berthaut, was encamped at St Maur for long enough with the *Mobiles*, who were commanded by that General, for me to have ample leisure to study the environs of the fort of Vincennes.'

'Let me see your map,' said the Marshal turning abruptly to General de Valdan.

The latter shrugged his shoulders, and at the same time

raised his two hands to show that he had not brought a map, and he in his turn applied to Jules Favre, who was no better supplied with a detail which one would have thought indispensable.

This rapid scene recalled to my mind a duel in which I was second with Count Exelmans. Each of the two groups of seconds was under the impression that the duel would be fought with the opposite side's weapons, so that when we arrived on the ground, a considerable distance from Paris, with the traditional landaus waiting under the trees, there was only one thing wanting to enable us to fight—the duelling swords.

Jules Favre had relied on the General, and in all probability the General had relied on Jules Favre.

Fortunately I had with me one of the maps which General Schmitz had given to each officer of the Staff; it never left me. I proved decisively that the camp of St Maur was neither a myth nor a dream, to the painful surprise of Marshal von Moltke.

The Marshal did not appear surprised that I knew the locality better than he did, but he seemed vexed that it had been proved before numerous witnesses that the map he possessed was incorrect. He experienced a shadow of a feeling of confusion. The line traced in red pencil which marked the limit of the German occupation was rectified.

And the fort of Vincennes was thus saved by 'General de Valdan,' so wrote Jules Favre.

This happened on the 26th of January. Nothing was as yet officially concluded, but matters were sufficiently advanced for one to state that the negotiations would terminate definitely, and that a rupture was impossible.

Jules Favre and I had been writing for nearly two hours on the first floor of the Jessé establishment. As my work was finished, I went down stairs to get some fresh air in the Chancellor's garden, and to stretch my legs, unaccustomed to office immobility. I had not been there more than a few moments, strolling along an alley at the bottom of the garden, when M. de Bismarck joined me, and asked me, with his customary courtesy, if, instead of turn· ing like a squirrel in the garden, I should not prefer to take a walk with him in the town.

I first of all looked at the Chancellor with a certain amount of astonishment, because, as a matter of fact, the armistice was not yet signed, and the promenade of Count Bismarck with an Orderly Officer of General Trochu assumed a political importance.

However, I hastened to accept, but I requested permission to go and ask the Minister how much time I had to myself. The Chancellor understood quite well that it was only a polite pretext, that I wished to let Jules Favre know, and that I did not wish to take upon myself to show a French uniform in Versailles side by side with a German uniform.

I put Jules Favre in possession of the situation in a very few words.

'Go,' he said to me. 'However painful may be the situation in which you find yourself, you must accept it. The Chancellor has his reasons. He no doubt wishes all Versailles, and therefore all Europe to know how matters are progressing, and that he no longer considers a rupture possible.'

M. de Bismarck was waiting for me down below, at the door leading out into the street. I drew back to let him pass, but he insisted that I should go out first. I record all these trivial things, because the smallest details of these days are indelibly engraved on my memory.

We were in the Rue de Provence. We turned to the right, and we emerged almost at once into the Boulevard de la Reine.

The Boulevard was crowded with German officers and ladies. It was the hour when the Prussian ladies who had joined their husbands came out to show themselves to the officers of the various Staffs. They treated M. de Bismarck with an amount of respect almost as profound and distinguished as is shown, almost everywhere except in France, to the members of the Royal Family.

This quite natural respect, about which there is no hesitation, did not astonish me. Brought up in Germany, I knew from having mixed with it, admired it, and envied it, the social hierarchy which reigns in that country, where the people do not seek to lure everybody to their nest, and where each class of society renders to the superior classes the same marks of deference which it receives from the classes below it.

Great was the surprise to see a French officer walking on the left of Count Bismarck and conversing with him. The news of this promenade, the meaning of which was grasped by everybody, spread with the rapidity of lightning. It was telegraphed to London, to Berlin, and to Vienna, that the Chancellor of the German Empire had been seen walking in a public place with the aide-de-camp of the French Minister of Foreign Affairs.

And on the following day how many mothers, wives, and daughters must have thanked God for this news of the speedy return of those dear ones whom each day they feared they should never see again!

In the evening, when we were setting out, and just as we were getting into our carriage, M. de Bismarck said to Jules Favre,

' Then we are agreed on all points, are we not ? '

' Perfectly,' replied Jules Favre.

' In that case it is useless to burn our powder any longer. I propose to you that the bombardment shall cease this very day. At midnight M. de Moltke is prepared to telegraph to all points to that effect. Do you agree ? '

' Ah ! Monsieur le Chancelier,' said Jules Favre, seizing the hand held out to him by the Count, ' you make me very happy. I dared not ask you for that, only, your Excellency, allow Paris to fire the last shot.'

' It is agreed. Adieu.'

That evening, though I was very tired, I determined to give myself the pleasure of being awake at that absolutely psychological moment, as the Chancellor called it, and I went for a walk on the quays. The batteries of Meudon and Châtillon were doing their utmost.

I remember hearing the first stroke of midnight as I was standing at the foot of the clock tower of the Palais de Justice.

The watches of the German army must have been well regulated, as well as our own, for before the second stroke of the bell sounded from the old tower, an imposing, solemn mournful silence reigned everywhere.

You may believe me or not as you please, but it seemed to me that something was wanting.

And I am not sure but that a goodly number of Parisians, already asleep in the gas-bereft town where nobody sat up to watch, did not awake, stirred by the silence of the atmosphere from their first sleep.

Just in this way do the dwellers in the neighbourhood of the markets, who are rocked to sleep all night long by the rumbling of the waggons of the market gardeners on the pavement, awake with a start amid the quiet of the country.

On the following day Paris knew that negotiations were on foot, and that an armistice was on the point of being signed. A few enthusiasts protested, gave utterance to desperate resolves, talked about a sortie, and of blowing the whole place up. Nobody attempted a sortie; nothing was blown up. In reality Paris had had enough, and was feeling the need of passing to some other exercise.

Before bringing the recital of these negotiations to a close with a dramatic and impressive episode, I wish to recount a detail which I should pass over in silence were it not that the personage whom it concerns has, since that period, made a great political fortune, and acquired a considerable position in the country.

Officially, the question of revictualling predominated over all the others; I say *officially*, because I am persuaded that very few people knew the exact truth in regard to the question of subsistence, and that we were not so much at the last gasp as was represented. The month of March was first spoken of as the extreme limit of our provisions. Then it was said that a mistake had been made, and that we could not hold out longer than the first days of January. Was a mistake really made? I do not think so. The proof of the correctness of my view is that plenty reigned in Paris before, in point of time, the provision trains could have reached the stations; and that, long after peace was concluded, I ascertained that almost everywhere there were stocks of spoiled flour, rotten potatoes, rancid bacon, &c., &c. I do not blame the Government for having anticipated the moment when bread would really have failed, and in default of other excuses a perfectly adequate explanation of the capitulation was to be found in the alarming increase in the mortality, especially among children, during the closing weeks of the siege.

Officially, therefore, the most considerable and most urgent question, the question which had brought Jules Favre to Versailles, being that of the revictualling of Paris, it was natural that the engineers and directors of the railways should go and make arrangements with the German authorities for the necessary restoration of the lines which had been cut, for the repairs of bridges and tunnels, and for the provision of rolling stock. This latter had been got ready beforehand by the Germans who, when the armistice was definitely signed, proved themselves absolutely exact and even foreseeing.

It was also natural that, in his capacity as Mayor of Paris, M. Jules Ferry should go to Versailles in connection with the revictualling. He went there several times, and I made a third with him and Jules Favre in the Emperor's *coupé* which had rendered us such signal service.

M. Jules Ferry was far more elegant than M. Jules Favre. Two Jules. Indeed the Jules abounded in the Government. Simon was called Jules, and Trochu himself was afflicted with that prenomen, somewhat too common among our powers that were, who had only that in common with Cæsar. M. Jules Ferry wore a short, tight frock-coat, light grey trousers (in spite of the season of the year), and lavender gloves. His figure was well made up.

Although on several occasions, when in our narrow vehicle, M. Jules Ferry thought fit to whisper in the ear of Jules Favre—a piece of doubtful politeness so far as the third passenger was concerned—I was fully aware that these two honourable gentlemen were principally preoccupied about the provincial elections, and the necessity that they should result in favour of the republican cause ; about the attitude of Gambetta, who did not appear to be at all enthusiastic on the subject of the armistice; and about the necessity of the *Garde National* being allowed to retain their arms—on this point M. Ferry was as pertinacious as Jules Favre ;—and lastly and principally, about the maintenance of the Republic.

I confess that I should have preferred to hear them converse a little less about their petty political combinations, and a little more about the grand dilemma which they appeared to·have completely forgotten—was peace to be concluded, or was the war to go on ?

I should have made them laugh if I had spoken to them of these things. For some time past, in common with the majority of Frenchmen, and with the regular army almost to a man, they had come to the conclusion that peace was inevitable.

It was all over, the military negotiations were concluded and the armistice convention had been written out in duplicate. Jules Favre carried off the copy by the German Colonel in order to submit it for final acceptance by his colleagues. The other, which I had written out, remained in the hands of the Germans.

After the Government had considered the matter at the Hôtel de Ville, Jules Favre brought away the convention, duly signed, in his paper-case, and directed me to take it to M. de Bismarck early on the following day. I need not say that although the missive entrusted to me was sealed, I knew its contents by heart, word for word, seeing that those contents had been dictated to me, and that I had assisted at the laborious birth of each one of its sentences.

While I was on my solitary journey to Versailles in the Imperial *coupé*, a mad idea crossed my brain, returned again and again, and speedily took up its abode there with disheartening obstinacy. It was that I should undertake a little additional negotiation at my own proper risk and peril.

' What have I to risk ? ' I asked myself. ' M. de Bismarck will never credit me with sufficient hardihood to suppose that the observations I am going to make to him, the modifications or additions I am going to solicit, have not been dictated to me by the Government. If my altogether patriotic stratagem is discovered, I shall be repudiated, blamed and punished by these gentlemen of Paris; and neither blame, nor repudiation, nor punishment will weigh the least with me in comparison with my desire to serve my country, and the glory of being of use to her. Well, a very exceptional opportunity of satisfying that desire and of gaining that glory now presents itself. Forward—I do not suppose they will shoot me. I know now how to carry on a diplomatic conversation. No doubt about that. I do not require to be shown how to proceed. People should never do anything in the presence of children.'

After having duly considered the *pros* and *cons*, after having reflected on what I was about to do, repeated my sentences, rehearsed my part in fact, I arrived at the residence of M. de Bismarck, firmly resolved to run the whole risk.

I was shown into the dining-room on the ground floor, which communicated with the anti-room by means of three or four steps. The Chancellor was busy, and I was requested to wait a few moments.

The table was laid for breakfast. A dozen covers were laid on a table-cloth stained in several places, the stains proving, what indeed I already knew from experience, that beer was not the only beverage indulged in by the warriors and diplomatists of the north.

The customary seat of the chief—so he was called by his pacific Staff—was marked by his campaign service and his silver cup.

It often happens that in moments of waiting and idleness, the strangest and most fantastic ideas cross one's brain. It is as if the mind, condemned to a forced repose, profited by the truce to wander about and explore—a moment of folly in which reason acquires new strength.

I thought to myself that it was eminently imprudent to allow an enemy to wait as I was waiting in a dining-room, an enemy whose reason might be affected by the misfortunes of his country, and who might very easily put a drop of prussic acid into the bottom of the drinking cup of the man who was on the point of snatching Alsace and Lorraine from our arms. The colossus would fall prone to the ground. The great thinker would be nothing but an inert mass, and starving Paris would be bending the knee before a corpse. It is quite true, I thought, that no good would come of it, because M. de Bismarck's successor would not have his genius and might possibly not have his moderation. It is also true that M. de Moltke would sacrifice to the enraged shade of his fellow labourer hecatombs of which history would never cease to speak. Decidedly it would be a bad speculation as well as a most cowardly attack.

I had reached that point in my philosophical-criminal reflections when I heard the shaking staircase of Madame Jessé creak. The door opened, and M. de Bismarck was before me.

'I was expecting you, Count,' he said. 'I hope everything is finished, and that you have, according to arrangement, brought the convention with you duly signed.

'I have brought it to your Excellency,' I replied; 'but in order to avoid loss of time and more useless journeys, I am not to hand it over until your Excellency has consented to the introduction into it of a few minor alterations. In case your Excellency does not consent, I must withdraw and await the arrival of M. Jules Favre.'

The Chancellor, who was already holding out his hand, showed me quite suddenly a countenance animated by an expression of irritated surprise.

'What is all this about?' he exclaimed. 'Everything was settled. Is M. Jules Favre absolutely bent on starving this capital, and allowing Europe to think that it is our fault?'

'M. Jules Favre,' I replied, 'has not changed his mind. He had to submit the convention to the Government. He has submitted it, and I have the honour to bring you the reply.'

'Come, come,' said the Chancellor, 'let us see what these alterations are, and whether it is possible to agree to them.'

'Here they are:—1st, The Government desires that, in conformity with the wishes expressed more than once by our plenipotentiaries in the course of the numerous discussions which have taken place on the subject, you will withdraw your stipulation that the guns now mounted on the fortifications of Paris shall be thrown over into the ditches. The Government asks you to consent to these guns being simply dismounted and placed in the roadway in rear of the ramparts. 2nd, That you will consent to the line of investment round Paris as set forth in the tracing by the French Head-quarters Staff, and that you will abandon the line finally marked out by the German Staff. 3rd, Lastly—and this is a *sine quâ non*—the

Government desires that, in opposition to what has already been agreed upon, the Army of Paris shall retain its colours.'

I stopped, frightened at my own audacity, and listening to my own words as if somebody else had uttered them.

M. de Bismarck's anger, which had been gradually rising, burst forth suddenly, and, banging the door which he had left half-open behind him, he said to me, emphasising his words and raising his voice,

'Do not these gentlemen understand that all this is forced on me by our Staff? That I personally have nothing to do in this particular matter? And that, as I have told M. Jules Favre, our officers are never tired of saying, 'Soldiers win the victories, and diplomatists spoil them?'

He walked up and down for several moments with such a wrathful expression on his face that I thought I had gone too far, and if it had not been for my ardent desire to succeed, I should have made up my mind to apologise.

'Wait here,' he said at last, 'I will go and speak to the Emperor.'

He put on his white cap with the yellow band, and with a determined step left the house.

I waited for two hours, a prey to the liveliest anxiety in regard to the result of my attempt. The breakfast hour had past a considerable time before the Chancellor, for whom I had never ceased to watch, returned, as calm now as he had been agitated before.

'I am very late,' he said, 'but it is all the fault of M. de Moltke. I had prevailed on the Emperor to accede to your requests; the Marshal interposed and begged his Majesty to refuse. The Emperor had therefore formally to signify his pleasure. All is now settled. The guns are not to be thrown over into the ditches. We will limit the investment to line No. 1 on the French tracing; and as for the colours, the Emperor's own words were, "You can inform the envoy of the French Government that we have enough trophies of our victories, and enough colours captured from the French armies, to have no need to add those of the army of Paris."'

I at once took my leave of the Chancellor. I felt as light as a bird, and I did not even pay any attention to the downright rudeness of the *employés* in the ante-room, not one of whom made room for me to pass. They were making me pay for the politeness they were compelled to show me when I was with the Chancellor. I shrugged my shoulders, and merely came to the conclusion that Henri Heine had seen clearly when he said, 'The German is born a fool, education makes him mischievous.' For in proportion as Count Bismarck is a personage of distinction and would remain one, to whatever nationality he might belong, and in proportion as the majority of the German officers were polished—so the Government officials, who do not belong to the aristocracy and, consequently, do not belong to the army, were by nature rude and uncivil.

Who was most astonished, on my return, at the boldness of my experiment and its unheard of success? My old chief, General Schmitz, to whom I went first of all to recount my adventure, and who undertook to inform the Government of it. The excellent General was very much moved; he embraced me several times, and such is the value of the esteem of certain men, that I considered his emotion and reception as the sweetest and most precious recompense of my efforts.

I did not return to Paris alone. Just as I was taking

my leave of M. de Bismarck, or rather, just as he gave me to understand that I was to go, with that grand manner incidental to sovereigns who know, by signs perceptible only to the initiated, how to convey to their visitors an intimation that they have ceased to please—just at that moment, dissembling the profound joy which filled my soul, and abusing for the last time the condescension that he had hitherto manifested towards me, I had the audacity to make an absolutely personal request.

'Your Excellency,' I said, 'I have come alone and I am not afraid of compromising my Minister by the propinquity of a few eatables.   Will your Excellency authorise me to introduce into Paris the first convoy of provisions, and permit me to wait in your garden while I send into the town for some bread, butter, and fowls.'

M. de Bismarck burst out laughing.

'I ought,' he replied, 'to have thought of sending you on that errand some days ago.'

Great God! What delicacies were to be had in Versailles for a hundred francs intelligently spent! And what a fortune I might have made if, instead of a *coupé* and a few louis, I had had at my disposal a large cart and a few thousand francs.

And to how many people I was able to bring happiness that day—people who were far from suspecting that the most precious things I brought back from Versailles were my bread, my butter, and my fowls.

And now, dear reader, be sure of one thing, which is that I should never have told you all this had it not been for the document signed 'Schmitz,' which you have read as a sort of preface to this volume, and to which I beg to call your attention if you have not already read it.

For I can quite understand the feelings which must be

roused within you by the individual who has just told you in so many words,

'You are not aware of the fact? Well, I prevented the guns being thrown over the ramparts into the ditches. I rescued from Prussian occupation several French towns, and, lastly, I spared Paris the shame and humiliation of surrendering her colours to the conquerors.'

If this individual has not in his hands the proof of his assertion he is and must be a fool.

In bringing to a close this journal, in which I have conscientiously and correctly noted the great and small events in which I took part, *quorum pars parva fui*, in those days which Victor Hugo has so justly called the Terrible Year, I think I ought to insert the last three letters I received from Jules Favre. They will go far to prove what men are, and what their gratitude is worth.

Very often, on our return from Versailles, after those terrible negotiations of which I was the sole witness, and those hopeless battles of which I was the sole spectator, the Minister of Foreign Affairs used to say to me,

'You are destined to render real service to your country, and before I leave the Ministry I shall give myself the satisfaction of placing you in a position where you may distinguish yourself.'

One day, as we were driving, Jules Favre reminded me with a laugh of an awkward position from which I had extricated him. In the course of an interview, the Chancellor had asked one of those military questions which are so far removed from being technical that they are familiar to everybody. The eminent lawyer did not know what answer to make, and, as he did very frequently, he hinted by kicking me under the table that I had better reply.

'Let me see,' he said to me ; 'where would you like me to send you ?'

'It seems to me,' I replied, 'that China would be active service, and that I might be of some service there, seeing that I speak the language of the country.'

'True, true,' said Jules Favre, slapping his leg with his right hand. 'Why did I not think of that before ?'

Later on, when he had had time to keep the promises he made, and which he gave without my having asked for them when there was no longer need of my humble existence, the attitude of the Minister changed.

I must confess that, in his book, Jules Favre has been good enough to thank me, and bring my discretion prominently forward. He was right, for, in spite of all that I have narrated, I am conscious that at this very time I am giving further proof of that discretion.

I will also add that I fully understand the desire to keep in the background the only witness of events so grave, of conversations so embarrassing ; and I understand too, that when once the peacock has paraded himself in the feathers of the jay—contrary to what generally happens— it is decidedly to the interest of the king of the farm-yard that the stripped fowl should go and hide himself in the forest.

The first of these letters is as follows :

> '*February* 7, 1871.

'MY VERY DEAR AIDE-DE-CAMP,

> 'I am not going to Versailles to-day. I may possibly go to-morrow. I will let you know.

> 'Yours sincerely, JULES FAVRE.'

This is the second.

> '*February* 10, *evening.*

'I am exceedingly touched by all your goodness, my very

dear Captain. I should not like to abuse your kindness and your fatigue. If, however, it will not inconvenience you too much, I shall leave my house at a quarter-past eleven to go to the Orleans railway station, and in any case I shall be very glad to shake hands with you.

'Thanking you again,

'Yours sincerely,·

'JULES FAVRE.'

That was the last journey we made together.

To tell the truth, and as one ought to be frank in all things, I was stupid enough to imagine that Jules Favre was still thinking of his 'dear captain' and his 'dear fellow.' I presented myself once or twice at the Foreign Office, but I was never fortunate enough to be received.

Seeing that, in order to take part in the war, I had actually broken off a diplomatic career which was just in its infancy, seeing that I should have merely considered it just and legitimate to join once more the broken thread of my destinies under the auspices of the man whose body I had covered with mine when he was trembling in front of the sentries of the *Garde Nationale*—I wrote him a long letter in which I reminded him of the services I had rendered, and the promises he had spontaneously made—

'The Minister of Foreign Affairs will have the honour of receiving Captain d'Herisson on *Saturday, March 18th*, at 5 o'clock.'

'Paris, March 17*th*, 1871.'

The 18th of March. Does not that read like a romance?

On that day Jules Favre returned to Versailles, but as the Germans were no longer there he had no need of me.

The usher of the Ministry of Foreign affairs had neglected to sign his name to the invitation. It was a misfortune, for the two letters from his master, with his own, would have formed an exact pendant for the letters of Metternich, and the communication from the usher of the Austrian Embassy.

A long time afterwards, however, accident threw me across the path of Jules Favre, who at once said to me,

'I am always thinking of you, my dear fellow. Your turn will come one of these days.'

I had already some knowledge of men. I knew how far I could count on them. It was fortunate that I did, because, if I had not known that, I should have been waiting my turn for the last fourteen years.

And now, dear reader, as you have followed me so far, I wish to recompense you for your trouble and your fidelity by giving you a little good advice.

If you love your country sacrifice yourself for her without hesitation. If she asks little of you, give it her; if she asks everything of you, still give it her.

But if, outside this patriotic immolation, you are a practical man — a citizen who does not care about being fiouted, or a private individual who knows the value of his time and trouble, never serve, never serve anybody, neither Republicans, nor Bonapartists, nor Royalists, nor any of those facetious individuals who aspire, so they say, to make your fortune.

They are all the same; no one of them is worth more than another.

Make use of them, that is legitimate, for they aspire to make use of you, but give particular heed to these common-sense words with which I bring my book to an end,

'Never devote yourself to anybody.'

FINIS

Lightning Source UK Ltd.
Milton Keynes UK
UKOW06f0312190717
305535UK00007B/59/P